The Holy Grail of Network Storage Management

The Holy Grail of Network Storage Management

Jon William Toigo

with illustrations by
Margaret Romao Toigo

PRENTICE
HALL
PTR

PRENTICE HALL
Professional Technical Reference
Upper Saddle River, New Jersey 07458
www.phptr.com

Editorial/production supervision: Patty Donovan (Pine Tree Composition, Inc.)
Cover design director: Jerry Votta
Manufacturing buyer: Alexis Heydt-Long
Publisher: Jeff Pepper
Full-service production manager: Anne R. Garcia

PRENTICE HALL PTR

© 2004 Pearson Education, Inc.
Publishing as Prentice Hall Professional Technical Reference
Upper Saddle River, NJ 07458

The publisher offers excellent discounts on this book when ordered in quantity for bulk purchases or special sales.
For more information, please contact:

U.S. Corporate and Government Sales
1–800–382–3419
corpsales@pearsontechgroup.com

For sales outside of the U.S., please contact:

International Sales
1–317–581–3793
international@pearsontechgroup.com

Printed in the United States of America
First Printing

ISBN 0-13-148968-2

Pearson Education Ltd., London
Pearson Education Australia Pty, Limited, Sydney
Pearson Education Singapore, Pte. Ltd.
Pearson Education North Asia Ltd., Hong Kong
Pearson Education Canada, Ltd., Toronto
Pearson Educación de Mexico, S.A. de C.V.
Pearson Education–Japan, Tokyo
Pearson Education Malaysia, Pte. Ltd.

CONTENTS

CHAPTER TEN The Cone of Silence   **178**

CHAPTER 11 Conclusion: Joining the Quest for the Holy Grail   **204**

GLOSSARY   **220**
INDEX   **269**

List of Illustrations

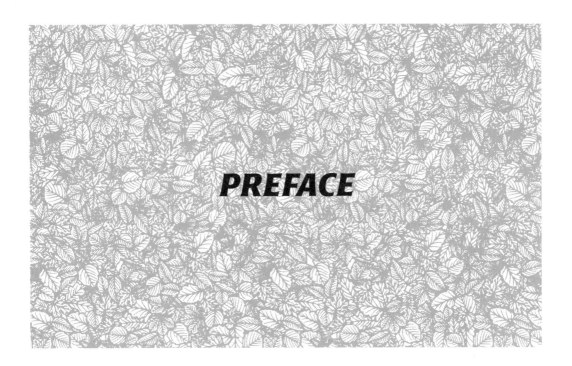

PREFACE

Nearly three years have transpired since the publication of *The Holy Grail of Data Storage Management*, an extraordinarily well-received primer covering the technology and trends in data storage. I would like to thank everyone who read the first *Holy Grail* book, and I am delighted to report that, since its publication, knowledgeable authors have published at least six additional titles around the same subject matter.

Most of the new titles contribute valuable information about the latest storage innovations and help contribute to the growing knowledge-base of contemporary storage technology. The net effect is that a long-ignored area of IT seems now to be getting the attention and historical record that it merits.

Our collective authors' egos aside, the success of all of these books is owed, in the final analysis, not so much to their content or presentation, but to the compelling nature of the subject itself. We should take no pride that our books have been successful, given the dire need that exists today for improved management of the burgeoning data being amassed in most organizations.

Over the past three years, many storage managers have reported to me that they are, quite simply, at wit's end—desperate to build storage infrastructure for their organizations that delivers measurable business value and also conforms to the budgetary and resource constraints imposed on all businesses by the current economy. They scour the trade press and bookstores for everything written on the subject of storage. They scavenge the presentations made by vendors and so-called industry experts at conferences, workshops, and trade shows for a hint about best practices and emerging standards. Basically, they seek any source of information that might provide guidance that will help them to achieve their goals.

Under the circumstances, I take no pride from ongoing royalties derived from the sales of the *Holy Grail of Data Storage Management*, though my publisher and my creditors are certainly delighted. As a veteran IT professional, and now as a CEO and founder of two companies charged with empowering storage consumers and developing data management as its own discipline within the IT field, I feel that I am simply doing my job.

So it is with this book. *The Holy Grail of Network Storage Management*, which you now hold in your hands, is not a revised and expanded version of my earlier book. In fact, this *Holy Grail* is not intended to be a primer at all, though I hope it will have the value of providing actionable information about some of the latest developments in storage technology.

This book is, pure and simple, an extended critique of contemporary storage technology and the industry that provides it. If I do my job correctly, this book will enable you to undertake successfully what is the most difficult and challenging task you face today: developing a critical view that will help you to filter out the vendor marketing hype that is so pervasive around network storage technology so that you can make better and more strategic design and acquisition decisions for the storage infrastructures you are tasked to build, support, and manage.

The original *Holy Grail* book provided a foundation in basic storage nomenclature, technology, and topologies that you need to begin building a true storage infrastructure. It is useful in understanding the content of this book, as well.

Above all, the earlier book emphasized the need to make the storage infrastructure that you design and build manageable. The book emphasized that, without management, you have nothing appropriately termed "storage infrastructure." Without effective management, you have only a morasse of equipment and cabling that will require the work of a growing (and increasingly unacceptable) staff to administer. The labor costs of unmanaged storage are the largest part of storage cost of ownership and will bankrupt your organization over time if unresolved.

In the years since the publication of the first *Holy Grail*, it became abundantly clear to me that another, very different kind of book, needed to be written. Knowledge of basic building blocks of storage and recognition of the primacy of storage management was not enough for those who were tasked with the role of storage planning and management to do their jobs effectively.

In fact, I came to realize that the title of storage manager provided an inadequate description of what you do for a living. Whether or not it is clearly stated in your job description, your work is not about managing storage devices. Rather, it is your mission to (1) provision storage capacity to meet the requirements of application data, paying close attention to the costs associated with data hosting, and, (2) to leverage any available architecture, topology, or device functionality to protect data from corruption or loss.

In the final analysis, you do not manage storage: You manage and protect data, your organization's most irreplaceable asset. You are not a storage manager, but a data manager.

As a data manager, the central challenge that you confront is the challenge of creating cost-effective and manageable infrastructure with the devices and management tools provided for your use by the storage industry. Unfortunately, the industry—apparently oblivious to real-world requirements confronting your shop, instead focused myopically on the advancement of proprietary, noninteroperable technology and market share improvement—isn't making your life any easier.

Month after month, you are besieged by marketing pitches from the vendor community pronouncing as the panacea for all that ails storage half-baked architectures and products that aren't quite ready for business primetime. Just sifting through the marketing hype to discern the underlying technological foundation so that it can be fairly and reasonably assessed can be a daunting task.

Perhaps the most hyped panacea of all in the storage world has been "networked storage"—a high-concept storage architecture whose manifestation in current products is so limited that it delivers very little of the business value proposition advanced by its own visionaries. It is a central theme of this book that none of what the industry currently terms networked storage is actually networked at all: All storage today is server-attached storage by another name. What's worse is that many of the impediments to building intelligent networked storage infrastructures trace their origins to this simple fact.

From this assertion, you may begin to perceive the difference between this book and its predecessor. What you are now reading is not a revised and expanded edition of the original *Holy Grail* primer. It is intended to help the reader to develop a more critical view of products and architecture in order to make better product acquisition decisions, build better infrastructure, and—just maybe—to negotiate better deals with those who are seeking to sell technology to the storage consumer.

I am reasonably sure that this book will not receive the same warm reception from the vendor community that was enjoyed by its predecessor. The first *Holy Grail* was widely adopted by vendors to provide basic storage training for salespersons and customers. From their perspective, it was a "feel good" book, underscoring the many worthwhile accomplishments of the industry up to that point and echoing the widely held platitude that improved storage management was needed. No products or architectures were critiqued or vendors criticized in the first book, which implicitly held that "storage is what it is."

In this book, the proverbial gloves are off. After nearly four years of working with clients who were endeavoring (usually with great pain) to deploy the industry's version of networked storage technology, participating in (and often eavesdropping on) standards groups and industry initiatives and associations, conducting informal chats with industry insiders about "known deficits" in their products, and synthesizing what had I learned in print and on-line columns read by nearly a half million storage technology consumers on a weekly and monthly basis, I have developed a somewhat different attitude than I had in 1999. This new view is reflected in the *Holy Grail of Network Storage Management*.

I now believe that, to arrive at a better understanding of storage technology so that it can be applied judiciously to meet business needs, storage managers need to start asking hard questions of their vendors, ranting and railing about all the snake-oil that is being sold, and generally making themselves into troublemakers from the vendor's perspective, while serving as true ombudsmen for the interests of their own organizations—the consumers of technology. Were this to happen in any kind of numbers, the result would be the beginning of a trend in which consumers demanded the kinds of features and functions they required in a voice so loud and so compelling that vendors would have little choice but to listen.

This "in your face" attitude is probably not what vendors have in mind when they claim that their best customers are educated consumers. It will be interesting to see how well this book resonates with the vendor community as its perspective on the industry is a might less cordial than the vendors are probably used to.

For you, the reader, I hope that this book will help you to puzzle out the issues of storage today and arrive at your own conclusions about the best technologies and architectures to pursue for your companies. This goal is shared by my consulting, training, and research & analysis practices, which were formalized in 2003 as Toigo Partners International LLC and The Data Management Institute LLC.

Please note that, as a living appendix to this book, a website has been set up at *www.stormgt.org*, for your use. If you want to dig deeper into the issues expressed here or that develop over the next four years (or however long it takes for me to convince a publisher that it is time for volume three in this series), please visit *www.it-sense.org* and *www.datainstitute.org* for access to the consulting and information services of Toigo Partners International and The Data Management Institute respectively.

So, let's commence the next leg of our quest for the *Holy Grail of Network Storage Management*. Thanks in advance for your interest and feedback.

Jon William Toigo

ACKNOWLEDGMENTS

This book is dedicated to the many consumers of storage technology with whom I have had the pleasure to meet and speak over the past four years. You have challenged me to move into the role of an active consumer advocate and provided positive and negative feedback on my positions over the years that have helped me to learn and grow. I hope that this dialogue will continue and will expand until your voice is clearly heard and understood by those who develop technology in the Wild West domain of data storage.

I also thank the many "fellow travelers" within the vendor community who have secretly encouraged this book, ventured "off-the-record" views and opinions, and occasionally provided hard information to the author in order to steer me toward a more informed perspective of what is really going on inside the industry. There are many good and honest people working within the development shops of storage vendors and they are laboring in earnest to redress customer problems with effective technology solutions. My criticisms of product shortcomings and hypocritical "marketecture" should not be taken to heart by these good people. Their very existence should give us all hope that the issues raised in this book are not intractable and that there is reason to hope that they will eventually be resolved.

I would also like to single out for appreciation my readers and advisors on this project, including Dean Morash, Randy Chalfant, Mike and July Linett, Michael Alvarado, Bruce Nelson, Deborah Jagoe, in Brazil, Oscar Ernst, and in Europe, Jean-Michel Guillou and Peter Martin: Thank you all for your valuable advice and feedback.

Russ Hall and Tim Moore, and later, John Vacca and Jeffrey Pepper, who together comprised the formal reader/editor contingent at Prentice Hall PTR, are also owed a debt of gratitude for their faith in this project and their helpful commentary on chapter content.

Additionally, I would like to thank the Quantum Corporation Network Storage University staff, Megan McGill, Anna Gough, Saret Britz and the rest of the folks of Terrapinn Party Limited in Australia and South Africa, Jennifer Sioteco and Lenny Heymann of Key3Media, Fritz Nelson and Kevin Cooke of CMP Publications, and the speaker selection folks at TechTarget, marcusevans, Storage Networking World, Storage World Conference, and Forum Stockage, for providing to me many opportunities to speak out over the years on the issues contained in this book.

Finally, I wish to thank my mother-in-law, Loretta "Hobby" Romao for her tireless assistance in keeping our toddlers, Isabella, Carrie Loretta, Vincent, and Mercedes, distracted long enough so Mom and Dad could finish the artwork and the text of this manuscript. Thanks also to my teenagers, Alexandra and Maximilian, for not getting into any of the trouble for which teenagers are notorious while this book was being written.

This book is dedicated to data managers everywhere.

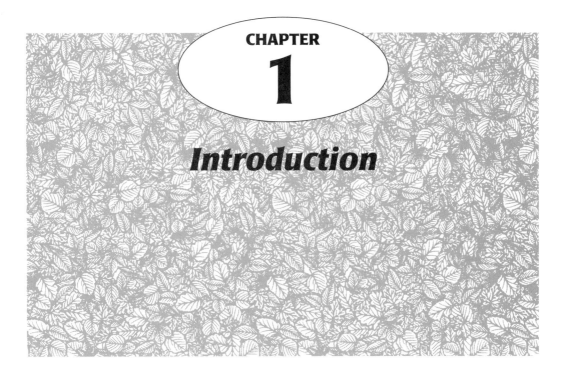

CHAPTER

1

Introduction

Given the high costs associated with enterprise storage in most companies, it might be easy to suspect that some dark and sinister hand is at work. By some analyst accounts, corporate IT departments are spending upward of 60 cents of every dollar budgeted annually for IT hardware to purchase storage platforms. This comes at a time when the per megabyte hardware cost for storage is declining at a rate of about 50 percent per year and the capacity of disk drives is growing (and has been since the late 1990s) at about 120 percent per annum. Given such trends, one might reasonably ask the question, "If storage is getting cheaper, why is it consuming more of my budget today than ever before?"

CONSPIRACY THEORY

If you had a conspiratorial mindset, you might suspect that there was a secret organization at work, a kind of storage vendor cartel laboring in the background to garner a greater and greater percentage of IT spending for the wares of its members. For the sake of argument, let's call them the Engineers for the Accelerated Total Depletion of Information Storage Components (EATDISC).[1]

With a bit of imagination, you can envision the group. Think organized criminal underworld, a la SPECTRE in the 1960s James Bond movies or the Mafiosi capo regimes in contemporary gangster films or cable TV's *The Sopranos*.

You might imagine this group meeting in some isolated alpine retreat, possibly situated in a facility carved out of a jagged rock face somewhere in the Colorado Rocky Mountains, where it would be near the development shops of many storage companies. Picture an assemblage of stone-faced men (and maybe one or two women) wearing $1,500 suits, all seated with their cigars and brandies around a great mahogany table. They listen attentively to one presentation after another, each one describing the progress of various nefarious programs and initiatives intended to bring about the global domination of IT spending by data storage technologies.

Imagine that EATDISC has cultivated "friends" in the technology trade press, where they purchase the bulk of the advertising, and in the industry analyst community, where they buy "friendly" coverage for a small sum of a few hundred thousand dollars per year—small, because it is an infinitesimal fraction of the $25 billion in revenues that disk-based storage was (conservatively) expected to generate in 2002, and smaller still as disk-based storage purchasing climbs to more than $30 billion by 2004.[2] For an investment of what amounts to pocket change, EATDISC virtually ensures that no negative press will surface about its members' products and that the two primary sources of information for end-users regarding their technology options are tightly controlled.

Imagine further that these powerful figures control vast cadres of value-added resellers (VARs) and integrators who recommend EATDISC products as "solutions" to their customers based not on how effectively they will meet actual application requirements, but what profit margin the recommended solution will yield to the reseller/integrator. Their rationale is simple: Why sell a customer one or two components that will deliver a rich, redundant, and manageable solution to his or her immediate problem when you could sell a complex, multicomponent storage area network (SAN) that the customer could "grow into" over time, and that, by coincidence, delivers immediate profits to the reseller and vendor?

Savvy customers would see through such a scam, you think? Not if the customer depends on a "trusted solution provider"—a reseller or integrator—to chart his or her strategic path.[3] Not if the customer has been convinced by analysts' reports and trade press articles that SANs are strategic. Not if the IT manager or chief technology officer or chief information officer finds his or her decision making undercut by vendor or re-seller salespersons who do "end runs" around the company technologists and cultivate sales directly with nontechnical chief financial officers or chief executive officers.

Imagine still further that the organizations responsible for developing "open storage standards" find their efforts stymied by their very openness, which permits representatives of EATDISC member companies to sit on, and in some cases even to chair, standards development committees. The vendor representatives could obfuscate progress on any initiative that might cost their firms "value discriminators," resisting common standards that might that contribute directly or indirectly to the erosion of their company's respective market share leadership. The irony of this situation is that, at the same time as the vendor representative obstructs progress on standards development, the representative's company can legitimately claim to be "actively engaged in the open standards development process," intent as it is upon providing less proprietary solutions for its customers.

Last but not least, imagine that EATDISC was as expert at manipulating the legal system as it was at manipulating data bits. What if large member companies leveraged loopholes in the patent and trademarks registration process to file "blanket patents" that covered all technological development in a given area—even development based on ideas not yet thought of—then used its legal authority to stifle innovation that EAT-DISC did not sanction?

In short, what if such a cartel worked earnestly behind the scenes to ensure that customer hearts and minds and dollars were continuously cultivated to support the acquisition of proprietary and half-baked technologies, premised upon the flimsiest and most untenable of business value propositions, that resisted common management and required forklift upgrades every one or two years?

Taken collectively, the above scenario would certainly provide an explanation for why something that is increasingly a commodity—like disk-based storage technology—is costing organizations more of their IT budget than ever before. Without a doubt, many industry events over the past few years would appear to validate some or all of the conspiracy theory advanced above.

But, of course, the existence of EATDISC is purely paranoiac fantasy. In reality, such a cartel would require levels of discipline and cooperation that the storage industry has never been able to manifest. The possibility of a real-world EATDISK runs afoul of long-standing fears among storage technology vendors that prevent such a cooperative cartel from ever appearing.

THE STORAGE INDUSTRY: FEAR OF STANDARDS
AND COMMODITIZATION

In point of fact, data storage remains one of the few areas of information technology characterized by a paucity of standards—whether open or *de facto*. In this, data storage stands in stark contrast to other technology sectors, where well-defined standards have either:

1. Been articulated by open standards organizations like American National Standards Institute (ANSI), Internet Engineering Task Force (IETF) and adopted across literally all vendor product lines, or
2. Imposed by a single vendor with a commanding market share leadership position (e.g., *de facto* standards).

An example of an open standards-based technology is the network interface card (NIC). In the NIC market, all manufacturers must adhere to a set of formal open standards if they want to sell their products. As a result of open standards, end-users can pick and choose products from the more than 100 products and still achieve their basic goal: connection to an Ethernet network operating the TCP/IP protocol suite, the dominant network protocol in the world today.

Because of open standards for Ethernet and TCP/IP, any NIC card will do the basic job of providing network attachment. Customers can, with confidence, buy a NIC from any vendor, install it in their desktop computer or server, and be sure that their system is ready to be connected to a network.

Of course, to differentiate their products from those of their competitors, some vendors "add value" to their NICs by adding features such as "Wake on LAN" or special TCP offload engine (TOE) chips, but the basic standards-based functionality is available whether the consumer buys the enhanced NIC or its less expensive "bare bones" cousin.

In the final analysis, consumers are the beneficiaries of open standards because such standards level the playing field between vendors, enable the "apples-to-apples" comparisons of different products, and provide customers with assurances of baseline compatibility that, in turn, frees them to consider options for purchase on the basis of feature, function, and price. The presence of open standards in the network space is owed to the work of a generation of network technology start-ups who sought to unseat a previous generation of proprietary network technology vendors, and also of a unified consumer voice that voted with their checkbooks for open standards-based products.

Standards breed commoditization, of course. And commoditization of technology exerts a downward pressure on product prices. That is why a gigabit Ethernet switch that cost $3,000 per port in late 2000 dropped precipitously to about $450 per port in late 2001 and today hovers at around $300. As more standards-compliant switches came to market that provided essentially the same business value, most customers preferred products that were less expensive to comparable products that were more expensive. The result of this purchasing pattern has been price erosion, another feature of open standards-based technology and one that nearly always works to the benefit of the consumer.

Another example of a technology segment "blessed" (from the consumer's standpoint, at least) by standards is the PC market. As of this writing, about 80 percent of personal computer operating systems (OS) bear the logo of Microsoft. The Windows OS is a *de facto* standard in desktop computing. Of course, Windows was never formally ratified as an open standard by an official standards body, but, by sheer presence in the market, the Microsoft OS dominates all contenders.

The result of a *de facto* standard is similar to that of an open standard in at least one respect: It fosters compatibility. The dominance of Microsoft, in turn, drives most independent software vendors (ISVs) to develop application software to run on the platform. For example, this tax season, an end-user can go to a local computer software store and select from among several personal tax preparation software packages from several ISVs, any of which will run on his or her Windows-based PC.

Whether or not you prefer the Microsoft platform is beside the point. The fact that nearly every desktop application software package will operate under the Windows operating system means that the application software products compete on a level playing field imposed by a *de facto* standard. Vendors must add features and functions to their products, or offer licenses under an attractive pricing scheme, if they want to compete. Again, the beneficiary of competition in a standards-based realm is the consumer.

Storage lacks both open and *de facto* standards. And the industry resists virtually any effort to impose meaningful standards (whether by a standards-making body or by one of its own members) that might compromise proprietary advantage for the vendor. Insights offered by many storage industry insiders underscore this position.

For example, a representative of one of the industry's largest disk array vendors tells the tale of how his management's biggest fear is that there will be a repeat, in the storage array business, of what happened in the disk drive business in the mid-1990s. In the late 1980s and early 1990s, disk drives featured proprietary technologies ranging from vendor-specific interfaces and low-level drive formats to specialized actuator arm and read/write head designs. This diversity ensured that Brand X products worked very differently from Brand Y and that consumers would be locked in to a particular vendor's technology. As a consequence, drive prices remained very high and margins were lucrative for disk drive manufacturers.

With the arrival of the Small Computer Systems Interface (SCSI) standard, however, this picture changed. SCSI provided a standards-based mechanism for communicating with storage devices and had the effect of standardizing drive electronics and interfaces. SCSI was not the only standard for disk drive interfaces—other standards emerged at about the same time, including IDE/ATA. However, the overall impact of standards was to reduce disk drive products to the level of commodity or stock items.

Prices eroded dramatically as low-cost, standards-compliant drives flooded the market from mass producers. According to the source, the greatest fear at his company—a large integrated disk array manufacturer—is that it could happen again. Originally, the taxonomy offered by researchers at the University of California at Berkeley to describe various Redundant Arrays of Independent Disks (so-called RAID levels) was suspected of introducing a commoditizing effect in storage arrays. However, as documented in *The Holy Grail of Data Storage Management*, vendors treated the UC-Berkeley definitions less as a standard taxonomy than as a useful point of reference for describing their varied implementation of disk redundancy schemes. Some even coined RAID levels to describe their products that weren't in the UC Berkeley taxonomy at all. However, this isn't the end of the story.

The same fear of standards-based commoditization has echoed and re-echoed in the public statements of leading storage industry spokespersons over the past couple of years. At a storage networking conference in spring 2001, the then-CEO for a market share leading company in storage arrays noted that the reason his company was transitioning from a hardware-focused to software-focused model was to leverage the only differentiator that remained to distinguish his products from those of his competitors: namely, intellectual property captured in the form of software on his company's arrays. Without software, said the CEO, there was no difference between his products and those of his nearest competitor: "We both just sell a box of Seagate hard drives." That statement underscored the fear of lost differentiation in the market as storage hardware became less proprietary and more commoditized.

As standards drive commoditization, vendors know that they must find new ways to realize proprietary technology-based margins from otherwise commoditized hardware technology. Sometimes, this takes the form of resistance to standards efforts altogether.

According to a spokesperson for a Fibre Channel "SAN"[4] switchmaker in 1999, "A real storage area network—one based on truly open standards and capable of supporting heterogeneous storage arrays (i.e., arrays from different product manufacturers)—will probably never appear in the market. If a real SAN did appear, Joe's JBODs (an abbreviation for Just a Bunch of Disks) would perform exactly the same as high-end, 'name brand,' proprietary arrays, which cost ten times as much. The 'name brand' vendor's customers would quickly realize that they had been paying way too much for storage."[5]

"Under those circumstances," the fellow continued, "do you really think that the leading vendor would allow his arrays to be included in an open SAN?"

The question crystallizes much of what has Balkanized early SAN standards development efforts, as well as bringing into sharp focus the concerns that vendors have about open standards and their commoditizing effect on products.

Another Industry Concern: The Rise of a Dominant Player

Arguably, the only thing that strikes more fear into the hearts of storage technology companies than open standards-based product commoditization is the fear that one of their peers will achieve such market dominance that it will be able to impose its own technology as a *de facto* standard on the entire industry—à la Microsoft in the desktop world.

Evidence of this concern can be inferred from the brief history of the Storage Networking Industry Association (SNIA). SNIA is a quasi-standards group comprised of vendors of storage technology products and services—the brainchild of several well-intentioned (and possibly idealistic) storage industry analysts and insiders who perceived a need, in the absence of standards for storage networks, to provide a forum for "co-opetition" (a blend of cooperation and competition) among storage vendors.

Among other things, SNIA was set up to foster informal agreements between vendors on their implementations of networked storage technology so that the entire storage networking initiative would not fall prey to petty vendor infighting. The interoperability difficulties in the Fibre Channel SANs of the late 1990s were proof positive to the founders that some sort of SNIA-like body was needed.

The fact is, however, that SNIA never received the full backing of the industry until a major storage vendor, EMC Corporation, announced its own competing alliance of companies, the Fibre Alliance, to advance the vendor's own view of how storage networks should work. Rather than allow a single vendor achieve the status of a broker of *de facto* standards, EMC's competitors turned their attention to SNIA and joined up with the fledgling organization in droves.[6]

This phenomenon repeated itself in 2002 when a number of vendors, troubled by the unilateral move of one of their peers (EMC, again) to advance its own model for universal storage management, decided to counter the initiative by supporting a common management approach under development at SNIA: Common Information Model/Web-based Enterprise Management (CIM/WBEM). Until that time, vendors had paid only lip service to CIM, making no real provisions for CIM-based management in their own platforms or products. However, the fear of an emerging *de facto* standard, in the form of EMC's AutoIS initiative and WideSky "middleware," compelled vendors to "take the pledge" at the Storage Networking World conference in Palm Desert, California, in Spring 2002 and to promise CIM-manageable platforms by year's end![7]

Whether or not the industry keeps its pledge to embrace a CIM-based management standard remains to be seen, of course. Cynics suggest that once the specter of single vendor dominance in universal storage management recedes, CIM developers at SNIA will see considerable backsliding among the newly converted. No one, after all, really wants a universal storage management standard.

In the past, those who suggested that consumers might benefit from an open cross-platform standards-based storage management methodology were met by cold stares from storage manufacturers—reminiscent of Anthony Hopkin's character, Hannibal Lecter, in the film version of the Thomas Harris novel, *Silence of the Lambs*. At the risk of belaboring the metaphor, in one scene from the popular film, the hero, a female FBI agent named Clarice Starling, passes a questionnaire to Lecter that is intended to gather information about the serial murderer's psychology for the FBI's behavioral science database. Hopkins, as Lecter, levels a cold, unwavering stare at Starling and asks in a calm and calculated tone whether she believes she can really "dissect" him with such a blunt instrument (i.e., the survey).

This is exactly the response that one could have expected from a storage manufacturer prior to the spring 2002 CIM announcement: It was heresy for anyone to suggest that there was enough common ground among all of the 17-odd thousand storage platform products in the market that would enable their management by a common management methodology such as CIM.[8] The very idea was as heretical to storage vendors as it once was to Compaq and other PC and server manufacturers when the Desktop Management Task Force (DMTF) first tried to apply the CIM strategy to PC management in the early 1990s.

THE ROAD TO UNIFICATION?

Of course, despite the deep-seated fears of commoditization and of the emergence of a single market share leader, there have been some cooperative development efforts—occasions when storage vendors seemed to rise a bit above the quagmire of storage industry politics. In some instances, cooperation between competitors was the result of self-interest and a response to clearly articulated consumer demands—particularly, when such demands emanate from *Fortune* 100 customers, who, analysts claim, collectively account for more than 60 percent of annual storage industry revenues.

An example of this dynamic was the development of Fibre Channel over IP (FCIP), a protocol for tunneling Fibre Channel–based storage commands and data between distant "SAN islands" using a TCP/IP network. In late 2000, several large enterprise customers—common to both Brocade Communications Systems, a Fibre Channel fabric switch vendor, and Cisco Systems, an IP networking technology goliath—demanded that their vendors work together to deliver such a tunneling protocol to interconnect small Fibre Channel SANs at geographically dispersed locations. An announcement of a joint initiative between the companies met surprised looks from attendees at the press conference where it was made. Only weeks before, spokespersons for Cisco, who advocated the use of IP networks, rather than Fibre Channel, to provide the plumbing for storage area networks, had criticized the Fibre Channel Industry Association's announcement of a forthcoming two-speed (or 2 Gigabit-per-second) version of its protocol, calling it "yesterday's bandwidth tomorrow." Cisco posited that 10-speed gigabit Ethernet, at 10 gigabits per second, would appear in the market shortly, mitigating the value of the accelerated FC protocol.

However, on an October morning in 2000, cooperation was the theme, and prior competitive utterances by the companies were described as water under the bridge. Representatives of Cisco and Brocade appeared together at the press event and described the synergies between the two companies and their desire to work together to meet the needs of their common customers. FCIP was developed from the initiative, referred to the IETF for consideration as a standard, and work began on creating a blade for a Cisco switch to support FC tunneling.

In June 2002, however, the relationship between the two companies was severed by Cisco with all the trappings of an ugly Hollywood divorce. The IP networking equipment manufacturer claimed that the goal of developing a tunneling protocol that could be supported on all Fibre Channel switches remained valid, but that the implementation of the protocol had been corrupted by Brocade, which had helped engineer the solution so that it would only work with its own switches. Still, an IETF open standards protocol was born of the initiative.

Another example of industry cooperation was BlueFin, a joint undertaking of several erstwhile storage market competitors intended to advance the cause of Fibre Channel SAN interoperability. Bluefin's creators (who comprised most major storage platform manufacturers in 2002, as well as several prominent storage management software vendors) held what could be described as secret meetings for about six months and, at a cost of nearly $500,000, produced an open standards-based mechanism that enabled the products of different vendors to "discover" each other in the same Fibre Channel SAN (fabric). BlueFin was hailed as a huge breakthrough in heterogeneous Fibre Channel SAN development, and one that laid the groundwork for subsequent management services that are not supported in the Fibre Channel protocol itself.[9]

The jury is still out on the true meaning and importance of BlueFin, which has since been turned over to SNIA for further development as "SMI-S," but it is reasonably certain that the vendors involved in its development were compelled to cooperate both by the slower-than-expected adoption rate of FC SANs and also by often-heard complaints of their largest customers, many of whom had fielded heterogeneous storage platforms over the years and saw the lack of support of Fibre Channel SANs for heterogeneous configurations as an impediment to implementation of the technology. Now, as then, few companies have been willing to do a "forklift upgrade" of their existing storage investment in order to deploy a homogeneous Fibre Channel SAN. Most savvy consumers vocalize deep concerns over the ultimate impact of homogeneous storage architecture: dependency on a single vendor.

These and other examples testify to the fact that, to storage vendors, the only thing more frightening than commoditization, and single vendor dominance, is consumer revolt. In the current economic reality, one in which cash-strapped consumers are putting off storage acquisitions and looking for ways to leverage storage networking and storage management technologies to curb IT costs, the pressure is on the vendor community to facilitate their needs. The cost of failure could be the decision by the consumer to give its business to an eager-to-please competitor—and competitors are in no short supply.

YESTERDAY'S RESELLERS, TOMORROW'S COMPETITORS

In fact, new storage start-ups are appearing at a more rapid pace than ever before. In many cases, these start-ups are not strangers to storage, but, to the contrary, are staffed and managed by former insiders or resellers of an established vendor.

As former insiders, the newcomers know the foibles of their previous employers and of their products. As solution architects and engineers, many resellers have the skills to develop comparable product offerings to those of leading vendors that offer full "backward compatibility" with the products of their former suppliers, while offering improved functionality at a lower price point.

Take, for example, the case of a Newark, Rhode Island-based reseller of NAS solutions. In 2002, the company moved from the role of reseller to the role of competitor in response to the draconian marketing practices initiated by equipment suppliers, who were themselves attempting to address the general economic slowdown. Today, the reseller's product is every bit as capable as the leading products in the NAS market, but at a fraction of the cost.

As happened over and over again after February 2001, the storage technology supplier, a publicly-traded firm, sought to improve its quarterly earning reports by redrawing its sales territories and reassigning its most lucrative customer accounts (heretofore managed by resellers) to its own internal direct sales force. The move, which cost the Rhode Island reseller considerable income, fostered a desire to create a competitive product that was "plug and pin" compatible with the supplier's product, but redressed certain "margin-enhancing" features of the supplier's product to cut its expense.

For example, the supplier was selling as part of its NAS solution disk drives priced at three times the cost of the drives on the open market. The supplier ensured that only its drives could be used with its network-attached storage "head" (the thin server component of a NAS) by placing a proprietary block format on the drives. Consumers were denied access to the drive formatting utility that could be used to format less expensive drives, readily obtained on the open market, for use with the vendor's platform.

By removing the special formatting step and using commodity disks, the reseller was able to reduce the cost for his "new" product, while at the same time ensuring that customers who already had an investment in his former supplier's products could preserve that investment and use their older drives and trays with his new NAS head. Such a scenario is repeating itself over and over in the industry today—to the chagrin of brand-name vendors.

While the business motives that drive some vendors to seize control of the most lucrative accounts from their resellers are understandable, the practice is somewhat short-sighted. Virtually every industry observer who has monitored the emergence of networked storage has noted the close link between NAS and SAN adoption rates and the sales education efforts of channel partners (resellers/integrators.) Of the 11,000 or so SANs deployed in the market at the time of this book, the preponderance have been sold to customers by reseller/integrators who have been better situated to educate consumers and to dedicate the necessary time to account cultivation than the minimalist direct sales forces that most equipment manufacturers would permit. Vendors ignore this relationship between channels and NAS/SAN adoption at their own peril. What's more, it is unwise to anger channel partners who possess the engineering talent and the knowledge of their products and access to the vendor's own parts suppliers, and who therefore have the ability to manufacture competitive products at reduced cost to the consumer.

A further gap in the wisdom of the vendors who "disrespected" their channel partners was evidenced by subsequent failure of direct sales in many cases. Direct sales forces are an expense that many vendors have found themselves unable to bear as the economy worsened. It was not unusual, therefore, to see renewed cultivation of channel partnerships in 2002, following massive layoffs of direct sales staff that the vendors could no longer afford to keep on the payroll.

In the final analysis, economic downturns have the twin effect of 1) bringing to the surface increased price sensitivity among consumers (and, in many cases, an increased willingness to try comparable products that cost less money) and 2) opening the door for plug and pin compatible products that provide viable alternatives for the established vendor's products. Some of the brand names of today, including EMC and parts of Hitachi Data Systems, were born of just such economic downturns in the 1980s that increased the vulnerability of dominant vendor IBM to competitive products.

The bottom line is that economic challenge breeds competition and competition, in turn, fuels consumer perceptions of commoditization by providing numerous "generic" alternatives for expensive "brand-name" technologies.

ABOUT THIS BOOK

All of the above simply sets the stage for the chapters that follow. The storage technology business provides a backdrop that explains some of the confusion that keeps the emergence of a true storage infrastructure, one defined by common management and automated, policy-driven intelligence, a "holy grail."

In the following pages, you will learn of the technological trends that are forcing storage into networked topologies and the challenges and opportunities that are created by this shift. In particular, you will look at the state of disk-drive technology futures, the inevitable outcome of limits to growth in disk-based storage and the drivers that this provides for a networked storage paradigm.

You will further examine the claims of networked storage advocates and evaluate their applicability in the face of current technology capabilities and limitations. Much of the hyperbole around networked storage is patently false: pure "marketecture" that consumers need to see for what it is in order to avoid ill-advised or ill-fated buying decisions. (Marketecture is the author's coined phrase describing an otherwise valid technological concept or solution that has been placed in the hands of a vendor's marketing department.)

You will focus on practical examples, drawn from the real world, to demonstrate what of the burgeoning network storage technology works, what doesn't, and what's needed. And you will look at the application-storage nexus in detail to describe best practices for developing effective storage strategy. As of this writing, the network storage industry appears to have created confusion in many minds about the proper focus for data storage, its design, and its management. Given the primordial state of current SAN technology, it is obvious that storage management strategies that focus on managing storage device capacity utilization and component operations are inadequate to the task of storage management. The application must drive the management of storage since it provides the metric that is ultimately used to discern how well the storage infrastructure itself is managed.

Finally, you will look at fruitful new areas of storage technology development, emphasizing object-oriented schemes for data classification and lifecycle management as the *sine qua non* of storage management.

Managing data in a networked storage setting is ultimately the only effective way to manage storage itself.

Bottom line: if you are looking for a primer about data storage component and platform technology, the author invites you to consult *The Holy Grail of Data Storage Management*, which is also available from this publisher. If you understand the components and you are ready to start becoming strategic about storage while solving immediate and evolving problems, those that contribute the lion's share of the cost to your constrained IT budgets, you are in the right place.

ENDNOTES

1. The idea of EATDISC first appeared in an October 2001 *Enterprise Systems* magazine column, written by the author.
2. These market revenue estimates are mean numbers derived from numerous industry analyst market estimates—each of which, by itself, strikes the author as suspect for a wide range of reasons.
3. Based on the author's research, reported in various trade press publications, U.S. government agencies and departments largely rely on integrators and resellers to define their strategic goals. While less prevalent in the private sector, the outsourcing of "strategic planning" to "trusted solution providers" appears to be a growing trend in the commercial sector, as well as organizations cutting their IT staff and management in response to the negative economic conditions prevailing at the time of this writing.
4. Using the terms Fibre Channel and SAN in connection is commonplace in the industry, though oxymoronical in technical terms. Fibre Channel is a serial storage interconnect that can be deployed in a switched fabric topology. It is not, however, a network protocol and cannot be used to create a network—only a fabric of point-to-point connections switched at high speed. Readers should be aware of this very important difference, which will be discussed in greater detail later in this book.
5. The name of the quoted party is being withheld at his request, though the author cited the speaker in a trade press article published in 1998. Since making the statement, the speaker's company has engaged in a strategic business relationship with the very hardware array manufacturer that was cited in the statement. The speaker asked to have his name removed from the quote (despite the fact that it is one of the more intelligent things anyone ever said about impediments to SANs in the industry) because, in the present business nexus, it was a "career limiting quotation."
6. EMC also joined SNIA, but has been accused from time to time of being an "undependable advocate" of SNIA initiatives—especially when they were at

cross-purposes to EMC's own interests. The same criticism can be leveled at virtually every one of SNIA's members at one time or another.

7. Taking the pledge is a description derived from various self-help groups popular around the time of the SNW announcement of CIM support. Developed by the author in a humorous column for Enterprise Systems magazine written shortly after the press event, it suggests that vendors approached the podium one after another, admitted that they had only supported proprietary management schemes up to that point, and pledged to support an open standards-based approach, CIM, going forward. As in most self-help programs, some "backsliding"—that is, deviation from the pledged path or course of action—is to be expected.

8. In fact, CIM advocates, such as Mark Carlson, a network storage engineer for Sun Microsystems who also oversees CIM development at SNIA, would argue that CIM is not a one-size-fits-all management method. Each device can have a unique Managed Object Format (MOF) that describes the customized features and functions unique to that device. Still, the industry resists the notion that any universal management method, including CIM, could ever capture the "secret sauce" diversity in 17,000-plus competing storage products. Conceding that it could might create the impression in consumer minds that no important differentiators existed between products bearing different brand names.

9. As per the previous note, Fibre Channel was not designed to serve as the plumbing of a SAN. It lacked, as documented in a Road Map whitepaper written by this author on behalf of the Fibre Channel Industry Association in 2001, "fabric services" for in-band device discovery, management, security, etc. that a real network protocol would have provided. BlueFin, if nothing else, adds an important fabric service that should have been provided in any real SAN plumbing solution from the outset.

The Data Explosion and Matters of the Disk

Read just about any treatise on data storage today—whether a vendor brochure, an analyst white paper, a pundit column, or an industry trade press article—and you will likely discover a recurring theme about unprecedented rates of data growth. The popular code phrase for the phenomenon is "the data explosion."

A strange kind of new mythology has grown up around the rate of data growth and its relationship to strategic storage planning and networked storage technology acquisitions. Those who promulgate this myth argue that data is doubling every year or so and that this trend is driving the adoption of storage area networks (SANs) by IT managers everywhere.

Proponents of the view—mainly, vendors of Fibre Channel SAN products—seem bent upon elevating the myth of a data explosion to the status of a self-evident truth. There is an old saw that a lie, told often enough, becomes the truth. FC SAN vendors seem to be depending on this axiom to build and bolster a business case for their products.

This chapter discusses the myth and reality of data growth within the context of networked storage. It is offered in the hopes of aiding you in cultivating a more critical mindset that may be of assistance as you sift through the value propositions and evaluate the products offered by vendors, analysts, and other information brokers for the storage industry.

THE DATA EXPLOSION MYTH

About the time of the publication of *The Holy Grail of Data Storage Management* (late 1999 to early 2000), analysts had just begun making the rounds of the storage industry tradeshow circuit to articulate their now-familiar rant about the data explosion that confronted contemporary business organizations. They contended that rates of data growth were predictable and exponential across all organizations. Depending on the analyst, the quantity of data generated by contemporary businesses was growing at an average rate of between 60 to 120 percent per year.

Some credence was given to these estimates by the selective reading of a study produced at the University of California at Berkeley, a study sponsored coincidentally by a leading storage industry vendor. The UC Berkeley study found that the total volume of digital information produced up to the year 2000 would double in 2002.[1] Researchers claimed that approximately two exabytes (10^{18} bytes) of electronic data had been generated by millennium's end (see Table 2–1), and that a rough doubling of this total volume would be seen by 2002.

Within the storage industry, the study was hailed as an academic validation of all the ballyhoo about the data explosion. Vendors seized on the "empirical evidence" in the Berkeley study to make their case for a data explosion, but ignored the fact that the researchers had carefully caveated their findings and had produced a lower estimate of data volume that was about a quarter of the total volume in the upper estimate. They further ignored another finding of the Berkeley professors that the preponderance of new data was *not* being generated by organizations nor stored on enterprise storage subsystems. Instead, private individuals were creating most of the flood of digital data in what the researchers called "the democratization of data" and were storing their JPEG camera images, their AVI and MPEG digital videos, their e-books, and their personal email on their own PC hard disks.

Thus, it was actually a rather selective reading of the Berkeley study that was used by vendors to reinforce claims about the data explosion. Nevertheless, the myth of the data explosion was subsequently harnessed to another purpose. Specifically, it was used to explain and to justify why

Table 2–1 University of California at Berkeley's Estimates of Digital Data Volume by 2000

Storage Medium	Type of Content	Terabytes/Year, Upper Estimate	Terabytes/Year, Lower Estimate	Growth Rate, %
Paper	Books	8	1	2
	Newspapers	25	2	-2
	Periodicals	12	1	2
	Office documents	195	19	2
	Subtotal:	**240**	**23**	**2**
Film	Photographs	410,000	41,000	5
	Cinema	16	16	3
	X-Rays	17,200	17,200	2
	Subtotal:	**427,216**	**58,216**	**4**
Optical	Music CDs	58	6	3
	Data CDs	3	3	2
	DVDs	22	22	100
	Subtotal:	**83**	**31**	**70**
Magnetic	Camcorder Tape	300,000	300,000	5
	PC Disk Drives	766,000	7,660	100
	Departmental Servers	460,000	161,000	100
	Enterprise Servers	167,000	108,550	100
	Subtotal:	**1,693,000**	**577,210**	**55**
TOTAL:		**2,120,539**	**635,480**	**50**

Source: Lyman, Peter and Hal R. Varian, "How Much Information," 2000. Retreived from http://www.sims.berkley.edu/how-much-info on 8/12/2003.

networked storage technology—SAN in particular—was a "must have" for businesses. Only through the consolidation and centralization of burgeoning digital information into a storage network, the vendors argued, could companies hope to meet storage scalability requirements imposed by the data explosion in a cost-effective way.

A key argument of the vendors held that a SAN was required to overcome the limitations to scaling imposed by the dominant storage topology of today: server-attached storage (SAS). Figure 2–1 depicts the difference between SAS and SAN.

With server-attached storage (sometimes called direct-attached storage, or DAS), increasing storage platform capacity required that more disk drives be added to the array connected to an application host. To accomplish this task, first, the applications hosted on the server needed to be quiesced and the server itself had to be powered down. Next, the attached

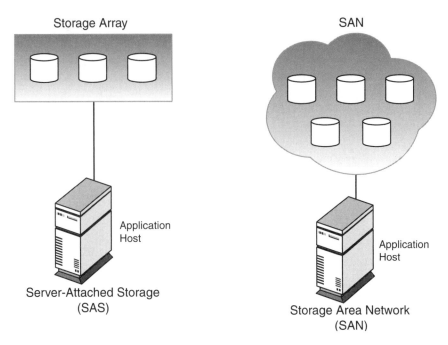

Figure 2–1   SAN versus SAS topologies.

storage array had to be upgraded with additional disks. Then, the host had to be powered up again, its operating system rebooted, and the volumes created on the newly expanded array properly registered with the server OS.

Scaling SAS in the manner described above, SAN vendors argued, created a great deal of costly downtime for organizations. Given the data explosion, such costs were bound to increase in frequency and duration. Clearly, said the vendors, an alternative—and "non-disruptive"—storage scaling approach was needed.

Fibre Channel SANs provided just such an option, vendors claimed. In a FC SAN, storage volume size could be increased without rebooting a single server, because storage and servers were separate. Just add more disk drives to a SAN volume, even while it was operating to process read and write requests from servers, and, magically, application server operating systems and their hosted application software would "see" the additional storage and begin using it.

There are many problems with the above description of volume scaling in a FC SAN, of course, and these will be fodder for discussion later in this book. For now, we will content ourselves with the argument of the vendors: that their dynamically scalable storage volumes made storage area networks THE mission critical storage infrastructure technology for coping with the data explosion.

On its face, this argument was both airtight and tautological. If you accepted the initial premise, exploding data growth, you had to concede the need for a highly scalable storage topology—a theoretical capability of a true SAN.[2]

DECONSTRUCTING THE DATA EXPLOSION MYTH

However, the first premise of the data explosion myth—"the predictable and exponential rate of growth of data in all organizations"—was, and is, a myth. The truth is that analysts have no way of knowing the average rate of data growth in organizations. They lack empirical data, and instead use data on the aggregated capacity of storage products sold into the market as rough guidance. In other words, the analysts are extrapolating trends from highly suspect data sets (vendor sales projections).

At a recent industry conference, this author had the pleasure of chairing a panel discussion that included several leading storage industry analysts. The event afforded an opportunity to query one analyst about the basis for his 100-percent-per-annum data growth rate projection. His first response was to "negotiate": "Okay, perhaps it is closer to 70 percent per year." Pressed further, he conceded that there was no exact way of knowing average rates of data growth, and that storage manufacturers themselves had provided much of his data. The audience chuckled, and the analyst, taken aback, added, "Well, I did poll a number of end-users who told me that the numbers seemed to be in line with the experience in their shops."

Since that time, analysts have protested over and over again that their data growth projections are validated by interviews with clients who are both end-users of storage technology and also subscribers to the analyst's reporting and analytical services. The problems with this argument are many.

- It is based on inductive reasoning: The practice of generalizing from a few specific examples is hardly a logical foundation for discerning trends. A deductive approach has long been preferred to an inductive approach for confirming the validity of any theory, especially in the absence of extremely large empirical data sets with a high degree of reliability. (Figure 2–2 shows the difference for anyone who missed logic class in school.)

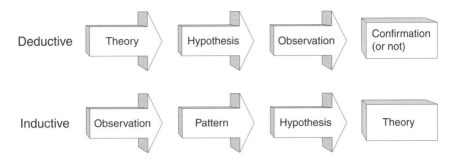

Figure 2–2 Inductive versus deductive reasoning.

- It depends on the accuracy of input from surveyed customers: Most IT professionals (and their solution providers) will tell you that the majority of businesses are clueless about actual rates of data growth in their storage environments. There is so much stale data, unnecessarily replicated data, junk data, and non-business-related data stored on corporate disk drives that data growth rate analyses, if indeed any are performed, reveal grossly inflated growth rates. Moreover, surveying end-users is a process that is notorious for being subject to corruption. Respondents will prevaricate for any number of reasons—to increase funding for preferred acquisitions, to appear "intelligent" to the interviewer, to justify or conceal bad decision making or poor acquisition choices, etc. So, end-user reports are suspect all around.

- The augmentation of consumer survey data with storage platform expenditure data proves nothing: Substituting storage platform expenditures/revenues for actual data growth assessments may seem like an acceptable practice to understand the data explosion, but it really isn't. In many shops, new storage platform acquisitions do not reflect data growth, but poor data management. For example, in the absence of effective storage capacity management and provisioning tools, applications may appear to need an ongoing infusion of additional disks mounted in the cabinets of standalone storage arrays. However, with effective provisioning tools, it may be possible for the high demand application to obtain additional resources from the storage platforms whose capacities are allocated to low demand applications. This, in turn, would forestall the need for more storage arrays. In such a case, the rate of data growth will not have changed, only the effectiveness of the use of existing resources. However, the rate of data growth would not be intuitively obvious if one looks merely at expenditures for new storage arrays.

The cynic might claim that the industry analysts worked in cahoots with storage vendors to create the specter of a data explosion. While such an allegation would be difficult to prove, it is interesting to note that the data explosion myth became the mantra of analysts at just about the same time that interest was waning in the analyst community's ongoing work in such "red herring" issue areas[3] as thin computing, first-generation application service provisioning, and "the dot.com revolution." It may have been a coincidence that the data explosion myth appeared at the very moment that the analyst community needed a new "cash cow"—an original hot topic to drive the sale of their information products and services. Certainly, for many industry analysis firms, the appearance of the data explosion was certainly serendipitous.

In point of fact, the only way for analysts to obtain good information on rates of data growth is to consult end users that have implemented exhaustive analyses of their current storage capacity utilization trends. This kind of data is rare because of the effort and cost involved in collecting it. Most companies have limited data to substantiate presumed rates of data growth and many report, after deploying storage topology discovery tools, that they found storage platforms nested away in closets and equipment rooms that they didn't even know existed!

The bottom line is that claims of a data explosion are largely unsubstantiated, an inference based on flimsy evidence. While it is doubtless that data is growing rapidly in many organizations, just how rapidly is a matter of conjecture—especially, in the absence of effective storage management.

At NASA's Goddard Space Flight Center, it took the earnest efforts of a team of researchers, armed mainly with tenacity and a mandate, nearly two years to produce a meaningful estimate of data growth (over 1 TB of new data would be added daily commencing in year 2000).[4] Data on capacity utilization trends was certainly difficult to come by in a complex environment like GSFC, and it required the allocation of scarce resources by Dr. Milton Halem, then GSFC's gifted and dedicated chief information officer, who was in need of the data to develop a strategic plan for cost-efficient IT growth and expansion. Few people in the public or private sector have exercised as much due diligence in finding out the facts of storage growth in their own environments.

The explanations for this deficit are several. Many have told this author that the software tools for ferreting out data growth trends are inadequate to the task, and that without the software, the job is simply too difficult to complete. Others have observed that it may not be data that is out of control, but end-users. Particularly with the advent of email, storage managers lack any effective way to police data growth rates because end-users have the ultimate control over what data gets saved and what data is discarded. Still others have decried the lack of consistent or enforced storage administration policies as the culprit behind unmanaged data growth: Chief Information Officers (CIOs) change every 18 to 24 months in many firms and each new executive brings in his or her own preferences as to vendors, technology, and policies. Moreover, in many organizations, the management of IT is not centralized at all, and corporate IT professionals complain that it is difficult or impossible to gain the cooperation of individual departmental or business unit managers—or individual system administrators—to come up with information on data growth or a set of policies for managing it.

In the final analysis, most organizations have no idea about the rate of data growth within their own shops. They only know that unmanaged growth is costing them money. Every time a server issues a "disk full" error message in response to an application write request, downtime accrues while technical staff add disk to their array or cart out another server with a new array attached.

FACT AND FICTION IN NETWORKED STORAGE

The panacea solution offered to the data explosion by the storage industry is summarized in the catch-all expression "networked storage." Networked storage is a "marketecture" term encompassing, at present, storage area networks (SAN) and network-attached storage (NAS).

In the writings of the industry (brochures, white papers, trade press articles, etc.), networked storage is often described as a revolutionary departure from traditional server-attached storage (sometimes called "server-captive" storage). In essence, it comprises topologies that separate storage platforms into their own infrastructure, enabling

- Storage scaling without application disruption,
- Enhanced storage accessibility,
- Storage self-management, and
- Intelligent and automatic storage provisioning and maintenance.

One of the first descriptions of networked storage appeared in a visionary white paper from Compaq Corporation, which was discussed in the previous *Holy Grail* book. With its acquisition of Digital Equipment Corporation in the 1990s, Compaq also acquired a conceptual design for networked storage called the Enterprise Network Storage Architecture (ENSA), which it promulgated in a white paper of the same name in 1997.

ENSA envisioned a utility storage infrastructure that delivered the capabilities enumerated above: scalability, accessibility, manageability, and intelligence. At least at first, Compaq did not leverage claims of a data explosion to justify the value of the ENSA infrastructure: ENSA simply provided an elegant and evolutionary strategy for enterprise data storage.

If anything, ENSA anticipated the diminishing revenues possible from an increasingly commoditized disk market and the need for vendors to "add value" to their storage platform offerings with software and services. The ENSA authors may also have anticipated the realities of superparamagnetism and its impact on disk storage itself.

It is a well-documented fact that disk drives have been increasing in capacity and decreasing in cost fairly consistently since the mid-1990s. According to industry watchers, disk capacity has doubled about every 18 months, while disk prices have been cut in half every 12 months (see Figure 2–3). This dynamic has been an engine of growth in terms of the quantity of storage products sold over the past decade, and has had the unfortunate side effect of encouraging consumers to address poor data management practices by throwing more and more inexpensive disks at the problems that mismanagement creates.

In 2000, however, an interesting fact about magnetic disk storage resurfaced: There were fixed limits to hard disk areal density (bits per square inch of data that could be reliably written and read from a disk platter), given conventional disk drive technology. These limits to magnetic storage capacity were imposed by a reality of physics called the superparamagnetic effect. And, at current rates of disk drive capacity improvement, the limits to growth in disk would be reached as early as 2005 or 2006.

Superparamagnetism is, simply stated, the point at which the magnetic energy used to hold data bits written to disk media in their recorded state becomes equal to the thermal energy generated by drive operations. Exceeding this limit would cause random bit flipping and make disk storage unreliable.

The specter of disk density limitations imposed by the superparamagnetic effect had been raised many times in the past by vendors. However, it had become so great a source of embarrassment when one manufacturer announced a fixed limit on disk size, only to be "corrected" by a competitor who claimed that its superior technology allowed the construction of a more capacious disk, that most vendors had decided not to talk about it in public.

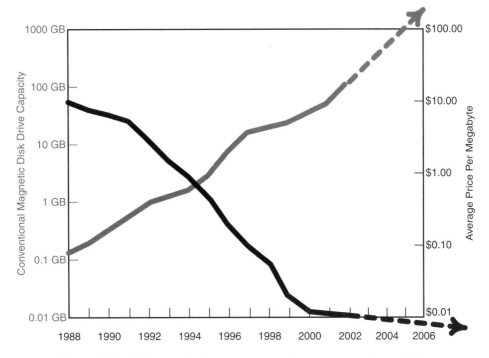

Figure 2–3   Disk capacity improvement and cost-per-megabyte decline.

However, in 2000, as I worked on an article on the subject for *Scientific American*,[5] leading manufacturers grudgingly provided their "best guess" estimates for the "superparamagnetic limit": 150 gigabits per square inch (Gb/in.²). This prognosis was unanimous among leading disk manufacturers, including Seagate, Hewlett-Packard, Quantum, and IBM. Barring some unforeseen breakthrough in media materials, the best areal density that could be obtained from current disk technology was fixed at 150 Gb/in.²—and, given the rates of disk growth (120 percent per year), that limit was fast approaching (see Figure 2–4).

Other exotic technologies, such as perpendicular recording, thermally assisted recording, near or far field recording (NFR/FFR), atomic force resolution, and even holographic storage, were in development at leading laboratories, but their introduction as products for general consumption was still at least a decade away, manufacturers agreed. Worst-case scenario: Conventional magnetic disk would run out of elbow room at least five years before alternatives would be ready for enterprise data storage "prime time."

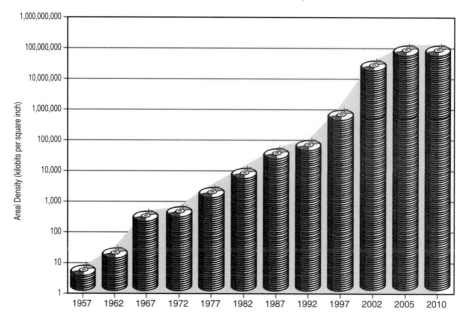

Figure 2–4   Data densities and the superparamagnetic effect.

It is likely that the early network storage visionaries, including members of the Digital Equipment Corporation brain trust who cross-pollinated the industry after the acquisition of DEC by Compaq, had superparamagnetism in the back of their minds. For disk-based storage to continue to scale once the superparamagnetic limit was reached, it would have to scale "outside the box"—whether that box was conceived as an individual disk drive or a cabinet of disk drives organized as an array. Put another way, network storage would be required to perpetuate the dynamic of 120 percent capacity improvement accompanied by 50 percent annual reduction in cost. It was an evolutionary solution to the problem.

FROM EVOLUTION TO REVOLUTION: THE MYTH OF THE FIBRE CHANNEL SAN

Unfortunately, the vision of networked storage articulated by the ENSA white paper authors (and other pioneers at Sun Microsystems and elsewhere) was coopted and recontextualized by the marketing departments of early SAN vendors in the late 1990s and early 2000s. Like many 20th Century revolutionary movements, the marketing forces behind Fibre Channel were not content to wait for the supposedly inevitable and evolutionary force of some unseen hand to bring about the shift to networked storage. Rather, like so many revolutionary zealots, they sought to stir up the hype around their preferred technology, to make a case for early adoption, and to help the inevitable revolution along. In short order, Fibre Channel SANs came to be characterized as a Clayton Christensen–style disruptive technology that "revolutionized" storage.

Vendors seized on the myth of the data explosion to promote solutions that bore little or no resemblance to the ENSA storage utility (or the comparable SAN architectures promoted by Sun's Project StoreX). Fibre Channel was pressed into service by a powerful industry association as the "plumbing" of a SAN, despite the fact that the protocol was, at least at that time, incapable of producing a true network by any valid definition of the term. Advocates of the Fibre Channel SAN, an oxymoronic name for a switched fabric of point-to-point connections, quickly became the dominant voice in forums where networked storage was being discussed. Despite its inherent limitations, vendors offered the FC SAN as "the only game in town" for addressing burgeoning data.

One myth, that of a data explosion, thus fueled a second: the myth of the Fibre Channel SAN. Today, FC SANs are represented as a *de facto* standard in network storage—one that separates storage from servers, and one that offers a real panacea for what ails enterprise storage with its nondisruptive scalability, universal accessibility, and improved management and security for enterprise data.

Analysts are contributing to the hype, offering that FC SANs are finding their way into the enterprise storage infrastructures of public and private organizations at a growing clip: Combined annual growth rates in the high 65 percent range are estimated for FC SANs through 2004.[6] By contrast, adoption rates for server-attached storage are tallied to be growing at "only" about 8 percent in the same period.

We could all learn a lesson about lying with statistics from the purveyors of these types of projections. Considering that the number of server-attached storage solutions deployed in the field is already enormous, and the number of deployed FC SANs remains quite small, analyst projections of comparative growth rates are deceptive. Metaphorically, if the Centers for Disease Control issued a statement that the number of persons infected with the common cold would increase by 8 percent this year, makers of cold remedies would delight at the prospect of millions of new customers. By contrast, if the CDC said that the number of persons infected by "Ebola Virus" would increase by 68 percent this year, the resulting number of new cases (about 10) would hardly create a murmur in the pharmaceutical industry and treatments for the disease would likely remain in the category of "orphan drugs."

So it is with FC SANs and server-attached storage platforms: According to some industry watchers, there were only about 11,000 FC SANs deployed as of 2001.[7] The preponderance had less than a terabyte of data, calling into question whether the FC SAN has achieved widespread acceptance as the *de facto* enterprise network storage topology at all.[8]

In the next chapter, we will further deconstruct the mythology around FC SANs and examine the evolution both of Fibre Channel standards and of IP-based storage networking protocols that portend to provide the plumbing for networked storage.

ENDNOTES

1. Lyman, Peter and Hal R. Varian, "How Much Information," 2000. Retrieved from *http://www.sims.berkeley.edu/how-much-info* on August 18, 2002.

2. In addition to its use for promoting SANs, the data explosion myth also resonated with many IT professionals because it provided a convenient explanation both for increasing server downtime and also for growing budgetary expenditures on storage technology. Ultimately, it provided a catch-all justification for virtually any problem confronting storage and server operations, even those that had no relationship whatsoever with storage capacity and its utilization.

3. In the mid-1990s, the analyst community had cultivated interest in a phenomenon it called the "thin client revolution." The Gartner Group, followed by other analysts, advanced the notion that the "fat client" Windows PC had become an unsupportable drain on corporate resources. Analysts promoted the concept of a dumb terminal device operating a Web browser and a Java Virtual Machine as an inevitable replacement for expensive-to-maintain, fat-client WINTEL desktops. This was among the first of a consecutive series of events in which the analysts, who were originally thought to watch and report on trends, instead tried to create trends for subsequent monitoring and analysis. After about two years of banging the thin client gong, the thin client revolution had fizzled, and even Gartner had to concede that it had been "something of a red herring." (They did so however in a paragraph written in a very small typeface and buried in the back pages of one of their less important subscriber newsletters: Their retraction was hardly made with the same measure of ballyhoo with which they had started the supposed revolution.)

4. Reported in Jon William Toigo, "Storage Area Networks Still on Washington Wish List," *Washington Technology*, September 11, 2000, *http://www.washingtontechnology.com*.

5. Jon William Toigo, "Avoiding a Data Crunch," *Scientific American,* March 2000, *www.sciam.com.*

6. Trend data in these ratios was reported in numerous analyst studies in 2000. More recent assessments by industry analysts are skewed only to reflect the current slowdown in IT spending by organizations.

7. See quote from Randy Kerns, a senior analyst with The Evaluator Group in Jon William Toigo, "Data Center and Storage Consolidation," A Report for Byte & Switch, July 17, 2002, *www.byteandswtich.com.* Since Kern's estimate was published there has been little trustworthy data on the size of the SAN market or how many SANs had actually been deployed. Most analysts count numbers of FC ports (on switches) shipped, or numbers of FC host bus adapters shipped, to support their estimates of SAN adoption rates. These numbers are inherently flawed as evidence of widespread SAN adoption. In fact, many companies that deployed early FC SANs have since "upgraded" them once or twice with newer, more capable equipment. Many FC ports are sold "in advance of requirements" because of problems and inefficiencies inherent in deploying SANs as a cascade of smaller switches. Moreover, FC HBA sales do not necessarily reflect SAN attachment. FC provides a high-speed point to point interconnect that can be used very effectively in building server-attached storage platforms as well as "storage area networks."

8. As this book goes to press, leading analysts have just declared that SANs have replaced SAS as the leading storage topology being acquired by companies today. Bases for this finding are unclear. Left unanswered are questions such as what is being measured and counted as a SAN. If analysts are counting numbers of host bus adapter (FC) ports, their conclusions may be flawed by the fact that Fibre Channel is increasingly used to connect direct-attached arrays (an application to which it is well-suited).

3

21st Century Oxymorons: Jumbo Shrimp and Fibre Channel SAN

In the last chapter, we looked at the marketecture around networked storage generally—and the Fibre Channel SAN, in particular. SANs originated as a conceptual topology for storage that provided network-based interconnections between servers and an intelligent storage infrastructure, sometimes called a "storage pool" or "storage utility."

Such a SAN was heterogeneous in nature, allowing for the any-to-any interconnection of servers with different operating systems to storage platforms from different vendors. The SAN was also intelligent, capable of recognizing the needs of applications requesting storage services and automatically provisioning applications with whatever storage services that they required. The enhanced manageability of a SAN gave it tremendous integrity as a highly available repository for mission critical data storage. And, SAN security would be more than sufficient to offset the increased risk that unavoidably accompanies increased accessibility.

Figures 3–1 and 3–2 depict the "Holy Grail" SAN as described in Enterprise Network Storage Architecture (ENSA) documentation from Compaq Computers and related writings of the late 1990s.

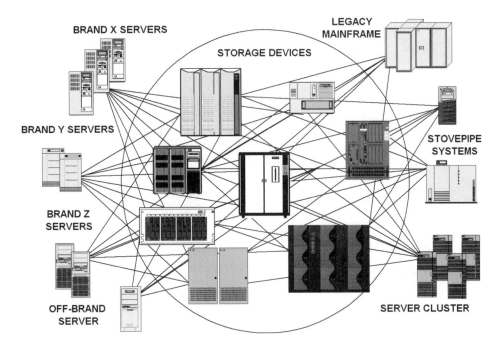

Figure 3–1   The Holy Grail SAN: Heterogeneous storage and server equipment with any-to-any network-based connectivity.

The ENSA SAN concept was truly visionary and captured the attention of storage technology producers and consumers. If it came to fruition, the SAN would establish data storage as its own infrastructure—creating a new service tier in the hierarchy of contemporary n-tier client/server computing. It could conceivably make storage infrastructure the solid, well-anchored foundation upon which networks, servers, and applications resided.

In the late 1990s, vendors and pundits alike said that the SAN was an intuitively obvious "next step" in computing. Storage was getting cheaper, with disk prices declining by as much as 50 percent per year. At the same time, however, the volume of data being stored was increasing—by more than 100 percent per year in some companies. That meant more and more storage needed to be fielded, and a lot of storage—like a lot of anything—carried with it a big price tag, both in terms of acquisition and deployment costs and labor expense.

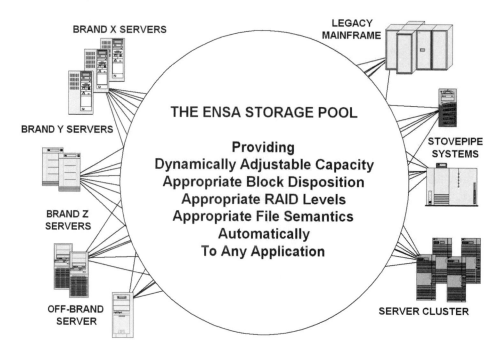

Figure 3–2   The Holy Grail SAN: A virtual storage resource pool.

SANS AND CAPACITY ALLOCATION EFFICIENCY

Early on, many advocates of the technology dismissed the huge acquisition and deployment costs of Fibre Channel (FC) SANs as inconsequential—especially when they were weighed against the enormous efficiencies derived from the networked storage topology. Vendors argued that an FC SAN would more than pay for itself by enabling improved capacity allocation efficiency and improved manageability.

The improved manageability of storage gathered into a FC SAN remains a myth that will be explored in greater detail later. The prospect of improved capacity allocation efficiency, however, had a strong appeal to most IT managers. To understand why, one only has to peek into any IT shop in which storage is directly attached to servers.

In virtually every IT shop, some servers have direct attached storage that tends to run out of disk space fairly often. When this happens, a "Disk Full Error" message is typically generated by the server operating system and returned to the application and/or end-user. The server administrator, who is typically responsible for performing all of the storage management and allocation in a distributed client/server setting, gets an earful from a disgruntled end-user, then spends an inordinate amount of time trying to rectify the problem by offloading files to free up space or adding more disk drives into the cabinet of the attached disk array.

Meanwhile, another server, usually located within a stone's throw of the problem server, goes merrily along about its business day in and day out without ever using more than 30 percent of its storage capacity (see Figure 3–3). The server admin looks longingly at the well-behaved server and array and wonders why there is no way to share the excess capacity on the good server's direct attached storage platform with the direct attached storage platform on the bad server, which is always running out of room.

Contained in that notion was a description of capacity allocation efficiency: the stuff, to paraphrase the Bard, that early FC SAN dreams were made of. To a one, FC SAN vendors promised that deploying a SAN would provide organizations with the ability to allocate storage capacity more efficiently across applications. Just "network" the storage into an FC SAN and *any* available capacity on *any* storage platform could be harnessed to create dynamically scalable "virtual volumes." Applications and end-users, and especially server administrators, would never see a "Disk Full Error" message again (see Figure 3–4).

From this value proposition of volume virtualization derived several others. For one, vendors claimed that enabling greater capacity allocation

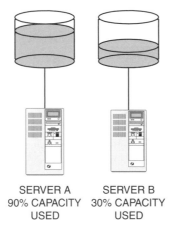

SERVER A   SERVER B
90% CAPACITY   30% CAPACITY
USED   USED

BEFORE
CAPACITY
OPTIMIZATION

Figure 3–3   Capacity allocation inefficiency in server attached storage.

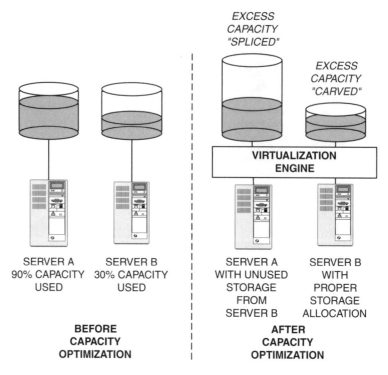

Figure 3–4   Capacity allocation efficiency with virtual san-based volumes.

efficiency with FC SANs would save customers money. FC SANs would actually pay for themselves by enabling older storage platforms to be kept in service for a longer period of time, deferring the need for new equipment purchases.

Additionally, since networked virtual volumes could scale readily, simply by adding more available capacity to an existing virtual volume as needed by the application, FC SANs would also eliminate the costly downtime brought about by the need to rectify disk space problems. This was, depending on the environment, another potentially huge cost savings of FC SANs—especially with estimates of downtime costs that averaged over $1 million per hour across all U.S. industries based on idle labor considerations alone. (See Figure 3–5.)

In the final analysis, the promise of capacity allocation efficiency made a compelling case for FC SANs. Unfortunately, it was not a valid one. The reason had to do with the nature of FC SANs themselves and with approaches advanced by the industry to create a virtual storage pool from devices interconnected in a FC fabric.

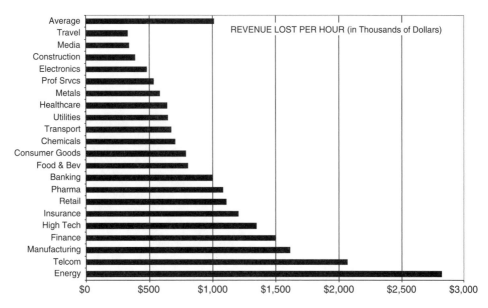

Figure 3–5 Downtime costs as a function of idle labor. (*Source: Performance Engineering & Measurement Strategies: Quantifying Performance Loss*, META Group, Inc., Stamford, CT. October 2000. Copyright © META Group, Inc. All rights reserved. Used with permission.)

THE "V" WORD

The key to capacity allocation efficiency in SANs was "volume virtualization," a technique for creating large and scaleable "virtual disks" or "array partitions" from multiple individual disk drives. In the late 1990s (and today), the creation of virtual volumes was mainly a function of disk array controllers.

Put simply, multiple individual disk drives within an array are aggregated into "virtual volumes" by means of firmware embedded on the disk array controller. This virtualization function was traditionally performed by the array controller for much the same reason that external software for building Redundant Arrays of Inexpensive (changed later to "Independent") Disks (RAID) found its way onto controllers: performance.

Like external software-based RAID, external software-based virtualization tended to incur a "write penalty" that became obvious during tape transfers or other large-scale data movements targeted to the disk drives in the array. The cause was simple: For each block of data directed to the virtual volume, the external software used to create the virtual volume needed to be interrogated to determine the appropriate physical disk target within the virtual volume for the write operation. Write commands amassed (or queued) quickly because of the inefficiencies of this process, and latency began to accrue that was sometimes referred to in the virtualization world, as it had been in the RAID world, as a form of the "write penalty."

Years earlier, in the case of RAID, engineers sought to surmount the write penalty by placing their RAID code into fast-executing silicon, wedded directly to the array controller. Combined with often-complex memory caches to queue commands and data, the write penalty was finessed by sheer engineering muscle.

In an effort to build the best RAID, vendors of high-end arrays made considerable investments in their proprietary controller designs—not knowing that they would later be creating a central obstacle to the realization of the SAN vision. With the advent of SANs and the desire to create aggregated volumes from disks, virtual disks and/or partitions implemented on different arrays by different controllers from different manufacturers, the obstacle finally presented itself. The proprietary differences in RAID array controllers contributed to the many problems associated with the formation of SAN-based virtual volumes from heterogeneous arrays.

Early on it was nearly impossible to create a virtual volume using disks or virtual disks/partitions, identified by Logical Unit Numbers (LUNs), from the arrays of different manufacturers. The controllers of different vendors simply did allow mix-and-match operation, and in a few cases, vendors used "warranty locks" to prevent such configurations. That is, the IT manager would void his warranty on vendor A's hardware if he/she included it in a SAN with vendor B's hardware or used the disk components of A in concert with B to create a virtual volume.

The challenge of array heterogeneity persists today. Until viable third-party virtualization software engines appear, the only way that true volume virtualization can be accomplished in a FC SAN is to purchase all the same brand of hardware from a single vendor (or vendor cadre). In other words, the storage devices connected to the SAN must be homogeneous. For most companies, accommodating this requirement would mean ripping out a lot of existing arrays and replacing them with the products of a single vendor—an option that fails to enthrall many IT managers.

Even in cases where IT decision-makers elected to "go homogeneous," the promise of automatic capacity allocation efficiency was rarely delivered. Most virtualization schemes enabled only the aggregation of

LUNs and did not permit "LUN carving and splicing." In other words, you could not take the unused capacity in one LUN (carve) and simply bolt it to another LUN (splice). The technology didn't exist. (See Chapter 7 for more information about the changing capabilities of SAN virtualization technology.)

By 2002, volume virtualization came to mean techniques for aggregating LUNs that had been defined at the time that homogeneous arrays were first deployed. Unless LUNs were defined at the level of the individual physical disk drive, LUN aggregation was never capable of providing the fine levels of granularity that real capacity allocation efficiency required.

Today, the state of capacity allocation efficiency, according to Fred Moore, a respected analyst and CEO of Horison Information Strategies, is abysmal.[1] According to Moore's calculations, storage capacity is allocated to about 60 percent of optimal efficiency in mainframe shops. In UNIX and Microsoft Windows shops, capacity allocation efficiency hovers at around 40 percent of optimal, and in Linux shops it is around 30 percent.

These allocation percentages show how much storage is potentially wasted in most facilities and underscore that we have quite a way to go to achieve the efficient allocation of storage capacity promised by SAN vendors in the open systems world.

Virtualization—the "V" word—has not materialized in such a way that it enables the creation of heterogeneous and dynamically scalable volumes that SANs were supposed to deliver. In the final analysis, the promise of capacity allocation efficiency, articulated by nearly all SAN vendors, has never been delivered.

CAPACITY UTILIZATION EFFICIENCY: ANOTHER GRAIL

Allocation efficiency is only the first step toward realizing an even more important goal of storage utilization efficiency. Utilization efficiency refers to the cost-effective distribution of data across storage platforms, based on different capabilities and price tags of storage platforms and the characteristics of the data itself. Utilization efficiency is required to ensure you get the most value from your storage investment while providing the right kind of storage for the data that occupy it.

The ENSA SAN promised utilization efficiency as a function of an intelligent storage pool. The storage pool would sense, in effect, the needs of the application and allocate not only the right capacity but also the right "flavor" of storage. A streaming multimedia application, for example, would be allocated the outermost tracks of disk platters because this was the longest contiguous storage space on the disk and would facilitate jitter-free playback of stored files. Similarly, a database with 15 elements would be allocated storage with a RAID level appropriate to each element—RAID 5 for some elements, RAID 3 for others, and RAID 0 (no RAID) for the rest—in order to optimize application performance.

What the ENSA pioneers were underscoring was a simple truism: It was not enough to simply provide an application with storage. Applications had specific requirements for the types of storage that they needed. This key point continues to elude many of those who portray SANs as simply "plumbing."

Capacity utilization efficiency goes beyond application requirements to include also the lifecycle requirements for data and practical considerations, such as platform cost. For example, many organizations store data to a high-end storage platform where its frequency of access or reference drops by 50 percent within three days, and by 90 percent within a month. Like it or not, the preponderance of data, including e-mail, fits this description in many shops. This characteristic or pattern of data utilization demonstrates how inefficiently we utilize storage capacity by allocating our most expensive storage to store data that isn't being referenced very often.

Clearly, it would be smarter to offload less-frequently referenced data either to a tier of inexpensive IDE/ATA storage arrays or to archival tape. Contemporary storage networking technology enables the interconnection of these devices into multitiered storage configurations. Lacking is the intelligence to do much with them.

Moore and others observe that, even if capacity allocation efficiency were somehow to be optimized, the cost efficiency of the storage infrastructure in most shops would continue to hover at around only 30 to 35 percent.[2] A combination of allocation and utilization efficiency is required to drive down storage costs effectively. Contemporary SANs deliver neither and therefore fail also to deliver on their promise of cost-efficient hardware utilization.

WHAT ABOUT MANAGEMENT?

In addition to cost-savings derived from improved hardware utilization efficiencies, SANs were also supposed to deliver significant labor-related cost savings through improved management. The ENSA SAN advocates predicted an intelligent and largely self-managing infrastructure whose growth could be managed easily by a fixed number of staff. This value proposition remains unrealized in current SANs.

By all accounts, using current tools and techniques, the most storage a single administrator can manage is approximately 300 to 500 GB. This number increases substantially when all storage arrays are homogeneous (as white papers commissioned from analysts by most array vendors often conclude). However, the reason has nothing to do with the storage topology. Rather, increased GB per administrator is a function of the efficacy of storage management software. If all deployed storage arrays are from a single vendor, the vendor's own configuration and management "point" software can be used to manage the products as a whole. The gain in GB per administrator has little or nothing to do with SANs, but with homogeneous infrastructure.

The management of heterogeneous FC SANs, by contrast, continues to be a "kludge." Part of the reason has to do with the lack of a "service" within the Fibre Channel protocol for performing in-band or in-the-wire management.

When it was first invented at IBM, the Fibre Channel protocol was conceived as little more than a serial storage interconnect replacement for a SCSI parallel bus. Designers are fond of saying that they did not set out to create a network protocol, just a serial interconnect. Thus, "IP stack-like functions," such as in-band management and in-band security, were deliberately excluded from the Fibre Channel protocol. The Fibre Channel Industry Association, in a draft white paper detailing the roadmap for the protocol in 2000, recognized this deficit and stated that it was working to add in additional services to make the protocol more "network-like" in the future.[3]

Whether or not Fibre Channel is, in fact, a network is a subject for debate among intelligent people in the industry. Howard Goldstein, a good guy and well-known storage consultant and trainer, offers a perspective that is somewhat contrary to this book. Out of deference to Howard, it is being printed here in its entirety.

"There are many myths in technology and many interpretations as well. One of these myths is the concept that Fibre Channel (FC) is not a network architecture. Some of this comes from the fact that many of the FC services are provided in a FC switch that in a historical OSI-like implementation operates at OSI Data Link Layer 2. In today's products, many functions that would be described at OSI Network Layer 3, Transport Layer 4, and other layers are often consolidated in single device."

"Take for example an integrated Internet Cable/DSL Firewall, DHCP-capable, Gateway, Router, and Switch one can purchase from the local computer store. This incorporates Internet Protocol Suite function at all 7 layers of the OSI Architecture but does this in the 4-Layer Internet architecture model."

"This view also comes from the incorrect assumption that OSI is the perfect network model and that all network architectures must layer and assign functionality based on this model. I can't tell you how many times I have seen this lead to incorrect comparisons between architectures and products in the storage-networking world. Comparing Gigabit Ethernet to Fibre Channel is like comparing the core of an apple to an entire orange."

"OSI approaches network functionality in a classic seven-layer model (see Figure 3–6). Each layer implemented by an OSI-compliant product follows the architected functionality of that layer. All of these OSI functions can also be found in the 5-Level architecture of Fibre Channel."

- OSI Physical Layer 1 media interface and bit transmission functions are found in FC Level 0 and Level 1
- OSI Data Link Layer 2 system port to system port frame transmission functions are found in FC Level 2. This Level 2 function

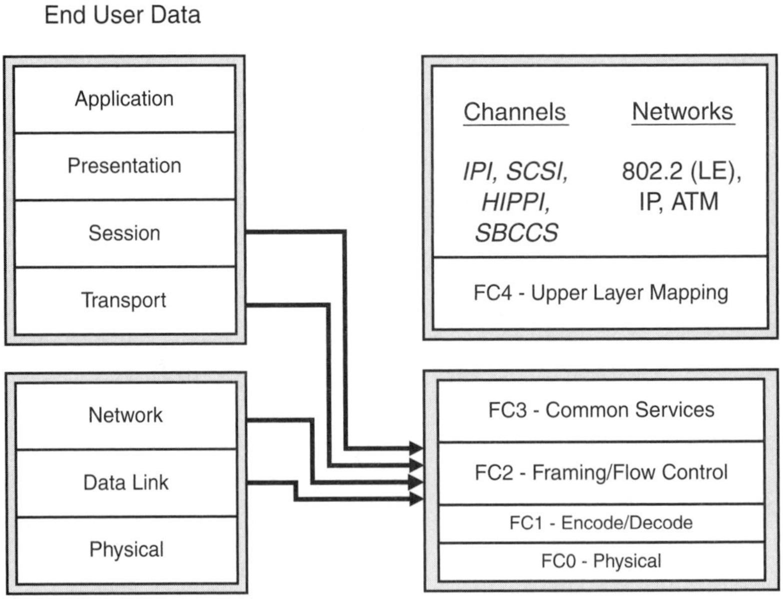

End User Data

Figure 3–6   Fibre Channel Protocol and the ISO Open Storage Interconnect Network Model. (*Source:* Howard Goldstein, President, Howard Goldstein Associates, Inc., Superior, Co., *www.hgai.com*. Reprinted by Permission.)

is implemented within a FC port found on Host Bus Adapters (HBA), FC Storage Adapters (FA), and switches.

- OSI Network Layer 3 routing functions are found from an End System point of view just above FC Level 2 port. From an interconnect topology Intermediate System perspective such as a fabric of switches, this routing takes place implicitly within the Fabric Controller services function of the fabric switch Generic Services architecture component. This uses the routing tables created by an OSI Network Layer 3 like protocol such as FC Fabric Shortest Path First (FSPF), a derivative of the Internet Layer 2 function such as the Open Shortest Path First (OSPF) protocol. If one had to put a number on it, it could be considered FC Level '2.5'.

FC Level 3 Common Services Level is not analogous to OSI Layer 3 but is a placeholder level for possible enhanced architected functionality like automatic failover, parallel I/O, hunt groups, etc. At the time of this writing, no FC Level 3 standards have been defined for these functions and that is unfortunate. Only proprietary implementations exist.

- OSI Transport Layer 4 End System to End System virtual interface functions are implemented with FC Level 2 as well.
- OSI Session Layer 5 application workflow management function can also be found in FC Level 2 through the use of FC Exchange and Sequence management.
- OSI Presentation Layer 6 syntax, data compression and data security functions are implemented with some of the newer FC Level 2 and '2.5' services such as Fabric Generic Services Security Key Distribution Service found in a FC switch or the proposed FC Security Protocol. Additionally, the fabric services include Zone management, configuration management, and others.
- OSI Application Layer 7 application support services such as X.500 Directory services has its parallels in FC Level '2.5' as well in the FC Extended Link Services and Directory service subcomponent Name Services again found in a FC fabric of switches.

"Desert cakes come in all shapes, sizes, layers and tastes. Each can be served on different occasions and for different purposes. Whether it is a 2-layer carrot cake, an 8-layer devil's food cake or a multi-tiered wedding cake, they all serve their designed purpose."

"Network architectures are like these deserts. Not all functions, even OSI functions need to be present to have robust network architecture. Fibre Channel provides Physical Transport Networking function by design. It implements all of the 7-Layer OSI functions in the mission it performs. I like to say that FC fundamentally is nothing more than the ability to provide the appearance of many private virtual SCSI Bus cables for every SCSI LUN accessed. It is a 'plumbing' platform to build on."[4]

Goldstein's perspective offers one of the most exhaustive efforts to rationalize the FC-as-network view of so many vendors in the FC community. According to him, even an effort to develop a channel interconnect can inadvertently lead to the creation of something else. He is fond of saying that, just as the fellow who developed "sticky notes" did not originally set out to develop a detachable/re-attachable glue, IBM invented a network architecture without meaning to. That alone does not invalidate the result as a network.

However, Goldstein does agree that certain services were not originally provided in FC that are taken for granted in other messaging networks. Even where enhancements have been made to the protocol through subsequent standards body development efforts, they have not been seized upon by the industry or implemented at all in a standard way.

In the absence of a native in-band management service, the FC SANs deployed today are actually a hybrid of a Fibre Channel protocol "fabric"—basically, a switched, serial, storage interconnect linking servers and storage devices and providing data transport services—and an IP network that also interconnects all SAN elements (server host bus adapters, switches, and storage controllers) to carry SAN management traffic (see Figure 3–7). In disagreement with Goldstein's conclusion, this author must conclude that it is oxymoronic for FC to ever have been used as the foundation for a storage *network*.

In fact, the lack of standards-based, in-band services in FC SAN implementations also accounts for the fact that heterogeneous FC SANs offer little improvement over heterogeneous server-attached configurations in terms of the number of GB that an individual storage administrator can manage. Until recently, those deploying heterogeneous SANs had enormous difficulty even with the low-level task of "discovering" heterogeneous devices in the same fabric. Vendors seemed to be going out of their way to ensure that a competitor's hardware could not be discovered or used by the switches of their preferred SAN switch-maker. SAN switch-makers seemed to be unwilling to recognize or interoperate with their competitor's switch product or with host bus adapters that were not part of their vendor cadre.

Today, there has been some improvement in this space, with HBA vendors agreeing to a quasi-standard device driver and some large array vendors cooperating to create "Bluefin," an object-oriented messaging interface specification that links distributed management applications with device management support and enables the discovery of different arrays in the same fabric. It remains to be seen how well these cooperative

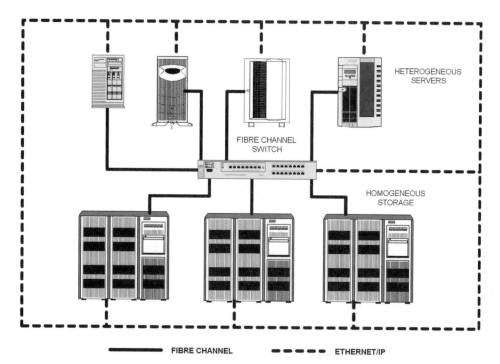

Figure 3–7   The FC SAN topology—A "kludge."

arrangements will stand the test of time and the proprietary forces driving the industry to greater and greater Balkanization. If the tenure of recent application programming interface (API) swapping arrangements between vendors is any indication of the life expectancy of such surrogate services, the management of FC SANs will likely remain a headache for storage administrators for the foreseeable future.

Even with discovery issues to some degree resolved, storage management—defined here as the cost-efficient provisioning of data across storage resources to meet the data-storage, data-access, and data-protection requirements as determined by business applications and end-users—entails significantly greater intelligence than contemporary tools provide. FC SANs, far from making storage management easier and reducing the labor costs associated with this activity, have actually contributed complexity and cost in most environments. The exceptions are homogeneous SANs created from the products of a select vendor cadre. However, in the final analysis, it is not the FC SAN that makes this infrastructure more manageable by fewer administrators, but the homogeneity of the configuration.

CONCLUSION

A later chapter in this book will cover the state of storage management software in greater detail. For now, it should suffice to say that Fibre Channel fabrics do not deliver on the business value proposition offered by SAN advocates. There are instances in which FC fabrics have enabled firms to scale storage nondisruptively behind applications, or to consolidate servers (and application software licenses) ahead of shared storage repositories, or to share large-scale tape libraries among multiple servers, or to accomplish other discrete objectives. However, these benefits have not been realized as a result of deploying a storage area network, per se. Any shared storage interconnect could have produced the same result.

By definition, FC SANs are not networked storage at all. They perpetuate a server-attached storage topology used in connecting storage arrays to servers for the past 40 years. FC SANs simply introduce a switch that enables, in the best of circumstances, connections to more physical storage devices from a single server HBA and connections over greater distances than were possible with the parallel SCSI bus.

Despite the hype, FC SANs have no inherent capability to improve capacity allocation or utilization efficiency or to improve management and increase the GB per administrator ratio. In many cases, they increase management cost and personnel resource requirements and, in the worst cases, introduce unpredictability and downtime into the computing environment that would never have been tolerated with more traditional storage topologies.

Used intelligently, however, FC fabrics can and do offer another topology for solving certain storage problems. Typically, they do so at considerable cost—including the cost to deploy and troubleshoot a switched fabric infrastructure that may be unstable in the face of heterogeneous gear and the cost to hire, train, and maintain a group of skilled Fibre Channel experts as part of the IT staff.

Try as one might to justify a Fibre Channel fabric using the value proposition of a SAN, reality is typically much different. Even those who have deployed "successful" FC SANs have discovered that they do not form a storage pool at all. Currently, FC SANs are little more than super-sized homogeneous disk arrays that must be "zoned" much in the way that a multiported array is "partitioned" in order to support the requirements of heterogeneous servers and the applications they host.

The topology is (hopefully) the last remnant of legacy server-attached storage and a bridge from older concepts of storage infrastructure to newer models. At least, that is what advocates of IP storage are saying, as we will see in the next chapter.

ENDNOTES

1. Fred Moore, CEO of Horison Information Systems, quoted in "Storage Management 2003: The 'Two Towers' Of Storage Pain—Part One: Provisioning," a white paper by Jon William Toigo, CEO & Managing Partner USA, Toigo Partners International LLC, April 2003.
2. Ibid.
3. This author, with the guidance of senior members of the FCIA, wrote the Fibre Channel Industry Association's Roadmap white paper in 2000. To my knowledge, the paper was reviewed, paid for, and never published.
4. Interview with Howard Goldstein, President, Howard Goldstein Associates, Inc., Superior, CO, *www.hgai.com,* June 2003.

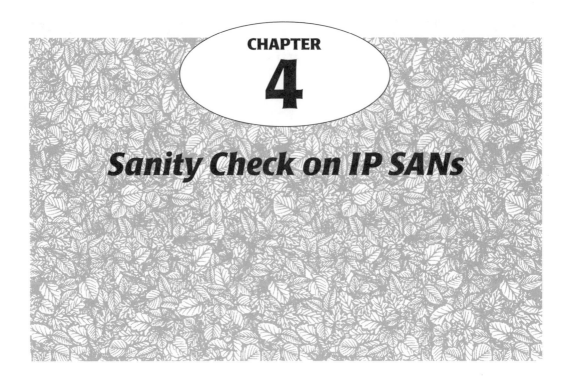

CHAPTER 4

Sanity Check on IP SANs

In the last chapter, we examined the Fibre Channel fabric and compared it to the ideal SAN originally described in the Compaq Computer Corporation's 1997 Enterprise Network Storage Architecture (ENSA) white paper, which provided the original definition of a storage utility infrastructure. The chapter surveyed the myths that were created around "Fibre Channel SAN" topology by a cadre of overzealous vendors and concluded that, while the Fibre Channel protocol could be used to create a serial interconnect fabric that could solve certain problems, FC SANs delivered none of the business value associated with ENSA-type SANs.

It was a classic case of oversell: Vendors correctly perceived how the SAN concept resonated with prospective customers and pressed the Fibre Channel Protocol, the fastest available interconnect for open systems storage at the time, into service as the plumbing for SANs. Despite the fact that the vendors themselves knew the protocol was unsuitable for building real networks and came up short in nearly every service category required for true cost-savings, FCP—and products built on it—provided the means to sever dependency on the parallel SCSI bus, enabled the attachment of more storage devices, and placed devices at greater distances from the server host.

More importantly, the "new" protocol and topology enabled a group of vendors that formerly specialized in selling mainframe channel extension products and ESCON director switches, and whose fortunes (like those of mainframe vendors generally) were hard hit by Y2K jitters and the flight from mainframe hosting that occurred at the end of the millennium, to breathe new life into their companies. To this day, most Fibre Channel switch vendors were yesterday's channel extension product vendors.

The truth is that vendors knew from the outset that the Fibre Channel protocol was not up to the task of building real ENSA-style SANs. Asking their representatives point-blank questions regarding the erroneous business value claims they were making about FC SANs usually produced wry grins and acknowledgement of the lack of important network services in FCP. The universal response was less apologetic or defensive than simple and direct: "Yes, we know all that, but we're the only game in town."

For a time, the mantra of the Fibre Channel Industry Association seemed to be that any technology, regardless of how half-baked, was ready for business "prime time" if businesses would buy it. Burgeoning data, plus a "bull market economy," created a need for more storage and a willingness among consumers to invest in just about any technology that was presented to them and contextualized as "the next big thing."

Vendors advised the critics of FC SANs (including this author) that they were lagging behind the trends. Supply-side industry analysts validated vendor claims of the solvency of FC SAN value, despite the fact that most had never seen a real FC SAN, and contributed to the not-so-subtle bending of technical terminology to mean anything a vendor decided it meant. In short order, the Open Systems Interconnect (OSI) definition of a network was cast to the wind, as was the ENSA description of a storage area network, as vendors applied the term to describe basically any interconnect topology, including the configuration of disk inside an array cabinet! A SAN became whatever a vendor said it was—a "marketecture" term with little or no technical meaning or relevance.

Just as Fibre Channel advocates were corrupting the meaning of SAN, a working group was being established within the Internet Engineering Task Force (IETF) tasked to develop a set of protocols for harnessing TCP/IP networks to become the plumbing for storage networks. The IP Storage Working Group was quick to dismiss arguments by the Fibre Channel Industry Association that IP could never serve as a storage interconnect. Protocol-specific issues, while technically nontrivial, could be surmounted, the group argued, and storage could be operated successfully as an application across an IP network.

By 2003, vendors in the storage industry were beginning to rally be-hind the newly completed Request for Comment (RFC)—IETF lingo for a standard—for SCSI over IP (iSCSI) and referring to FC fabrics in casual conversation and conference presentations as "legacy SANs." Some were the very same vendors who had just completed deployments of "legacy" Fibre Channel SANs for their customers!

Like FC SANs, current IP-based SANs also fail to deliver on the ENSA SAN vision. However, IP SANs move closer to the goal by utilizing a full-service network with a robust set of services as the plumbing for storage I/O.

IP SANS AND METCALFE'S LAW

In theory, IP SANs will outperform on a cost/value basis their Fibre Channel fabric cousins within a comparatively brief period of time. Ven-dors arguing this position cite Metcalfe's Law, which states (1) that the value of a network increases as the number of nodes connected to the net-work increase, and (2) that growth in terms of network cost flattens out as more nodes are added. (See Figure 4–1).

It is assumed that using IP as a storage interconnect will produce the same results as we have seen in local area networks. This remains to be seen. Another question that arises is which IP storage standard will predominate.

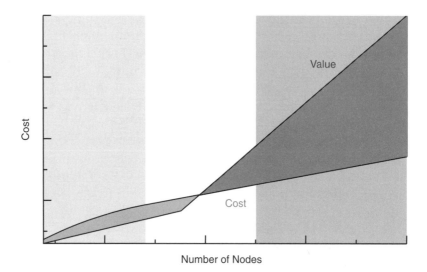

Figure 4–1   Metcalfe's Law.

The IP Storage Working Group actually produced three distinct IP storage protocols. One is iSCSI, a mechanism for encapsulating SCSI commands and data into TCP and transporting the resulting packages across an IP network (see Figure 4–2). A second is Fibre Channel Protocol over Internet (iFCP), a method for encapsulating Fibre Channel protocol traffic under TCP and transporting it between Fibre Channel gateways in two or more FC Fabrics. The third approach, called Fibre Channel over IP (FCIP), involves the tunneling of Fibre Channel Protocol traffic between "island SANs" across an IP network link.

This "alphabet soup" of IP storage protocols is explained by the differing underlying assumptions behind each specific approach. FCIP was the product of a temporary alliance forged out of necessity between FC SAN switch vendor, Brocade Communications Systems, and IP networking giant, Cisco Systems. In late 2000, the two companies, which had only weeks before taken turns dismissing each other's roadmaps for SANs, made an unexpected announcement that they would work together to devise a protocol for tunneling FCP across IP. The grudging agreement was the result of demands from several key customers of both companies that had deployed small FC fabrics and did not want to incur the expense of deploying additional FC links in parallel to their existing IP networks to interconnect the SANs.

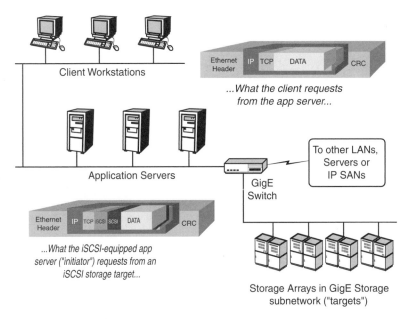

Figure 4–2 SCSI encapsulation in iSCSI.

FCIP was contextualized by Cisco (off the record, of course) as a tactical measure. Its benefit was straightforward: dual use of IP infrastructure to move storage as well as LAN message traffic. Its inherent shortcoming was also obvious: Joining two or more SAN islands together using FCIP created the equivalent of one giant SAN. Local identities of the SAN islands were lost. And, in the process of joining the fabrics together by this method, a customer ran the risk of creating a fabric that wouldn't work at all. The same issues that created pain for technicians in local multiswitch fabric deployments—from switch interoperability difficulties, and zoning scheme conflicts, to HBA firmware-related problems and constraints—would present themselves when joining remote fabrics across an IP-based local, metropolitan, or wide area network (LAN, MAN, or WAN). The distances involved in the overall infrastructure would compound the resolution of these problems.

Regardless of these deficits, work proceeded and the FCIP protocol was created, supported by a Cisco Systems switch blade—and later given RFC status by the IETF. A scant 18 months later, the relationship between Cisco Systems and Brocade Communications Systems was broken off with all the acrimony of a Hollywood divorce.

Cisco cried foul when Brocade purportedly engineered the protocol for compatibility only with Brocade's switches rather than with all Fibre Channel switches. Each company went its own way, but—also in good Hollywood fashion—neither was willing to give up the last name "Systems."

In contrast to FCIP, iFCP was a protocol championed by a cadre of vendors who sought to bridge the FCP world and the IP world by introducing the concept of a IP-FCP gateway. The solution was viewed as eminently practical by companies such as Nishan Systems, and anticipated the SAN landscape that exists today.

Like FCIP, iFCP provided a way of transporting data to and from Fibre Channel storage devices using TCP/IP. Advocates describe it as the best of both worlds with TCP providing congestion control as well as error detection and recovery services, and FCP providing a robust serialization of SCSI commands and data. iFCP also enables the merging of existing SCSI buses and Fibre Channel fabrics into the Internet.

The iFCP protocol can be used as a wholesale replacement for FCP, enabling the construction of FC fabrics using Ethernet. However, it is more often proposed for use as a supplement to existing FC fabrics and as an alternative to FCIP. Advocates observe that using iFCP to interconnect "island FC SANs" provides a more robust solution than FCIP tunneling for companies that have already deployed FC fabrics. The iFCP solution

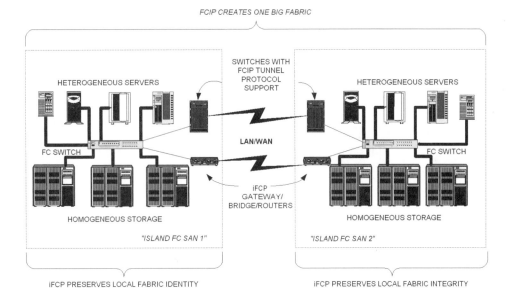

Figure 4–3 FCIP and iFCP architectures.

preserves the integrity of each SAN island's switch and zone scheme, and is less prone to general failure after a connection is made (assuming that iFCP gateways are compatible) (see Figure 4–3).

At this point, iFCP is being positioned as a migration tool for companies that are electing to move from FC fabrics to pure iSCSI-based over time. Switch-makers are beginning to support both iFCP and iSCSI protocols, a sign that FCP's star is slowly fading.

WHAT, WHEN, AND WHERE iSCSI

Advocates of iSCSI represent the protocol as pure SAN: SCSI operated as an application across a true network protocol. They extol the advent of a true SAN that leverages existing protocol services for in-band services such as security (IP has the Ipsec family of protocols) and management (IP offers Simple Network Management Protocol or SNMP). They avoid discussing the vicissitudes of IP networking from the standpoint of storage I/O requirements.

On its face, TCP/IP networking is not terribly efficient. As much as 25 percent of network bandwidth is consumed by protocol overhead. This is one reason why pundits and analysts are fond of linking their prognostications about iSCSI SAN adoption to the evolution of underlying Ethernet protocols. In a word, iSCSI is expected to come into its own in the market once 10-gigabit-per-second gigabit Ethernet (10-GbE) achieves widespread adoption (late 2004 or early 2005, depending on the analyst one reads). Even at 75 percent efficiency, 10-GbE pipes are thought to be adequate to support the throughput and latency requirements of even the most demanding storage application.

Moreover, since 10-GbE switches are expected to be deployed in the "core" (as opposed to the "edge") of enterprise networks—that is, they will likely be rack-mounted in the company data center—advocates claim that iSCSI will displace Fibre Channel fabric switches that have already been deployed there. At least, this was Cisco Systems' position in 2000.

As of this writing, a different (and more confusing) set of messages about iSCSI is being heard from the industry. At conferences and trade shows, even frothing-at-the-mouth iSCSI bigots have been ratcheting back the tone and volume of their pitches. Rather than positioning iSCSI as a forklift replacement for legacy fabrics, even Cisco Systems has adopted a conciliatory position: FC fabrics and iSCSI SANs will coexist for the next several years.

This is partly a reflection of the economy. During the current challenging economic period, many vendors have changed their messaging from the more freewheeling "replace every 12 to 18 months to capitalize on technology innovation" to the more conservative "buy and hold for five to seven years to realize strategic value." Intel has backed away from its Infiniband/Virtual Interface Architecture server roadmap, which would have pushed customers to replace their existing Intel servers with a next-generation product, in favor of a strategy predicated on deriving value from existing products over a longer timeframe.

So it is with current messaging around iSCSI. Rather than pressing companies to replace their just-installed FC fabrics, iSCSI SANs are being contextualized alternatively as a mechanism for connecting outlying servers to the core Fibre Channel storage fabric and/or as a "SAN for the rest of us"—that is, for small and medium-sized companies or for departments or business units within large organizations. As with Intel's VIA server roadmap, the iSCSI roadmap appears to be taking its lead from the economy and conservative purchasing patterns that it encourages.

However, these marketing messages raise a number of questions in the minds of consumers. The first is straightforward enough: Why is the value of iSCSI always discussed in the context of Fibre Channel? Very few FC SANs have ever been deployed. The technology never took hold the way the vendors (and their paid pitchmen within the analyst community) hoped it would. So, why is iSCSI always discussed in the same breath as FC SAN?

In truth, iSCSI is just another way to connect storage with servers for block-level operation. Constantly comparing iSCSI with FC SANs has a limiting effect because it makes people believe that there is only one way to implement the protocol. While iSCSI could be used to build a SAN, it could also be used as a long-distance IP-based storage interconnect, facilitating remote backup or mirroring or SAN interconnection. It could also be used to enable a block channel on a NAS device, encouraging the evolution of a NAS/SAN hybrid.

Moreover, the connections in a SAN are thought to be always on, but iSCSI enables servers and storage devices to interact when necessary, and it doesn't necessitate that an active connection always exist between them. This opens some new possibilities for storage device sharing that do not require the complexity or management hassles of a full-blown SAN.

Another question that deserves critical attention is this: If iSCSI is initially targeted at smaller organizations or departments, what is the "killer application" that will drive its adoption? The bulk of early FC fabric deployments were predicated on a need to share expensive, enterprise-class, tape libraries among multiple storage arrays.

The need for efficient backup resonated with large IT shops, but vendors appear to doubt that iSCSI will play in large corporate data centers in the short term, at least. Even Cisco has backed away from its projection that iSCSI would cause the "SAN-ification" of all the storage in all of the Fortune 500 companies—in part, because of issues with the performance of the current version of the protocol, and possibly because Cisco now sells both FC and IP switches.

Thus, if iSCSI is targeted to small- and medium-sized IT environments that do not own large tape silos, will backup still be the driving force or "killer app" for its adoption? Until an application is identified that would drive smaller shops away from tenured server-attached and network-attached storage (NAS) configurations, it would seem that vendors might be wasting their time with an iSCSI play.

Other questions around iSCSI go to the core value proposition of protocol, specifically the assertion that provides a more manageable and secure foundation for building SANs. While iSCSI will enable the use of protocols like SNMP and IPSec (standards within the TCP/IP suite) to provide in-band management and security for storage, the question remains whether anyone will actually use these protocols.

During a presentation in Boston, one storage manager observed, "If we had wanted to use SNMP and IPSec, wouldn't we have leveraged them as part of the out-of-band IP network that we already use to manage servers and storage devices in an FC fabric?" The point is well taken. The trade press has carried many articles recently about the reluctance of organizations to implement IPsec, because the protocols impose some significant and labor-intensive administrative requirements, or SNMP, because of the protocol's inherent lack of security. If these protocols are not widely used in safeguarding or managing IP LANs, why would anyone argue that they will add value to IP SANs?

Moreover, despite the claims of vendors that iSCSI SANs are less mysterious than FC fabrics—that is, that the IP protocols are more familiar than is the Fibre Channel protocol—more than one storage manager has questioned the meaning of this statement. An attendee at a recent tradeshow wondered aloud, "Wouldn't storage administrators be required to learn Cisco's IOS switch operating system, and does this really impose any less of a learning curve than the need to learn the rarified details of Fibre Channel?"

Another valid and pragmatic question is how vendors will convince their channel partners, resellers, and integrators to sell iSCSI solutions—especially if FC alternatives will yield a much higher profit margin. While one would like to believe that the intrinsic nobility of resellers and integrators would cause them to sell the solution that best meets client needs, instead of a solution that best lines their own pockets, the proliferation in the field of inadequate solutions based on poor technology suggests that this is not the case. Ultimately, resellers and integrators will decide which technology options are placed in front of their customers. Channel sales organizations (as these groups are sometimes called) have long been identified as the makers and breakers of technology—particularly in complex sales that require substantial "face time" with customers to conclude.

WHY IP SANS?

Ultimately, the question of why IP storage seems to be answered by the burgeoning requirements for block-level storage scaling. When introduced to market in the late 1990s, SANs reflected a continuing bifurcation of the storage market. SANs provided a scaling mechanism for block-level applications such as databases, while NAS provided "elbow room" for files. Recent events, such as the announced substitution of an object-oriented database for a file system in Microsoft's forthcoming operating system—code-named "Longhorn"—combined with similar structural changes in popular databases from IBM (DB2 Open Edition) and Oracle

Corporation, suggest that scaleable block architecture may become *de rigueur* for all storage in the future.

This is not to say that IP SANs provide a "one size fits all" solution to application storage requirements. The very proliferation of protocols and topologies suggests a diversified solution set that may map to the different requirements of different applications. Just as different RAID levels are preferred by different elements of an Oracle database to obtain optimal performance, so, too, different storage protocols and architectures may be required by different applications. For example, for streaming data applications, such as tape backup, iSCSI may actually be a better match than Fibre Channel, owing to the support in Ethernet for "Jumbo Frames." Independent tests have verified that the use of Jumbo Frames (extended Ethernet frames that range in size from the standard 1,518 bytes up to 9,000 bytes) can deliver a 50 percent increase in throughput with a simultaneous 50 percent decrease in CPU utilization in streaming tape applications. Alternatively, and this is likely to raise arguments, applications requiring a specific class of service support (an available but rarely implemented capability of FCP) might be well-served by a Fibre Channel interconnect.

Ultimately, the decision over which protocol to use with which application must consider a number of variables including application performance requirements, cost, available support resources, management and security requirements, and data growth rates. Without minimizing the differences between iSCSI and FCP, it needs to be clearly understood that interconnecting servers and storage using either of these protocols is largely irrelevant to the SAN value proposition. Plumbing is just plumbing. Intelligence—some would say, management—is required to create an infrastructure from the aggregation of disk drives, cables, switches, and HBAs. Without it, you do not have an infrastructure, just a morass of hardware and cabling.

What SAN plumbing does provide, in addition to protocol-specific features, is the foundation for building resilience and provisioning efficiency into storage. The IP storage model arguably provides a better foundation because of its tenure. We have a better understanding of techniques and methods for designing IP LANs to achieve optimal performance and to minimize risk, knowledge that can be transferred readily to build high-performance, fault-tolerant IP storage networks. There is no equivalent tenure in Fibre Channel.

Added to this is the ubiquity of IP. Storage, like any other application, gains part of its value from its accessibility by those who need it. IP networking, in its many manifestations, enables broad geographic accessibility.

Ubiquity and tenure also conspire to make IP storage networking components cheaper, product development times shorter, and vendors coffers bigger. At the time of this writing, the research and development budget at Cisco Systems was greater than the budgets of the top five Fibre Channel switch-makers combined. This fact bodes well for the ability of IP SAN technology to keep pace with changing storage technologies and changing business requirements. It is also a practical explanation for why IP has buried virtually any rival technology that has crossed its path.

CONCLUSION

The marketecture around IP SANs and FC fabrics persists. Claims are repeatedly made by vendors in each camp about the superiority of their preferred protocol and topology that are not born out in reality. For example, nothing about IP storage makes it any more secure or manageable than FC storage. Moreover, neither IP storage nor FC storage truly breaks with the SCSI protocol or with the concept of a LUN that derives from the days of the parallel SCSI bus. Neither protocol fixes the problems created by the proprietary controller architectures of array vendors. Neither furthers in any significant way the creation of a common storage model. Neither delivers, on its own, the intelligence required to provision storage automatically to applications that need it. And, neither IP storage nor FC storage solve the ultimate conundrum: how to make data self-describing so that management tools can be created to realize not only capacity allocation efficiency, but also capacity utilization efficiency.

A final note about IP storage: It is a more elegant solution than FC if only because both the data path and the control path are handled through the same wire. In the past, elegance counted for something. In today's cost-constrained IT environments, it just might count for something again.

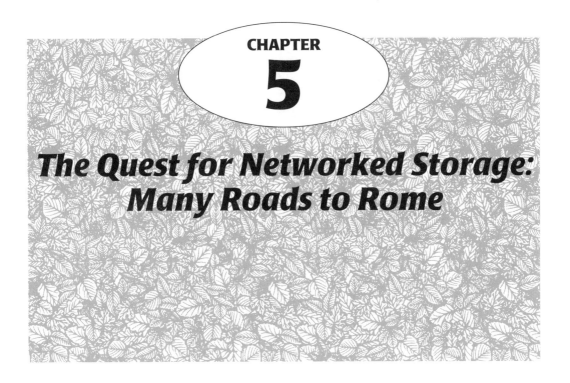

The Quest for Networked Storage: Many Roads to Rome

The preceding chapters have illuminated the information gap that persists around networked storage. Erroneous impressions of storage networking technology, fostered by an abundance of vendor marketing hype, bear little resemblance to the actual capabilities and limitations of products and topologies that are grouped under this broad category.

This chapter moves the discussion out of the realm of marketecture into the realm of storage architecture. In order to begin assessing how current storage technology, networked or not, may be harnessed to solve real world problems, you need to look beyond the hype and at the particular storage requirements manifested by applications themselves.

THE ZEN RIDDLE OF STORAGE NETWORKING

Networked storage is something of a Zen riddle today. On the one hand, it can be argued rather persuasively that all storage is already networked, whether that storage is provided by disks installed inside a server chassis, or mounted in arrays connected to a server via a SCSI parallel cable, or accessed across a LAN using a network file system protocol, or interconnected with other arrays and servers using a Fibre Channel switched fabric.

The justification for this claim is simple: In the prevailing open systems computing architecture of today, client/server, virtually all clients (applications or end-users) access data via servers that are themselves connected within a local- or wide-area internetwork (including the Internet). As shown in Figure 5–1, the overwhelming preponderance of storage requests are made and fulfilled across IP-based networks. So, effectively speaking, all storage is already networked.

Conversely, it can be argued that no storage today is truly networked storage. The case can be made that it is inappropriate to use the term "networked storage" to describe any of the current classes of storage products and topologies. In point of fact, all of the so-called networked storage products perpetuate server-attached models.

For example, network-attached storage (NAS) is little more than a thin server operating system bolted on to a storage array. In even its most deliberate manifestation, in which the NAS operating system is custom-developed by its manufacturer (see Figure 5–2), the NAS thin server is basically a general purpose OS kernel that has been "optimized" to perform certain networking and storage-related tasks. Some inexpensive NAS de-

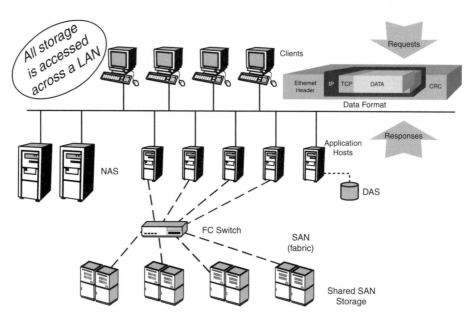

Figure 5–1   Zen riddle: All storage is networked . . . across an IP network.

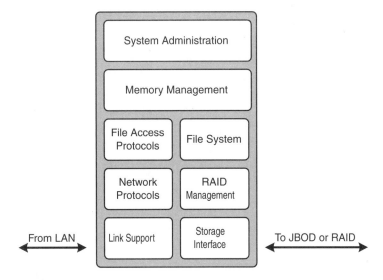

Figure 5–2 Network-attached storage operating system components.

vices, in fact, utilize general-purpose operating system kernels embedded on off-the-shelf silicon chips as their "brains." Any way you view it, the NAS appliance is server-attached storage.

The same argument, that networked storage is a misnomer, holds true in the case of storage arrays arranged in Fibre Channel fabrics. While it is true that Fibre Channel enables more devices to be interconnected and made accessible to a server than does its progenitor, the parallel SCSI bus, and, by consequence, that this capability enables nondisruptive scaling of the storage platform (within vendor-specific limits), the implementations made of FC fabrics today are not, technically speaking, networks. Placing a Fibre Channel switch between a server-attached storage device and its server host does not create networked storage, but merely switched, server-attached storage (see Figure 5–3).

The distinction may seem to be an unimportant one until you require network services that are not usually implemented as a part of the function set of Fibre Channel Switches, such as standards-based in-band security or management. You must create workarounds to provide the necessary functionality.

As argued in the previous chapters, FCP itself was never intended to be a network protocol and contemporary FC fabrics are not networks in the traditional (International Standards Organization) definition of the word. A fabric cannot be substituted for a true network if storage is to be detached from a server and network-enabled.

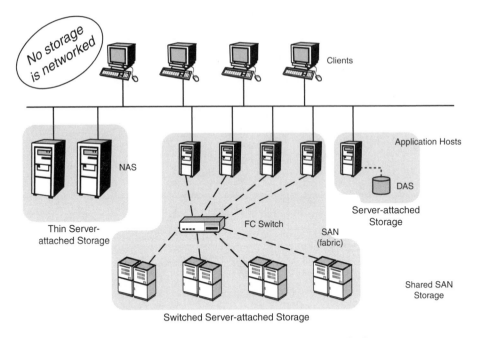

Figure 5–3   Zen riddle: No storage is networked.

Of course, the arguments advanced by both the "all-storage-is-networked-storage" and the "no-storage-is-networked-storage" crowds fly in the face of "conventional wisdom," which has been purchased at a price of tens of millions of marketing dollars spent by storage vendors annually. These perspectives also call into question the nice neat categories used by leading IT research and analysis companies to describe the storage industry. Even the moniker of the leading industry advocate, the Storage Networking Industry Association (SNIA), must be taken as part of the hype.

In the case of analysts, many of whom derive significant income streams from the vendor community, networked storage has become embedded as a product category. In an apparent homage to the "natural system" advanced by Carolus Linneaus (also known as Carl Linné), analysts have set forth a taxonomy for the storage world consisting of two "kingdoms": server-attached storage and networked storage. Within the networked storage kingdom, they define two major phyla: NAS for file-oriented storage, and SAN for block-oriented storage (see Figure 5–4).

If one accepts that the distinction between networked and server-attached storage is largely specious, the more interesting aspect of this

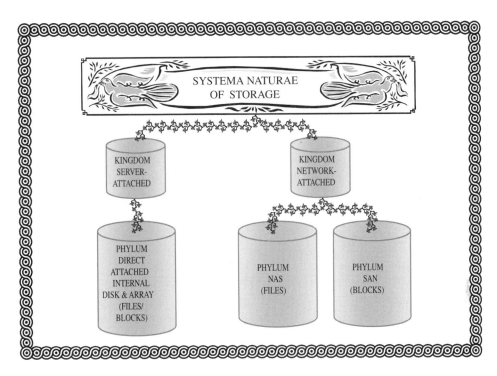

Figure 5–4 A contemporary storage taxonomy.

taxonomy is the bifurcation it introduces between platforms optimized for block-level and file-level storage. Since no formal distinction exists in the world of server-attached storage, this division of storage platforms within the networked storage world may be worth exploring.

BLOCK AND FILE

At first glance, the division of networked storage platforms into block-optimized and file-optimized types might appear to have been driven by real architectural differentiators. At the protocol level, for example, NAS relies on network file system protocol, FC fabrics use an encapsulation of SCSI across a serial interconnect. It remains to be demonstrated, however, whether these technical differences justify the segregation of disk and block and the platforms that support them.

Traditionally, all storage was simply block storage. That is to say that, for most of the computing era, we used internal disk drives and disk arrays to store all data, whether block or file. Disk drives provided a common location for writing both the raw block output of databases as well as collections of blocks described with "metadata"—what we refer to as files.

As two-tier client/server computing gave rise to three-tier architectures consisting of client, application server host, and database server, server administrators deliberately delegated to some disk platforms the task of file storage, and to others the task of database, or block-level, storage.

Over time, IT decision-makers came to prefer using "fast" storage platforms, delivering what vendors described as high performance I/O, to accommodate the block storage requirements of high-volume, transaction-oriented applications. On the other hand, less expensive platforms offering commensurately lower I/O performance were often deployed to handle file system storage.

There was little to distinguish these platforms from each other save for their read/write performance (a function of controller design, buffer memory, and type and size of disk drive) and, of course, their price tags. Truth be told, any data could be written to any platform: It was up to the IT decision-maker to select the product that he or she believed best met the needs of the application—and did so at an acceptable price.

With the advent of NAS and SAN, this differentiation moved from the realm of preference to the realm of design. NAS was designed to store files. It leverages standards-based protocols such as the Network File System (NFS), Common Internet File System (CIFS), or the Hypertext Transfer Protocol (HTTP), to enable the extension of file system–based storage across multiple storage platforms.

Initially, NAS provided "elbow room" for file storage: an efficient one-stop-shop alternative to configuring a general-purpose server with internal disk or external arrays and configuring it for use across a network. In short order, NAS came into vogue as a platform for email hosting, partly because of its simpler deployment and lower cost, but also because of innovations such as "snap shots"—a technique for backing up inode[1] pointers that facilitated point-in-time recovery of data. Many large email service providers both within large enterprises and on the web claimed that, given the propensity of early email server software to fail at random, point-in-time recovery was a key feature of NAS.

NAS, however, did not remain the pure file system play that it was touted to be by its advocates. In 1999, Microsoft announced that its Exchange Server 2000 would no longer support NFS- or CIFS-based access alone. To address failure rates and to support new software architecture, Microsoft needed to establish, in addition to a network file system connection, a block-level connection to the storage device.

So entrenched was the view of "NAS-as-file-server" and so embedded was the file server concept in product architecture, even "brand-name" NAS vendors trembled when Redmond announced its new email server (and underlying SQL database server) and excluded virtually all NAS products from the list of supported storage platforms. In the end, they had no alternative but to comply with Microsoft's change of direction and added the necessary block channel support.

So, to enable its use with SQL Server, NAS became, like all other storage platforms, both a block- and file-system-oriented storage device: a so-called "hybrid." This evolution is discussed in greater detail below.

SANs, by contrast to NAS, first appeared as a solution for off-LAN tape backup. According to some observers, upwards of 75 percent of early SANs were deployed to establish back-end connections to a shared tape library. Not only did such a strategy provide shared access to expensive tape libraries, but it also attacked the problem of shrinking backup windows that had long plagued LAN-based tape backups in open systems environments.

The vendor community, however, saw another "killer application" to drive SANs—namely, SANs were touted to provide a nondisruptive storage scaling solution for block data storage associated with very large databases. At first, this was the meaning assigned to the expression: "storage utility." Ultimately, however, SANs proved to be more like arrays of arrays, with SAN zoning substituted for "old fashioned" array partitioning.

Can you store files on a SAN? Of course: Files are collections of blocks, after all. But, to use a SAN (or any other platform) for file storage, some means must be provided to manage and control file access by applications and end-users. As of this writing, storing files to a SAN (or any other platform in which storage capacity is shared among multiple hosts with multiple operating systems) requires the file management services of application hosts. And, because of differences in the semantics of different file systems used by different operating systems, files must be segregated on shared storage platforms so that the files used by one OS file system are kept separate from those used by another. This has traditionally been accomplished on shared direct-attached arrays through the use of partitions. With SANs, the same logical partitioning of storage can be accomplished using zones.

As of this writing, the development of SAN file systems is ongoing at IBM and elsewhere. In keeping with the FC SAN tradition, many approaches support only one flavor of server operating system or a single vendor's storage platform. For now, it is less expensive and difficult to use FC SANs for OS-neutral block storage, rather than file system storage. Storage architects and consultants prefer NAS to SAN when it comes to file system storage.

Interestingly, however, developments at Microsoft and elsewhere may be changing this position within the next two or three years. Microsoft's next operating system, code named "Longhorn," substitutes an SQL database and binary objects for a traditional file system. Such an approach, long advocated by database software vendors such as Oracle and IBM, has the potential to reunify "bifurcated" storage by returning to the concept of all storage as blocks. Adoption of the "new" approach and its impact on the file systems of UNIX and Linux operating systems remains to be seen.

Another interesting development is Houston, Texas-based NuView's StorageX offering. StorageX provides a means to aggregate file systems into a common or global "namespace." A global namespace was originally conceived as a logical layer that sits between clients and file systems for purposes of aggregating multiple, heterogeneous file systems, and presenting file information to users and applications in a single, logical view, with obvious benefits for users and administrators. Users (and applications) are shielded from physical storage complexities, while Administrators can add, move, rebalance, and reconfigure physical storage without affecting how users view and access it.

With a global namespace in place, the administrator can perform data management and data movement tasks in less time, without disrupting user access to files. When files are moved, links in the namespace are automatically updated, which reduces manual administration and ensures continuous client access to date. Figures 5–5 and 5–6 depict the "before" and "after" images of a representative implementation of global namespace technology.

The potential of the technology, however, goes beyond simple file system pointer aggregation. It might well become a platform for delivering value-added functions that directly support data migration, server consolidation, and disaster recovery. By tightly synchronizing these services between servers and storage devices with the metadata server, NuView's architecture is non-disruptive and preserves existing server OS and storage controller investments. Ultimately, the vision of the designers seems to be the creation of a file broker service, similar to a directory server in a distributed client/server application, that enables storage to scale horizontally (i.e., by deploying many storage devices) just as efficiently as—or even more efficiently than—scaling it vertically (i.e., by creating bigger volumes).

In the StorageX approach, the choice of deployment of files to SAN, NAS, or DAS is determined simply by the security, accessibility, and performance requirements of data itself—as well as platform cost parame-

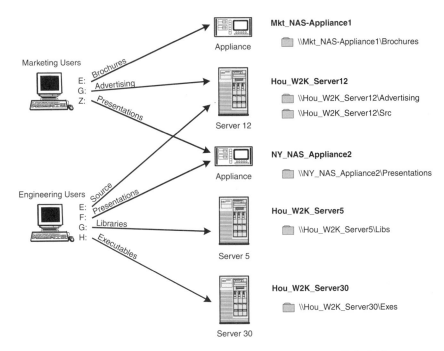

Figure 5–5 Before the implementation of a StorageX Global Name-
space—Hurdles for File (Data) Management and File (Data)
Movement increase as storage platforms increase. (*Source:*
"Global Namespace—The Future of Distributed File Server
Management," a white paper from NuView, Inc., Houston,
TX, *www.nuview.com.* Reprinted by permission.)

ters. As depicted in Figure 5–7, the physical hosting of files is already irrelevant from the perspective of its inclusion in a global namespace.

NAS/SAN HYBRIDS

The purported section between file and block in networked storage may also
be healed by the convergence of SAN and NAS architecture in hybrid storage products. As shown in Figure 5–8, a traditional NAS platform consists of
a "head unit" that offers physical connectivity to both the IP network (the
"front end") and to "trays" of disk drives (the "back end") configured into a
JBOD or RAID array. The back end could scale within practical limits imposed by the number of accesses made to the storage across the IP network
and the disk handling capabilities of the back end array bus and controller.

Given the traditional design of NAS products, capacity scaling was
conceived as a "horizontal" process. That is, when storage capacity re-

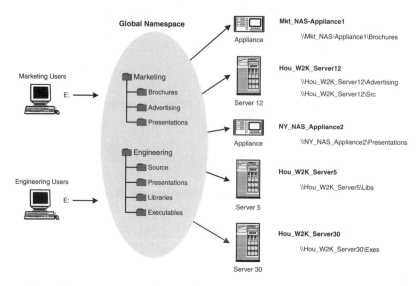

Figure 5–6   After implementation of a StorageX Global Namespace—
A single point of access and management. (*Source:* "Global
Namespace—The Future of Distributed File Server Management," a white paper from NuView, Inc., Houston, TX,
www.nuview.com. Reprinted by permission.)

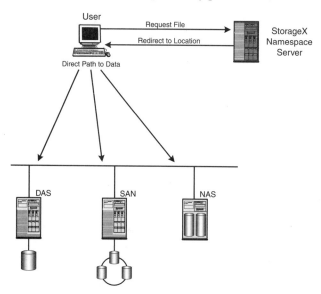

Figure 5–7   An Inclusive and Non-Disruptive Approach—A Global
Namespace Brokers Requests for Files to Back End Storage,
Regardless of Topology. (*Source:* "Global Namespace—
The Future of Distributed File Server Management," a
white paper from NuView, Inc., Houston, TX, *www.nuview
.com.* Reprinted by permission.)

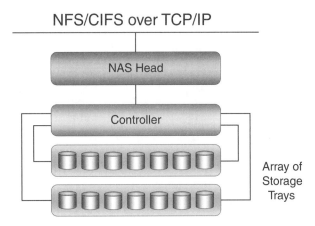

Figure 5–8 Traditional NAS design.

quirements exceeded the practical limitations of a single NAS appliance, users were advised to purchase another unit and install it on the network. This scaling approach worked reasonably well in small- to medium-sized environments where NAS was deployed for file storage "elbow room." However, as a scaling approach for files in larger shops, it created problems with respect to data management, as suggested by the NuView StorageX offering described above.

On the device management front, first-generation NAS suffered from the same problem confronting all storage: The more devices that were fielded, the more unwieldy the situation was from a management perspective. It wasn't until the early 2000s that leading vendors began fielding multiplatform management products to enable customers with hundreds of appliances to oversee and manage them from a single console. Smaller NAS vendors never provided a multibox management scheme, and instead used off-the-shelf web engines to enable their products to articulate web pages that provided access to configuration controls and status information. More than one storage administrator, confronting this proliferation of device-generated web pages, complained that the task of storage management had been reduced to the drudgery of "surfing the web"—traveling from one device web page to another to obtain management information.

The dilemma of multisystem management was a partial driver for more robust and "vertically-scaling" NAS appliances. A more capacious NAS, in theory, could reduce the number of appliances that needed to be managed . . . or even fielded in the first place.

The other driver for vertical scaling (the ability to add more storage behind a NAS head) was the burgeoning data storage requirements of email, and, to a lesser extent, other databases that were being hosted on NAS. These applications were difficult to distribute across multiple NAS appliances as their data exceeded the capacity of a single unit. Adding in the multibox management issues, NAS became an increasingly problematic hosting platform for growing data repositories.

In 2001, work began on addressing the vertical scalability of NAS (and other direct-attached storage arrays). Vixel Corporation, a Fibre Channel fabric switch-maker that had found its position in the market marginalized by the more popular FC switch vendors of the day, led the charge to deliver chip-based FC switches that could be integrated into storage arrays to enable a fabric interconnect among disk drives inside the array. Vixel chips and others found their way into NAS in late 2001 and early 2002, affording the capability to attach a greater number of drives to NAS heads, and increasing NAS capacity vertically in the process. This architecture (see Figure 5–9), combined with improvements in the NAS OS, effectively merged NAS and SAN technology to create a highly scalable appliance well-suited to certain applications, including e-mail.

The approach, while affording an increase in capacity, did little to address the practical constraints imposed on NAS storage by the protocols used to read and write data stored to those devices. Experts estimated that upwards of 70,000 instructions needed to be processed in order to open a file or bit location on a NAS disk using the Network File System (NFS) protocol. As a result, the more concurrent accesses made to the NAS appliance, the slower it operated. Moreover, the more capacity you added to the NAS, the more likely you were to see increased concurrent access attempts. So, latency became a constraint on NAS scaling.

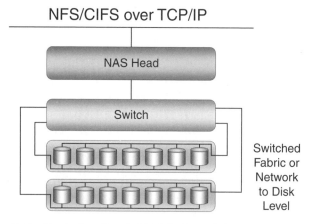

Figure 5–9   Vertical scaling in NAS facilitated through FC switching.

Various approaches are being tried as of this writing to rectify the situation. Some vendors seek to place most NAS OS functions into faster-executing silicon and to add large memory buffers and caches in order to facilitate improved request handling speeds and feeds. In the early 2000s, work was done on the creation of a zero copy protocol called the Direct Access File System (DAFS) that would enable memory-to-memory mapping between initiators of I/O requests and their storage targets. This protocol, plus the work being done on Remote Direct Memory Access (RDMA) over TCP/IP, promise to dramatically reduce latency by reducing the number of steps required to request, process, transfer, process, and use data from storage platforms.

While zero copy protocols continue to develop, so does the hybridization of NAS and SAN. To facilitate high-performance database hosting on NAS appliances, architectures are in the works to enable, not only network file system protocol connectivity, but also network block protocol connectivity, on the NAS head. Such a hybrid might take the form of the platform described in Figure 5–10.

In the figure, the back end of the appliance is vertically scalable using FC fabric or iSCSI network switching. The head end has been enhanced to support traditional NFS-, CIFS- and HTTP-based file access, and also iSCSI access for block storage. This enhancement effectively reunifies block and file storage in a single storage platform, a trend that began with

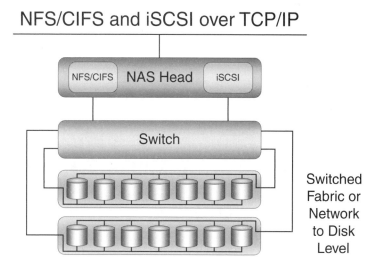

Figure 5–10 NAS/SAN hybrids with Network File System and Network Block Protocol accessibility.

Microsoft's introduction of Exchange Server 2000 (which required a block channel), and that will likely be underscored by the increasing substitution of object-oriented databases for traditional file systems going forward.

CONCLUSION

The division of so-called networked storage into block-optimized and file-optimized categories has always been less rooted in design than in architectural preference supported by vendor marketing. In the final analysis, all data is block data, but certain storage platform attributes—RAID, scalability, protocol support, I/O performance—have always guided the selection of storage platforms by smart storage planners who seek to match storage product capabilities to application performance requirements.

NAS/SAN hybrids may well become the preferred storage platforms going forward. If vendors were to modularize or "componentize" platform capabilities and features, selecting the right kind of storage for a particular application might become as simple as selecting a full meal from an a la carte menu.

In point of fact, the SAN has not delivered the intelligence that enables it to recognize applications and to deliver to them automatically the right amount or "flavor" of storage. The promise of the Enhanced Network Storage Architecture (ENSA) that started the SAN phenomenon in the late 1990s has yet to be realized. In its absence, storage administrators must still undertake the tedious and labor-intensive process of matching storage product capabilities to known application performance requirements. A modular NAS/SAN hybrid may provide a mechanism for doing so.

ENDNOTES

1. Inodes are data structures that contain information about files in Unix and derivative file systems. Each file has an inode and is identified by an inode number (i-number) in the file system where it resides. Inodes provide important information on files such as user and group ownership, access mode (read, write, execute permissions) and type. Inodes are created when a file system is created. There are a set number of inodes, which indicates the maximum number of files the system can hold.

6

Making Storage Platforms Smarter

In the previous chapter, we examined the recent division of data storage technology into block- and file-optimized platforms. We determined that, if such a division ever had any real value beyond that of "product differentiation" for vendor marketeers, it was quickly disappearing—especially in the face of ongoing developments in operating systems and in NAS/SAN hybrid platform architectures.

Ultimately, it is the storage planner's job to select the best storage platform to meet application storage requirements within the constraints of budget and other factors. No *Systema Naturae* articulated by any analyst house provides an adequate substitute for careful evaluation of the many available alternatives. Nor can marketecture ever substitute for the close scrutiny of the storage-related determinants of application performance.

In the final analysis, the design of a storage infrastructure has less to do with the platform components themselves than it does with their capability of the overall platform to deliver to applications a level of service required for peak performance. The components you select must work together to create an interoperable, manageable, resilient, secure, and accessible infrastructure that provides a strategic business value to your organization.

That some technologies are occasionally elevated to the status of "strategic" by vendors, analysts, or the trade press is strictly a function of marketecture. There is nothing intrinsically advantageous about a SAN or a NAS appliance or any other storage device. Being the first person to own a SAN doesn't impart special status to a storage manager. Like all technology, networked storage is a tool that can be used to help businesses achieve business objectives. The best technology is the one that delivers the most business value for the least money.

While this observation may seem rather obvious, you might be surprised how many storage managers still think of FC SANs as the pinnacle of storage technology. Successful industry marketing has positioned the FC SAN as a kind of status symbol, a goal toward which all storage professionals must aspire.

The simple fact is that what passes for a SAN today can be likened to a "boutique resort" in Southern California. The resort may be noteworthy for the celebrities who have visited but also notorious for being only half-completed, short on services, and overpriced in the extreme. Bottom line: Most current-generation SANs are a place to send your data on vacation, assuming you have the money and lack the wits to spend it wisely.

On the other hand, contemporary SANs might provide a certain fit in certain applications. For example, attaching servers and storage devices in an FC fabric in order to share the data protection afforded by a tape library may have a certain risk reduction value, but only if it can be demonstrated that there are also cost-savings and business enablement values to be achieved in doing so and that these values cannot be realized by any other means. (By the way, vendor claims about the inherent value of FC fabrics for tape backup are increasingly questionable given the mounting evidence that Ethernet, with its Jumbo Frames, actually provides a more efficient transport for tape backup streams.)

Creating a FC fabric may also provide business value by enabling the consolidation of server software licenses or the nondisruptive scaling of storage capacity behind a storage-hungry database. However, many other storage topologies may offer the same value at a lower total cost of ownership and must be explored carefully.

The point is that no storage topology is inherently superior or inferior to any other. Sometimes *not* selecting a FC SAN is the smartest approach. Storage architecture isn't about selecting the trendiest technology but selecting the technology offering the best return on investment and the lowest total cost of ownership. Whatever infrastructure you design, whether or not it includes a SAN, will accord you kudos or disparagements based on the business value it delivers.

THE SOURCES OF STORAGE INFRASTRUCTURE VALUE

Storage infrastructure delivers value both as a function of its design or architecture and as a function of device capability and intelligence. Smart architects know that some value is derived from infrastructure design: The more you can truly network storage, the more you can enable other value-producing processes.

For example, creating a back-end network of storage devices sets the stage for capacity utilization efficiency via some sort of hierarchical storage management. Migrating less frequently accessed data to less expensive and less high performance storage repositories can yield considerable business value.

Back-end networking might also enable improved data sharing with less replication, or improved replication for disaster recovery purposes at a lower cost. This assumes of course that the arrays and other devices deployed in the back end are able to comprise a stable and interoperable whole.

The point is that networked storage does not deliver any of these capabilities by itself. It can, given careful attention to details such as manageability, interoperability, and security, provide an enabling infrastructure that other processes require to accomplish the goals that the architect has defined.

In addition to process enablement, the other source of value in storage infrastructure derives from the capabilities of the storage devices themselves. We all are aware that storage components offer various performance capabilities. Some offer additional features that elevate them from the status of dumb peripheral devices to active peers in data handling, control, and management.

Efforts are afoot within the industry today to "add value" to traditional storage peripherals by enhancing their "intelligence." In the case of SAN switches, for example, many vendors have struck up alliances with storage virtualization and storage management software developers to embed their software tools directly on the switch hardware. "Fatter" or more intelligent switches, according to advocates, will deliver advantages over server-based management software or virtualization software appliances such as single point of management, streamlined licensing, and so forth.

Similarly, within the realm of tape and optical peripherals, an industry initiative[1] has been launched to add value through the implementation of intelligence "modules" providing enhanced "network awareness" and "self-management" to the devices themselves. Network awareness translates to the capability to sense changes in bandwidth availability and the corresponding automatic adjustment of memory buffers so that tape drives in a library can operate at their rated speeds. Self-management means different things to different vendors in the coalition, but all vendors appear intent upon adding basic error condition sensing and process restart to their platforms, presumably offloading this task from storage managers except in the case of nonrecoverable faults.

In general, these efforts by vendors to enhance their products with new "intelligence" features are driven by several objectives. One is the desire to prolong the utility of tape and optical, technologies that are under substantial (and largely unmerited) pressure from new, inexpensive magnetic disk-based data replication and protection solutions. Another goal is to create product differentiation—and potentially to lock customers into proprietary product technology—in an increasingly commoditized market.

The worst-case outcome of some of these efforts is the creation of products (like WAP phones in the portable telephony market) that integrate so many functions that they perform no specific functions particularly well. The enhancements may also lead to the perpetuation of proprietary barriers to interoperability between the products of different vendors.

At best, the enhancements may contribute to the simplification of storage management or, at least, provide additional useful information for storage managers when troubleshooting problems in the infrastructure.

In the final analysis, intelligence is not an intrinsic attribute of contemporary storage products. Human planners must build intelligence into the storage infrastructure through the selection of the best component technologies organized in the most efficient topologies to meet the requirements of applications.

Interestingly, this architectural decision-making process increasingly begins at the level of the disk drive. Arguably the lowest common denominator of storage componentry, and a technology that has undergone substantial commoditization over its nearly 50-year history, the magnetic disk has been thrust into the forefront of storage design decision making by a combination of engineering and economic factors.

BARRIERS TO GROWTH IN DISK AND CONSEQUENCES FOR PLATFORM DECISION MAKING

Of key importance in current disk drive technology is the limit imposed by the superparamagnetic effect (SPE) on areal density scaling in disk media. As previously mentioned, SPE refers to a relationship between the magnetic stability of disk storage and the thermal properties of disk subsystems. When the magnetic energy holding bits in their recorded states (0 or 1) becomes equal to the thermal energy generated by the disk drive in operation, random "bit flipping" can occur, making disk-based data storage unreliable.

SPE has become an issue because of the manner in which disk technology has achieved its phenomenal storage density improvements through the years. Vendors have increased areal density—defined as the product of the number of tracks per inch on a disk multiplied by the number of bits per inch—by packing more and more bits more and more closely into a track and by squeezing tracks closer and closer together on the same platter (see Figure 6–1). Of course, this has been accompanied by steady improvements in the sensitivity of read-write heads to enable the reading of the diminished magnetic signal of smaller and smaller bits against the backdrop of electromagnetic noise generated by the drive itself. The question that is being asked over and over today is how densely bits can be packed before SPE imposes a finite limit to capacity.

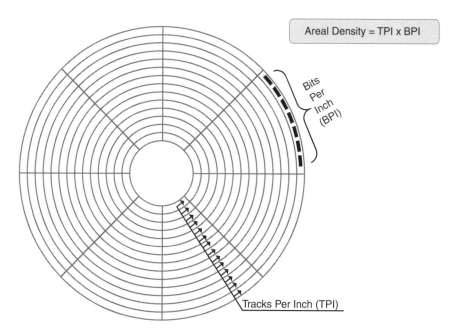

Figure 6–1   Areal density: Tracks per inch (TPI) × bits per inch (BPI).

According to engineers at IBM, HP, Seagate, Quantum and elsewhere,[2] the SPE is just another engineering parameter—not so much a "limit," as a media property that must be addressed as part of disk drive design.

Experts have optimistically noted that the presumed "limit" imposed by SPE has been set—and broken—more times than the mythical MACH barriers were established, then surmounted, by Chuck Yeager and other aircraft test pilots in the 1940s and 1950s. Indeed, public pronouncements of the limits of areal density scaling had all but disappeared by the 1990s, owing to the many times that vendors, who had declared areal density limits, were made to appear foolish or inept by rivals who had found a way to exceed the limit.

Initially set at 2 kilobits per square inch (Kb/in.^{2}), the SPE "barrier" was overcome by vendors time after time by improving disk drive components so that more bits could be reliably written and read within the same fixed space of the disk platter. As late as 1998, industry rule of thumb held that superparamagnetism would limit disk areal density to about 30 gigabits per square inch (Gb/in.^{2}). This would have been a more frightening concept at the time, given that areal densities of high-end disk drives were already hovering at 10 Gb/in.^{2}, but no vendor was willing to make a public statement about an SPE-imposed limit.

In 1999, IBM demonstrated a significantly higher areal density in its Almaden Research facility. About a year later, they bolstered their laboratory test results by adding "Pixiedust"—Ruthenium—to their platter coating, enabling 100 Gb/in.^{2} densities.[3]

Today, the "SPE demon" is thought to live out at about the 100 to 150 Gb/in.^{2} range, providing substantial "elbow room" to assuage the concerns of companies whose appetite for data storage seems boundless. However, the future of areal density improvement is not terribly bright beyond the 150 Gb/in.^{2} Moreover, even with such a generous runway for growth, if current capacity expansion trends continue, SPE-related limits will be reached before 2010.

According to most experts, areal density improvements beyond 150 Gb/in.^{2} will not be achievable without the application of entirely new technologies, many of which will require either significant breakthroughs in enabling process technologies or discoveries in materials science. To understand the improvements that will need to be made to current disk drives in order to reach even the anticipated 100 to 150 Gb/in.^{2} areal densities, it is useful to look at the disk drive as it has evolved to this point.

Readers of the first *Holy Grail* book will recall that the modern magnetic hard disk (see Figure 6–2) consists of a stack of disk platters—each comprising an aluminum alloy substrate with a magnetic material coating—onto which data is written in the form of linear tracks of magnetic bits. The platters are rotated counter-clockwise by a spindle motor at speeds of between 3,600 and 10,000 rotations per minute (RPM). Data is recorded to and retrieved from the spinning media by means of read-write heads that "fly" above the media at heights measured in microinches.

With most current disk drives, heads are positioned precisely over tracks on both sides—or "faces"—of the media through the use of servo-motor-controlled actuator arms. Microelectronics are used to control the operation of the drive, to convert detected magnetic states into useful signals, and to provide an interface between the drive and the computer system or systems that use it.

The basic design of the disk drive traces its origins to IBM's RAMAC drive, which was introduced in 1956. The RAMAC offered random access storage of up to 5 million characters, weighed nearly 2,000 pounds, and occupied the same floor space as two modern refrigerators. Data was

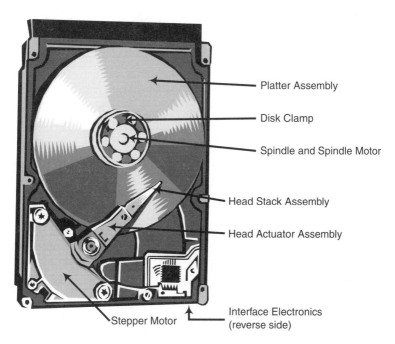

Platter Assembly

Disk Clamp

Spindle and Spindle Motor

Head Stack Assembly

Head Actuator Assembly

Interface Electronics
(reverse side)

Stepper Motor

Figure 6–2   An exploded view of a contemporary disk drive.

stored on fifty, 24-inch diameter, aluminum disk platters that were coated on each side with magnetic iron oxide. The magnetic coating of the media was derived from the primer used to paint San Francisco's Golden Gate Bridge.

In the 40-plus years that followed, innovations in the technologies of disk drive subcomponents and in signal processing algorithms led to dramatic increases in storage capacity and equally dramatic decreases in the physical dimensions of drives themselves. According to industry spokespersons, improvements have been largely realized through the scaling of drive components, which have enabled more bits to be written to more tracks on the media.

The statistics are stunning. There has been a 5-million-fold increase in magnetic disk storage capacity since the first disk drive. The growth rate accelerated in the 1990s. From 1991 until 1997, capacities increased annually at a rate of approximately 60 percent per year. In 1998, the rate of increase was 80 percent per year. In 1999, the rate of capacity improvement was at 130 percent. Currently, capacity is doubling every nine months.

It is no coincidence that areal density improvements have been seen at roughly the same times as drives featuring new read-write heads were introduced to market. As a practical matter, to increase areal density requires both the capability to write data to smaller and smaller areas (called domains) of the disk and to read the magnetic patterns from those domains efficiently.

Traditionally, bits are recorded on a disk by flying a write head over domains and altering the magnetic polarity of the grains of magnetic material located in the domain. Reading the bits is a function of positioning the read element of a read-write head at a position where it can successfully interpret the magnetic state of the domain and convert it into a useful signal. Over time, the precision and sensitivity of read-write heads, positioning electronics, and media itself have improved to enable smaller and smaller domains to be used to store bits.

Many early disk drives used ferrite heads to induce magnetic changes in media. Beginning in 1979, ferrite heads gave way to thin film inductive heads, a new approach that applied silicon chip-building technology to head design and production. Thin film heads enabled closer head fly heights and the reading and writing of more densely packed bits.

Thin film heads themselves were displaced in the early 1990s as other head designs offering the capability to read even smaller-sized bits appeared on the scene. The year 1991 saw the introduction of a new head design from IBM, based on the magnetoresitive (MR) effect, which revolutionized the industry.

MR head design used a traditional inductive head approach to write data to disk media, but it added a read element whose resistance changed as a function of an applied magnetic field. This application of the magnetoresistive effect, which was first observed by Lord Kelvin in 1857, enabled a major breakthrough in areal density. By increasing the sensitivity of read heads to the minute magnetic fields generated by smaller bit domains, smaller bits could be used effectively for data storage.

While older thin film read-write heads continued to be used by many manufacturers through 1996, drives based on the newer MR heads technology and incorporating additional improvements in servo control and media coating eventually came to dominate the market. In 1997, IBM introduced another read-write head innovation—the gigantic magnetoresistive (GMR) head—that enabled areal densities to climb even higher.

GMR heads improved upon MR heads by layering magnetic and non-magnetic materials in the read head to increase its sensitivity to even weaker magnetic fields, and by extension, to smaller bit sizes. According to one IBM insider, "tweaks" to the company's GMR head structure, a manmade component, are being counted upon to aid the vendor in achieving capacity expectations of 100 Gb/in.^{2} within the next six years.

MEDIA MATERIALS ARE KEY

While areal density improvements are enabled by read-write head improvements, media materials themselves provide the actual keys to realizing smaller bit sizes and true density improvements. Currently, bits are long, but narrow. To fit more bits on a disk, many manufacturers are looking for media that will support squarer bits. The problem engineers confront is that the smaller the grain size in the magnetic media coating, the less capability the grains have to hold a magnetic field or to resist heat.

Thermal stability is a key limiter of areal density improvement, most industry insiders concur. Heads can be made more sensitive, they can be flown closer to media to improve signal detection, and they can be improved in terms of tracking. Ultimately, however, the material properties of media—how few grains can be used to obtain the best mix of coercivity (magnetic hardness) and resistance to temperature—exert a limiting influence on density scaling.

Currently, a minimum of about 1,000 grains of magnetic material are required to store a bit of data. To make a bit smaller, one of three things must happen. Either 1) new materials must be found that will hold a detectible magnetic charge and resist SPE using fewer than 1,000 grains;

2) new materials or processes must be created that provide grains that are all uniform in size thereby creating a smaller domain; or 3) new signal detection technologies need to be discovered that will detect a magnetic charge using fewer grains.

In lieu of these improvements, experts say, the current bits per inch (BPI) limit for available media is right around 500,000 to 650,000 BPI. However, BPI is only one determinant of areal density; the other is tracks per inch (TPI).

In its quest for higher areal densities, the industry has looked for ways to write bits into a greater number of narrower tracks. The results of this approach are the drive geometries we see today, which offer TPI capabilities of about 20,000 TPI.

Expanding areal density by increasing TPI of a disk is not, however, a panacea for disk capacity growth. The number of tracks per inch that can be created on disk media is limited by several factors. These include the accuracy of the head position sensing system and resolution of the head recording elements. Significant improvements in the areas of head design, actuator control, and signal decoding will be required to pump up the TPI side of the areal density equation.

With current technology, tracks must be separated from each other by gaps of 90 to 100 nanometers in width to avoid the effects of fringe fields generated by write heads during the recording process. In the words of one expert, "Most write heads look like a horseshoe that extends across the width of a track. They write in a longitudinal (circumferential) direction, but they also generate fringe fields that extend radially. The fringe field causes side writing and side erasure, which is actually desirable and necessary to completely erase and overwrite old information. However, it also imposes a limit on how close tracks can be to one another since you do not want the fringe field generated while writing one track to accidentally erase data in an adjacent track."

More precise "head trimming" processes could lead to further TPI improvements. For example, experts say, a focused ion beam could be used to trim the write head and to narrow the width of the track that a writer writes. However, the read head, which is a sandwich of elements, poses a more difficult problem. The precision of the manufacturing process becomes much more important and much more difficult.

Getting to 100 Gb/in.^{2} will require disk TPIs of 50,000 to 150,000. With tracks that are only 0.17 microns wide, not only will head design be an issue, so will actuator design. Secondary actuators will be required for heads to follow tracks accurately.

Finally, new technologies, such as turbocodes, will be required to separate the weak signals generated by smaller bits from background noise and to decode them accurately. Current methods for signal processing require a 20-decibel signal-to-noise ratio. With current media and channels, the industry is at least 6 decibels short of being able to work with the signal-to-noise ratio that would apply when dealing with the bit sizes entailed in disks with areal densities of 100 to 150 Gb/in.^{2}

Design constraints are well understood, and industry insiders suggest that they are confident that materials and read-write technology improvements already in development will support the realization of drives with 100 to 150 Gb/in.^{2} areal densities. However, this optimism is caveated with the concession that a materials breakthrough will be required to move conventional magnetic disk storage technology much beyond that point.

CAPACITY VERSUS PERFORMANCE AND OTHER ECONOMIC REALITIES

Of course, capacity improvements do not provide the full picture of the future of disk drive technology. In addition to capacity improvements, performance improvements must also be considered. The speed with which data can be accessed from disk is increasingly important to end-users and may also be a determinant of the useful life span of magnetic disk drive technology.

Industry observers claim that moving to secondary actuators with high-capacity drives will be required not only to read and write narrower tracks more accurately, but also to facilitate better overall drive performance and throughput. The increasing rotational speed of drives, intended to improve drive access times, also necessitates the implementation of secondary actuators (called fine motor actuators) for every head in order to obtain the same (or improved) rate of performance from faster and more capacious disk drives.

Other enhancements required for improved performance will include smoother disk media with greater head texturization in order to facilitate decreased read-write head fly heights and more accurate reads of smaller bits. New fluid dynamic bearings will also be needed to replace steel or ceramic bearings that both wear out and emit audible noise when platters spin at speeds greater than 10,000 RPM.

According to most industry insiders, we are at the beginning of a true bifurcation of storage technology—not, as marketeers would have it, between platforms optimized for files and others optimized for blocks— but between disk drives optimized for speed and disk drives optimized for capacity. Signs of such a split are already here.

According to one industry insider, data transfer rates are increasing at 40 percent per annum, compared to the 130 percent improvement in disk storage capacity. In the past, disk drives were not bought based on performance, but on price.

Traditionally, most consumers preferred a bigger drive at the lowest possible cost, even if it offered lower performance. They didn't want to pay extra dollars in most cases to obtain a performance improvement. The return to the drive manufacturer for a 30 percent performance improvement was only about a 10 percent increase in its list price.

However, new demands are being seen for faster drives: in the business enterprise computing market, where high performance disk arrays are commonly deployed, and also in network-attached storage, where data needs to be shared and accessed by a number of users or servers. Some industry insiders project that at least two types of disk storage platforms are in the offing: one comprised of small form factor, high-performance/low-capacity disk to address the needs of high-speed transaction processing systems, and the other comprising large-capacity/low-perfomance disk to address the need for data that is less frequently accessed but that requires disk-based storage none the less.

Despite the current debate that is raging over the relative suitability of high-performance SCSI/Fibre Channel-attached arrays versus lower cost ATA and Serial ATA arrays (see below), the bifurcation of disk described above is still in the future. Economics will have a major role to play in the speed at which new, more capacious disk drives will enter the market.

ECONOMIC REALITIES

Just getting to 100 to 150 Gb/in.^{2} will, most observers agree, require solutions to many economically (as well as technically) nontrivial problems. A survey of the hard disk market to date confirms his view.

The introduction of thin film read-write heads to displace ferrite heads took nearly 10 years. Six years were required to introduce MR head-based products, while the move from MR to GMR heads took between 12 and 18 months. Vendors agree that the rapidity of changes to existing magnetic disk drive technology have been closely tied in the past to the nature and extent of disruptive changes to established manufacturing processes represented by the new technology.

Going from thin film inductive heads to MR heads entailed a number of new processes, ranging from how the media is sputter coated, to the manufacturing of an entirely new head design with different servo controls and a number of other integration issues. Delays were inevitable. By contrast, the change from MR to GMR head-based drives occurred much more quickly. While the GMR head was a radically new design, most changes were to the head fabrication process itself, which facilitated the transition. GMR heads yielded about a 2 to 3 percent performance improvement, but a 100 percent growth in capacity, which accounted for the quick adoption of disk drives integrating the technology in the market and helped to further bolster the speed of product introduction.

Vendors claim that the introduction of 100 Gb/in.^{2} magnetic disk drives will be an incremental one. There will likely be a reduction in the 130 percent per year compound growth rate in disk drive capacity improvement as the effort proceeds to bring new capacity expanding features on line—possibly returning to 60 percent annual growth rate by 2005. However, demand for greater capacity seems likely to continue unabated.

Interestingly, together with increased demand for capacity, there is also an expectation that the cost per GB of storage will continue to decrease with new technology. This poses a conundrum for the disk manufacturers. On the one hand, to remain competitive with possible disk replacement technologies, they are compelled to reduce the number of read-write actuators in their disk drives, rather than increase them, and to pursue other cost-savings techniques. On the other hand, these expectations also insulate the disk industry from potential competitors offering fast, high-capacity replacements for magnetic drives going forward.

In the words of one insider, "The trend is definitely toward cost reduction, which will make it very difficult for nondisk technologies to get on the tracks. To succeed, they will need to show a profit quickly and be able to compete on a cost per GB of storage with magnetic disk. More likely, they will need to carve out their own niche by appealing to a specific set of application requirements."

The same words could be applied to magnetic disk itself. For a 150 Gb/in.^{2} disk to succeed, it will need to deliver the same (or better) cost-efficiencies as current generation products. So, some method will need to be found to offset the cost of the additional technology required to create the new disk. Otherwise, the products will sell to a niche market defined by a subset of applications and their specialized storage I/O requirements.

BACK TO ARCHITECTURE

As the trends in disk storage technology suggest, the design of a storage infrastructure involves more than the simplistic selection of a topology such as NAS or SAN. If the most fundamental components of storage, disks themselves, are changing and growing more specialized in their feature set, functionality, and price, imagine how much more complexity exists as these technologies are configured into arrays and provisioned to applications! From this perspective, it should be clear that there is no substitute for the intelligence of the designer in selecting and implementing the right technologies to meet the needs of business processes and the applications that support them.

Above the level of the disk drive is the issue of disk interface protocols. As mentioned above, protocols are also an area of considerable development.

Today, most storage device attachments in the open systems world are made using one of two protocols. The first is the Small Computer Systems Interface (SCSI) and its derivatives such as Fibre Channel and iSCSI. Serial Attached SCSI, Fibre Channel, and iSCSI perpetuate the use of the SCSI command set and other SCSCI conventions but obviate the use of the physical parallel bus interconnect of traditional SCSI. The other dominant interface is Integrated Drive Electronics/Advanced Technology Attachment (IDE/ATA), used predominantly for internal disk attachment in PCs and smaller servers. IDE/ATA is receiving new attention by array manufacturers as Serial ATA (SATA) is brought online as an interface for creating general-purpose arrays of inexpensive disk. Table 6–1 summarizes and compares these evolving standards.

Industry insiders and pundits are currently having a field day debating the relative merits of SCSI and SCSI-derivative storage arrays versus

Table 6–1   SCSI and IDE/ATA Evolution

Interface	Distance	# Devices	Bus Width	Data Rate	Miscellany
SCSI-1	25 meters	8 devices	8-bit	5 MB/s	25-pin connector
SCSI-2	25 meters	8 devices	8-bit	5 MB/s	50-pin connector
Wide SCSI	25 meters	16 devices	16-bit	5 MB/s	168 cable lines to 68 pins
Fast SCSI	25 meters	16 devices	8-bit (but doubled clock rate to 10 Mhz)	10 MBps	
Fast Wide SCSI	25 meters	16 devices	16-bit	20 MBps	

Interface	Distance	# Devices	Bus Width	Data Rate	Miscellany
Ultra SCSI	25 meters	16 devices	8-bit	20 MBps	
SCSI-3 "Ultra Wide SCSI"	25 meters	16 devices	16-bit	40 MBps	
Ultra2 SCSI	25 meters	16 devices	8-bit	40 MBps	
Wide Ultra2 SCSI	25 meters	16 devices	16-bit	80 MBps	
Ultra160				160 MBps	
Ultra320				320 MBps	
Ultra 640/1280				640/1280 MBps	Future clouded by Serial Attached SCSI (SAS)
Fibre Channel	10 km (extendable to 100 km with special optical adapters)	126 devices per loop; theoretically, 16 million nodes in a switched fabric	Serial interface: copper or optical	1 to 4 GBps, 1000 GBps planned	
Serial-Attached SCSI (SAS)	6 meters	128 devices, 16 thousand maximum with Expanders	Serial interface	150, 300, 600 MBps	
iSCSI	No distance limitation	No device attachment limitation	Serial interface, TCP/ Ethernet transport	75% of IP network bandwidth practicable	
ATA, also known as IDE	40cm	Supports one or two hard drives	16-bit interface and PIO modes 0, 1 and 2		Parallel cable 40 pin

(continued)

Table 6–1   *Continued*

Interface	Distance	# Devices	Bus Width	Data Rate	Miscellany
ATA-2 (Marketed as Fast ATA and Enhanced IDE or EIDE) ATA-3			Supports faster PIO modes (3 and 4) and multiword DMA modes (1 and 2).		Supports logical block addressing (LBA) and block transfers. Minor revision to ATA-2.
Ultra-ATA: (Also called Ultra-DMA, ATA-33, and DMA-33)				33 MBps	Supports multiword DMA mode 3
"ATA/66"				Doubles ATA's throughput to 66 MBps	
Ultra ATA/ ATAPI-6 "ATA/100"				An updated version of ATA/66 that increases data transfer rates to 100 MBps	
Ultra ATA/ ATAPI-7 "ATA-133"				133 MBps	
Serial ATA (SATA or S-ATA)	1 meter			150–300 MBps	Serial ATA is a serial link—a single cable with a minimum of four wires

ATA and SATA arrays. Champions of SCSI interfaces boast that the tried and true technology provides faster data transmission rates (up to 80 megabytes per second) than IDE/ATA ports and note that SCSI ports enable multiple device attachment, whereas ATA does not.

It is worth keeping in mind that, although SCSI is an ANSI standard, it comes in many "flavors" (including a number of variants that are sponsored by vendors rather than codified as formal standards). So, anyone who has managed storage over the past 20 years is probably aware of the fact that two SCSI interfaces may be incompatible, even at the level of connectors.

The reach of SCSI has been dramatically extended by wedding the command set to serial transports, such as Fibre Channel. From a 25-m transmission range with traditional SCSI, Fibre Channel extends the distance between devices to 10 km, or to 100 km with special optic transceivers.

In addition to distance improvements, serial Fibre Channel operates at much higher speeds than parallel SCSI. Fibre Channel currently offers a 2 Gb interconnect, and 10 Gb links are on the drawing board.

Fibre Channel also supports up to 126 devices per arbitrated loop, or a theoretical capacity of more than 16 million nodes in a switched fabric. This capability dwarfs the 16-device-per-channel connectivity capability of traditional SCSI.

Substituting a serial channel for a parallel bus is also the thinking behind Serial Attached SCSI (SAS). SAS offers many features not found in traditional storage solutions such as drive addressability up to 4,032 devices per port, and reliable point-to-point serial connections at speeds of up to 3 Gb per second. Through the use of "expanders," as shown in Figure 6–3, topologies can grow to as many as 16,000 devices.

Like Fibre Channel and high-end parallel SCSI drives, SAS interfaces support dual porting, a useful feature for fault-tolerant array design. The smaller size of SAS device connectors enable full dual-ported connections on smaller 2.5-in. hard disk drives, a feature only previously found on larger 3.5-in. Fibre Channel disk drives. This is considered very important when catering to applications that require redundant drive spindles in a dense server form factor, such as contemporary blade servers.

SAS uses a 64-port expander to take advantage of its enhanced drive addressability and connectivity capabilities. One or more SAS host controllers can connect to a large number of drives, or other host connections or other SAS expanders. Vendors claim that this scalable connection scheme enables SAS to be used to build enterprise-class topologies that can support multinode clustering for automatic fail over or load balancing[4] (see Figure 6–4).

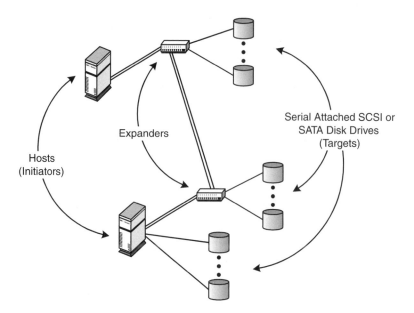

Figure 6–3   SAS topology with expanders.

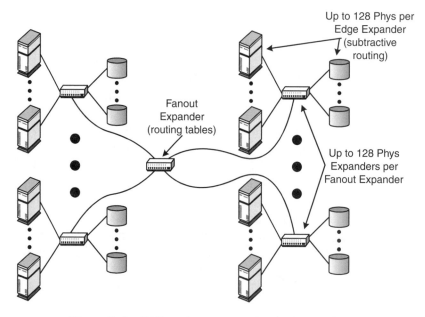

Figure 6–4   SAS maximum expander device topology.

Finally, iSCSI takes the SCSI command set and operates it as an application across a TCP/IP network. Supporting a Gigabit Ethernet interface at the physical layer, the protocol removes distance restrictions and device connectivity constraints altogether. And by leveraging a true network interconnect, rather than a serial channel interface, iSCSI provides the means to separate storage from servers once and for all and to enable the establishment of storage as its own infrastructure within the client/server hierarchy.

In an iSCSI connection, when an operating system receives a storage request from an application, it generates the SCSI command, then encapsulates the command in an iSCSI wrapper packet. This packet is directed to a target device across the network, where it is received, the SCSI commands are extracted, and the SCSI commands and data are sent to the SCSI controller and then to the SCSI storage device. The device response (more SCSI commands and data) are repackaged and transmitted to the requestor using the same protocol.

iSCSI was developed by the IETF and became an official standard in February 2003. To date, there are no storage devices explicitly tooled with an iSCSI interface. This necessitates the use of off-drive software and hardware to package and unpackage SCSI commands, which are typically wedded to controllers and host bus adapters.

In a sense, iSCSI adds to the existing processing burden of packaging and unpackaging of network message traffic between hosts that accounts for the fact that only about 75 percent efficiency is achieved with IP network messaging (including iSCSI). In other words, a 1 GB pipe dedicated to iSCSI traffic will yield an effective 750 MBps throughput, a 10 GB pipe, 7.5 GBps, and so forth. The balance of the bandwidth is lost to "overhead" processing.

In most cases, the overhead burden is irrelevant in actual operation—assuming that network bandwidth is adequate to application demands. To reduce the TCP/IP stack processing burden on servers, expediting technologies such as TCP Offload Engines (TOE) are being added to adapters, controllers and switch/router blades (see Figure 6–5). At least one host bus adapter vendor is also seeking to offload the iSCSI command packaging and unpackaging stack as well.

The bottom line is that high-end SCSI (SCSI 3 and above), Fibre Channel, SAS, and iSCSI interfaces provide the *crème de la crème* of connectivity and array building interfaces for meeting the needs of performance and data intensive applications. Vendors emphasize the dual porting of drives, their manufacture to higher standards of precision and durability, and their flexibility in terms of speed and distance, in arguing for their deployment into demanding enterprise environments.

At the other end of the spectrum are inexpensive disk drives, known as ATA drives, originally targeted to smaller systems and PCs. ATA is a

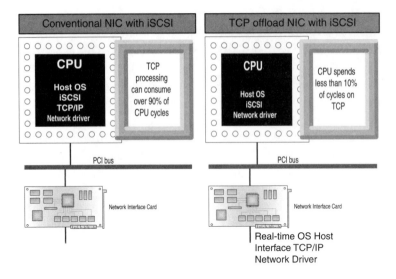

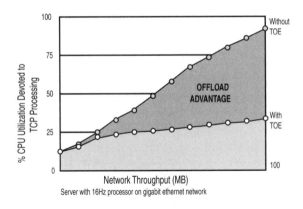

Figure 6–5   TCP offload engines lessen server CPU load.

disk drive implementation that integrates the controller on the disk drive itself.

There are several versions of ATA, all developed by the Small Form Factor (SFF) Committee. Over time, ATA technology has been enhanced to support steadily improving disk drive data rates, but it has consistently utilized a short length parallel bus—the notorious "ribbon cable" inside every PC—for connecting one or two drives to the computer motherboard. This reflects ATA's pedigree as an internal storage attachment method.

In the late 1990s, vendors perceived that new usage models for PCs and small servers, including digital video creation and editing, digital audio storage and playback, file sharing over high-speed networks, and other data-intensive applications, were placing new demands on hard drive throughput that would require further changes to the ATA bus. To keep pace, manufacturers began work on a serial implementation of the parallel Ultra ATA interface that promised to extend the roadmap for ATA beyond the theoretical limits of the Ultra ATA bus.

Serial ATA builds upon (or replaces, depending on who you speak to) the latest revision of the Ultra ATA specification in development by the ANSI-backed INCITS T13 committee, the governing body for ATA specifications: ATA/ATAPI-7 specification, an update of the parallel bus architecture that provides up to 133 MBps (see Figure 6–6). Serial ATA (SATA) introduces a four-wire cable replacement for the 40-wire ribbon cable of parallel ATA and delivers 150 MBps throughput with a roadmap of future enhancement out to 600 MBps over the next 10 years.[5]

Where Ultra ATA technology supported up to two drives—a master and a slave—per channel via a shared bus, serial ATA uses a point-to-point connection topology, meaning that each source is connected to one destination. Each channel has the capability to work independently so that there is no contention between drives and thus no sharing of interface bandwidth. This connection strategy also negates the need for master/slave jumper settings on devices.

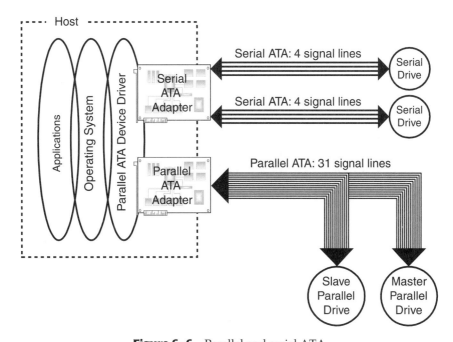

Figure 6–6   Parallel and serial ATA.

Other technical advantages of the SATA 1.0 interface cited by vendors[6] include:

- Point-to-point connection topology ensures dedicated 150 Mbytes/sec to each device,
- Thinner, longer cables for easier routing and better cabinet airflow,
- Fewer interface signals require less board space and allow for simpler routing,
- Better connector design for easier installation and better device reliability,
- 32-bit CRC error checking on all data and control information,
- Hot-swap capability,
- Support for low power consumption drives.

The capabilities in SATA 1.0 set the stage for a second-generation standard development process, SATA II. Announced at the spring 2002 Intel Developers Forum (IDF), a working group comprised of APT, Dell, Intel, Maxtor, and Seagate began developing a Serial ATA II specification, described as a superset of Serial ATA 1.0. This specification is being developed in two phases to meet market demands.

Phase 1 improves the use of Serial ATA devices in server and network storage applications. Phase 2 adds additional features for the entry-level and mid-range server segment and provides the second-generation speed increase (from 150 MBps supported by Serial ATA 1.0 to 300 MBps) for both server and desktop.

This effort parallels the development of Serial Attached SCSI (SAS), which has, as a stated development goal, compatibility not only with SAS drives and devices, but also with lower cost-per-gigabyte SATA drives. In late January 2003, the SCSI Trade Association (STA) and the Serial ATA (SATA) II Working Group announced a partnership to enable SAS system-level compatibility with SATA hard disk drives. This collaboration, as well as cooperation among storage vendors and standards committees, promises to facilitate the definition of compatibility guidelines to aid system builders, IT professionals, and end-users to better tune their systems to optimize application performance and reliability and to reduce total cost of ownership.

The anticipated result of this parallel effort is that products will begin to appear in the market by 2004 that support both drive types in the same array (see Figure 6–7) or topology (see Figure 6–8).[7] Advocates argue that this will provide flexibility to system builders to integrate ei-

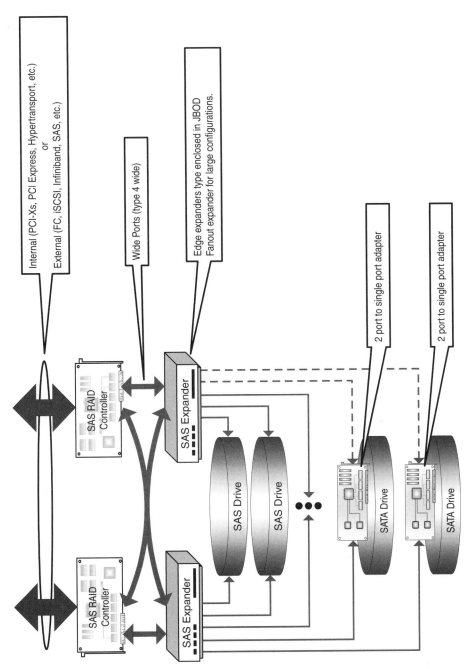

Internal (PCI-Xs, PCI Express, Hypertransport, etc.)
or
External (FC, iSCSI, Infiniband, SAS, etc.)

Wide Ports (type 4 wide)

Edge expanders type enclosed in JBOD
Fanout expander for large configurations.

2 port to single port adapter

2 port to single port adapter

SAS RAID Controller

SAS RAID Controller

SAS Expander

SAS Expander

SAS Drive

SAS Drive

SATA Drive

SATA Drive

Figure 6–7 Building a fault-tolerant RAID array with SATA and SAS.

93

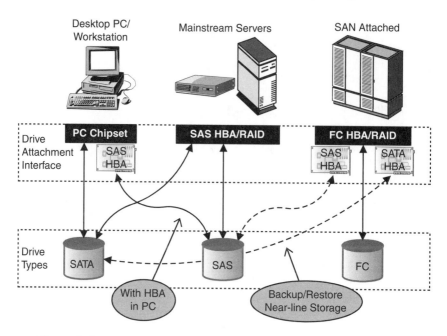

Figure 6–8   SATA, SAS, and Fibre Channel: One View of the future
enterprise storage landscape.

ther SAS or SATA devices, capitalizing on reduced costs where it makes
sense, and consolidating two separate interfaces into one.

Vendors of early products in this space are keen to assert that most
storage requirements can be met adequately by SATA (and in the future,
SAS/SATA) arrays. They claim that companies are paying dearly for
high-performance parallel SCSI or serial Fibre Channel platforms when
cheaper alternatives are now coming to market.

DISK AND ARRAY SELECTION CRITERIA

Today, arguments for and against platforms based on "high-end" (Ultra-
SCSI, SAS, FC and iSCSI) and "low-end" (UltraATA and SATA) drives
and interfaces are appearing in the trade press and on conference agendas
that are equal parts marketing hype and techno-babble. The situation is
creating confusion for many planners as they seek to establish an intelligent foundation for their storage infrastructure.

In the selection of disk and interface technologies for your next array
purchase, the following criteria will help sift through the marketecture:

1. The application is king. To select an appropriate technology for storing application data, the nature of the data and its characteristic access, security, and protection requirements must be identified and understood. Table 6–2 describes some typical characteristics of modern applications.

2. Data protection is paramount. The data that is being stored must participate in some sort of data protection strategy. For mission-critical data, most organizations seek to architect some sort of real-time redundancy into storage associated with the data. This will usually require dual-ported drives that can be attached to two, rather than one, controllers in an array as a protection against single point of failure (see Figure 6–9). Higher-end drives are dual-ported: typically, lower-end drives are not. However, an important caveat raised by many ATA array builders is that fault-tolerant arrays can be readily con-

Table 6–2   Typical characteristics of application data

Application	Read Intensive	Write Intensive	I/O Intensive	Throughput Intensive	Random Access	Sequential Access
Online Transaction Processing	X	X	X		X	
Data Warehousing	X		X		X	
File Services	X			X	X	
Medical Imaging		X		X	X	
Web Services	X			X	X	
Multimedia Video	X			X		X
Document Imaging		X		X		X
CAD and GIS	X		X		X	
Backup/ Restore		X		X		X
Archive		X		X		X

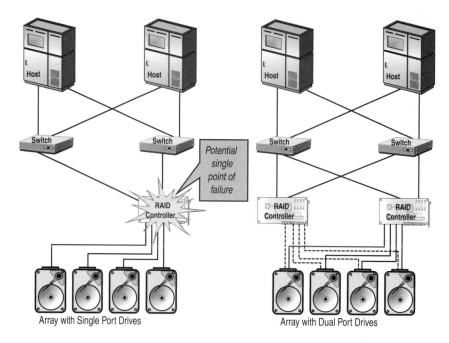

Figure 6–9   Dual-ported drives for high availability.[8]

structed using double the number of single-port drives and specialized controllers that still cost less than the total price of an array comprised of dual-port drives (see Figure 6–10).

3. Data integrity is key. For critical application data storage, protection
   is required to ensure that data written is data read. Top vendors have
   adopted "long blocks" in their high-end drives: sector information is
   supplemented with an appendix that does block checking to validate
   the address and contents of the sector (see Figure 6–11). This is an
   important stopgap against firmware and hardware errors.

4. Mean Time Before Failure (MTBF) must be considered. High-end drives are designed to provide a service life of more than 1 million
   hours before failing. Engineers design the drives for 24-hour/7-day
   operation (8760 hours/year). The drives in personal computers are
   designed for an 8-hour/5-day (2080 hours/year) duty cycle and typically demonstrate greater vibration as a function of their design, contributing to an abbreviated MTBF as well as greater frequency of
   write aborts and read retries.[10]

5. Performance requirements must be considered. Vibration can also
   impact speed of drive operation as seek times are protracted. That is

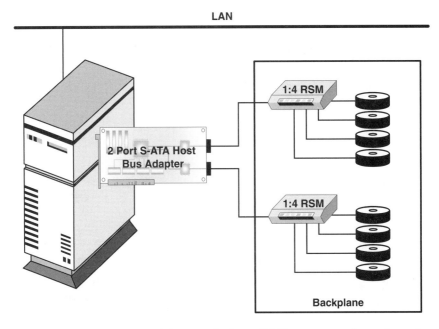

Figure 6–10   Single-ported drives in high availability array configuration using routing/switching/multiplexing (RSM) technology.[9]

part of the explanation for why high-end drives tend to provide 40 percent better performance than lower-end units. The other part is a combination of features of high-end drives engineered into units specifically to up performance. Better motors, more precise actuators, better electronics, and enhanced firmware providing such features as sorted work queues all contribute to much improved drive performance at the high end.

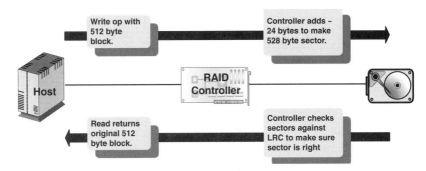

Figure 6–11   Long blocks for data integrity.

6. Warranty provisions may also be important. Put bluntly, high-end drives tend to have better warranties—testimony to the vendor's belief that longer MTBF will minimize warranty replacement expense.

From the criteria above, it may seem that high-end drives are the preferred foundation for any storage infrastructure. They might well be if cost were not an issue. In the real world, however, budgets do not permit the universal hosting of all data on the most expensive platforms.

Cost efficiency is gained by first matching a drive and interface to application data characteristics, then using practical parameters such as budgetary constraints to cull the list of possibilities. For virtually any application, there is an optimal storage solution and a number of less optimal ones from the standpoint of pure technology that may be better suited from a business value standpoint.

In the current industry view, disk and interface technologies may be viewed as forming a matrix bounded by performance and capacity characteristics (which are inversely proportional to one another) on one side and SCSI or ATA on the other—rather like the one depicted in Figure 6–12.[11]

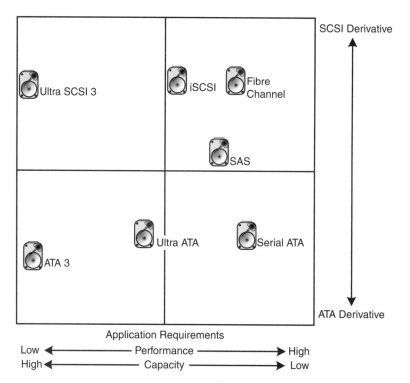

Figure 6–12   Industry matrix model of disk/interface solutions.

Another approach, most often championed by vendors of SAS and SATA, is to base disk and interface selection on the frequency of data change. If data is relatively nonchanging (read more often than written or updated), lower-performance, high-capacity disk may be preferred.[12] Conversely, for data that changes frequently, high-performance disk may be the better solution. Simplistic as this division might seem, it has the advantage of clarity without engaging in hyperbolistic infighting over one interface protocol or another.

STORAGE INTELLIGENCE BEGINS WITH INFORMED AND PRAGMATIC DEVICE DECISIONS

Of course, many additional factors beyond price and performance may enter into a decision about which type of disk or array to buy. Return on Investment analyses and anticipated service life will be factors in some cases, as will the manageability and "secret sauce" functionality that vendors add to their disk arrays through controller firmware. These are the subjects of subsequent chapters.

For now, it should be clear that the intelligence in a storage infrastructure is not an intrinsic quality of a particular topology or technology. From the standpoint of platform design, the intelligence in a storage repository is the direct result of proper analysis of application storage requirements and component characteristics.

Bottom line: The storage infrastructure is only as smart as you make it. There are no "angels in the architecture" without a few "devils in the details." It is the burden of the storage architect to evaluate options from the standpoint of business value and to select those that make the most sense.

It all begins with the data.

ENDNOTES

1. The Tape Automation Coalition (TAC) was being formed by Hewlett Packard, ADIC, Quantum Corporation and a number of other vendors at the time of this writing.
2. Jon William Toigo, "Avoiding the Data Crunch," *Scientific American*, May 2000.
3. Not to minimize IBM's accomplishment in any way, the company discovered a way to push back the data storage industry's most formidable barrier—the

areal density limit—by adding a few atoms of "pixie dust" to its platter coating process. Following on a long list of accomplishments in hard disk development, IBM was first to mass-produce computer hard disk drives using the new type of magnetic coating, and effectively quadrupled hard disk data densities. Known technically as "anti-ferromagnetically-coupled (AFC) media," the new multi-layer coating used a three-atom-thick layer of the element ruthenium, a precious metal similar to platinum, sandwiched between two magnetic layers. That only a few atoms could have such a dramatic impact caused some IBM scientists to refer to the ruthenium layer informally as "pixie dust." AFC media is now shipping in IBM's Travelstar notebook hard disk drive products with data densities of up to 25.7 gigabits per square inch. In time, IBM plans to implement AFC media across all of its disk drive product lines and hopes to reach areal densities of 150 Gb/in.[2] within the next two years.

4. Marty Czekalski, Vice President, Director—SCSI Trade Association, Technical Marketing Manager—Maxtor Corporation, "Serial Attached SCSI," March 5, 2003, *www.serialattachedscsi.com*.

5. Serial ATA Working Group, "Serial ATA White Paper," November 7, 2000, *www.serialata.org*.

6. Serial ATA Working Group, "Serial ATA (SATA) in Servers and Networked Storage," June 7, 2002, *www.serialata.org*.

7. Harry Mason, Director, Industry Marketing, LSI Logic and President, SCSI Trade Association, "Serial Attached SCSI: The Universal Enterprise Storage Connection," March 5, 2003, *www.serialattachedscsi.com*.

8. Suggested by SCSI Trade Association Presentation by Seagate Technology, "It's More than the Interface: Selecting the Right Drive for Your Application," August 20, 2002, *www.serialattachedscsi.com*.

9. See Serial ATA Working Group, "Serial ATA (SATA) in Servers and Networked Storage," June 7, 2002, *www.serialata.org* for more models of Serial ATA topologies and arrays.

10. SCSI Trade Association Presentation by Seagate Technology, "It's More than the Interface: Selecting the Right Drive for Your Application," August 20, 2002, *www.serialattachedscsi.com.*

An additional insight about the value of MTBF as a criterion for disk drive selection is offered by John R. Vacca, himself an author and IT Consultant with Tech Write in Pomeroy, Ohio, and a technical reviewer for this book. Says Vacca, "MTBF is an excellent characteristic for determining how many spare hard drives are needed to support 1000 PC's, but a poor characteristic for guiding you on when you should change your hard drive to avoid a crash. MTBF's are best determined from large populations. How large? From every point of view (theoretical, practical, statistical) but cost, the answer is 'the larger, the better.' There are well established techniques for planning and conducting test programs to develop specified levels of confidence in a hard drive's MTBF. Establishing an MTBF at the 80% confidence level, for example, is clearly better, but much more difficult and expensive, than doing it at a 60% confidence level. As an example, a test designed to demonstrate a hard drive's MTBF at the 80% confidence level, requires a total hard drive-time of 160% of the MTBF if it can be conducted with no failures. You don't want to know how much hard drive-time is required to achieve reasonable confidence levels if any failures occur during the test."

"What, by the way is, 'hard drive-time?' An important subtlety is that 'hard drive-time' isn't 'clock time' (unless, of course, your hard drive is a clock). The question of how to compute hard drive-time is a critical one in re-liability engineering. For some hard drives (living thing) time always counts, but for others the passage of hard drive-time may be highly dependent upon the state of the hard drive. Various ad hoc time corrections (such as "power on hours" (POH)) have been used, primarily in the electronics area. There is significant evidence that, in the mechanical area, hard drive-time is much more related to activity rate than it is to clock time. Measures such as 'Mean Cycles Between Failures (MCBF)' are becoming accepted as more accurate ways to assess the 'duty cycle effect.' Well-founded, if heuristic, techniques have been developed for combining MCBF and MTBF effects for systems in which the average activity rate is known."

"MTBF need not then be 'Mysterious time Between Failures' or 'Mislead-ing Time Between Failures,' but an important system characteristic which can help to quantify the suitability of a system for a potential application. While rising demands on system integrity may make this characteristic seem 'un-natural', remember you live in a country of 330 million 10-million-hour MTBF people!"

11. Figure 6–12 is very simplified. There are, of course, new disk drives appear-ing in the market daily that span categories shown here. For example, some vendor will doubtless provide a high performance disk with high capacity using the SAS interconnect and may also offer a high performance/low capacity SAS drive to support other applications such as notebook computing. So, these categories are by no means "cut and dried." Planners will need to read all specifications carefully.

12. Jon William Toigo, "SCSI versus Fibre Channel: Picking The Right Protocol," Enterprise Storage Strategies Newsletter, June 5, 2003, *www.esj.com*.

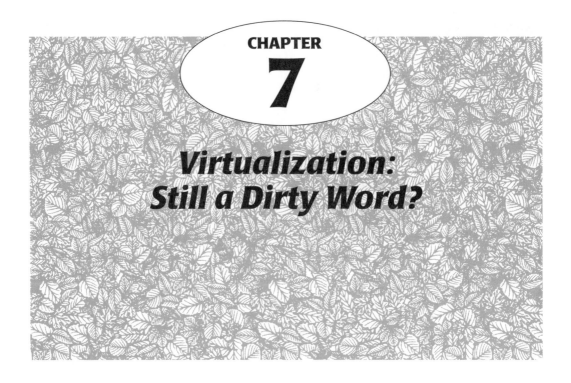

CHAPTER
7

Virtualization: Still a Dirty Word?

As discussed in the previous chapter, selecting the right disk and interface to meet the access and usage characteristics of applications is a basic element of intelligent storage architecture design. The differences in disk and interface performance—and price—also guide their inclusion in disk array platforms.

Arrays may vary in complexity from simple JBODs (just a bunch of disks), to more complex RAIDs (redundant arrays of independent disks) that afford a certain degree of internal protection against disk faults, to intelligent, multiported repositories that are increasingly acting as peer computers in a peer-to-peer I/O processing topology. The trend in the industry appears to be the delivery of arrays with the capability to scale their storage capacity dynamically through the use of an internal switch fabric. An increasing number are using Fibre Channel switches embedded in silicon chips to capitalize on the device connectivity capabilities of Fibre Channel fabrics inside the array, while relying on controller (or "head") intelligence to provide the operational management and control for the configuration.

Given the impending limits to magnetic disk areal density growth imposed by the superparamagnetic effect, the argument could be made that more capacious arrays, and ultimately networks of arrays, will be required to continue the pattern of increasing disk capacity at decreasing cost per megabyte that has long served as an engine of growth in modern information technology. To continue to scale disk beyond the areal density limit, multiple physical disk drives must be aggregated and presented as a single volume to operating systems and applications. A disk volume is an abstraction or simplification referring to a collection of blocks of storage. It is a virtual disk.

A BRIEF OVERVIEW OF VIRTUALIZATION IN IT

Virtualization has long been a part of IT infrastructure. In the mainframe world, host systems could be segregated into logical partitions or LPARs, each capable of running its own operating system and applications. Each LPAR was a virtual machine, behaving like an independent entity for all intents and purposes, despite the fact that it shared the same physical platform as every other LPAR.

In the early days of PCs, users could augment their slow-performing floppy disk drives by purchasing memory and constructing a virtual disk to which data could be written and read, albeit at much higher speeds than physical targets. "Vdisks" were fairly common in the late 1980s, with chip manufacturers garnering substantial income from memory cards that competed in terms of price with the expensive, pre-standard, hard disk drives of the day.

Even in the realm of networks, virtualization found a role. To extend storage devices and other peripherals further away from their host backplane connection points than manufacturers deemed possible, channel extension vendors devised a number of virtualization-based techniques. One approach involved "spoofing" through the installation of intelligent controllers at the local and remote sites (see Figure 7–1). These controllers, called channel extenders, emulated the communications of the peripheral devices locally, provided wide area network communications access for the I/O traffic, and emulated the host at the remote side so that overall system performance was insulated from the distance-imposed latency of the far-flung configuration.

From this brief survey, it is obvious that the use of virtual abstractions has served purposes ranging from performance improvement (virtual disk) and fault tolerance enhancement (RAID), to improved topological flexibility (channel extension), to improved resource allocation (LPARs). In these roles, virtualization enables architectural design goals to be achieved

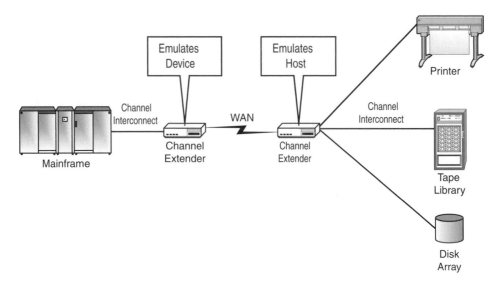

Figure 7-1   Channel/device emulation in a wide area channel extension configuration.

using a fixed complement of hardware. Without it, we would need to
replicate configurations, or in some cases build specialized devices, for almost every application we field or process we invent or support.

Virtual abstractions may also be used to conceal complexity by making many elements appear to be a single element. A file, for example, is a
simplified reference to a set of physical blocks containing data used by an
application. File systems are a kind of virtualization.

Virtualization may also be used, as in the case of LPARs and certain
tape virtualization techniques, to "multiply" fixed resource by making a
single element appear as a separate and unique resource from the perspective of multiple processes or elements. One leading vendor of tape offers a platform today that identifies itself to all servers as whatever brand
of tape the servers prefer. When it receives input streams from each
server, it captures the data, schedules and prioritizes it, and formats it for
storage on whatever type of library that is physically connected to its back
end: In effect, it multiplies the number of tape devices available to servers.

SANS AND VIRTUALIZATION

So, if virtualization is a pedigreed concept in computing architecture and
one that has enjoyed such widespread use in the IT environment, why is it
that virtualization has become a "dirty word" within the context of stor-

age area networking today? Many vendors are reluctant to use the term to describe software technologies that they are promoting for use in managing SAN infrastructure. Survey after survey reflects consumer disdain for the term "SAN virtualization."

There are many possible explanations for the phenomenon, which has stymied the marketing efforts of even the leading vendors in the storage space. Many vendors and analysts suggest that virtualization is too confusing to resonate with consumers. Like the term SAN, virtualization has been bent and twisted by marketeers so that it seems to mean different things depending on the vendor to whom one speaks. The only two points of universal agreement when it comes to virtualization are 1) that it is essential to have virtualization in order for SANs to deliver on their value proposition and 2) that there is absolute disagreement about the best strategy for realizing it.

SANs require virtualization if they are to deliver on their value proposition of reduced storage-related downtime and improved capacity allocation efficiency. SANs promise to reduce downtime by dynamically scaling storage behind an application so that applications never encounter a disk-full error message.

This value proposition is an extension of a claim long made by vendors of high-end arrays. As a function of controller intelligence and microcode, arrays enabled many physical disk drives to be joined together and presented as a single disk volume (typically identified by a Logical Unit Number or LUN) to the operating systems of connected servers. Increasingly, array vendors provided configuration tools to IT technicians that would enable them to add more physical disks to a LUN or to combine two or more LUNs to make larger volumes.

While these capabilities were useful, they often ran afoul of constraints within server operating systems themselves. Some operating systems identified volume capacity at the time of boot-strapping (start-up) and needed to be quiesced, powered down, then rebooted, to identify and begin using newly expanded volumes. This process disrupted normal operations and became more painful as IT shops began operating on "Internet time"—365 days per year, 24 hours per day, 7 days per week.

In the parlance of storage area networks (SANs), which may themselves be conceived of as very large disk arrays (or, more confusingly, as "arrays of arrays"), virtualization is used both as a verb, referring to the process of creating scalable volumes from storage nodes connected in the SAN fabric, and as a noun, a device or software component that provides a role comparable to that of a controller in a single disk array. In general, SAN virtualization refers to techniques for combining or aggregating LUNs.

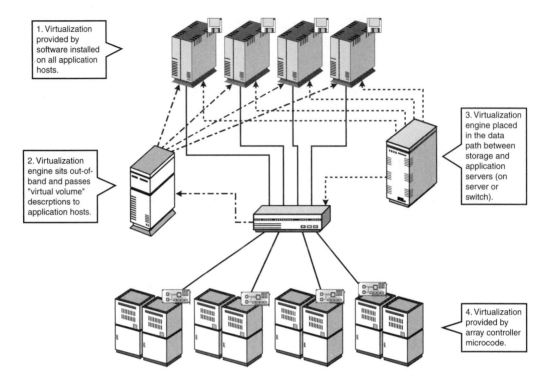

Figure 7–2   Options for locating virtualization intelligence in a SAN.

Vendors differ in their preference for locating this aggrandized array controller functionality in the SAN. Figure 7–2 surveys the popular options: on the host, in the wire (in-band) on a switch or intelligent appliance, out-of-band on a server or appliance, or at the array controller.

HOST SOFTWARE-BASED VIRTUALIZATION

Some vendors have opted to base virtualization functionality on server hosts in the form of a low-level software layer. This approach (shown in Figure 7–3) has several precedents. File systems, arguably a form of virtualization (see above), tend to be components of operating systems and operating systems are typically responsible for "virtualizing" their internal server disks and, in some cases, direct attached arrays by applying formats and partitions to physical drives.

In most cases of host-based virtualization strategies, software is used to re-map physical drives (and drive aggregations presented to the server

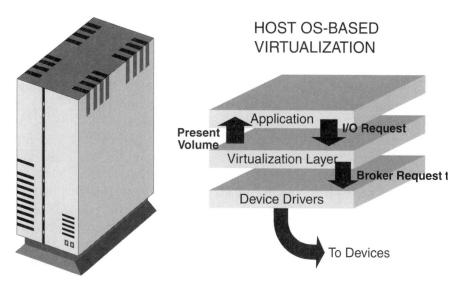

Figure 7–3   Host-based virtualization.

as "volumes"). In so doing, the software presents its own virtual volume entities to the application layer of the server environment. In operation, read/write commands issued by applications are "brokered" by the virtualization software, and I/O is passed to the appropriate device drivers for actual disk resources.

Additional software functionality enables virtual volumes to be "enlarged" (that is, more physical resources can be assigned or shared with the existing virtual volume) or "reduced" (physical resources can be subtracted from the volume) to adjust capacity to meet application needs.

The problems with this strategy are potentially several. For one, the operation of the virtualization layer consumes server processing cycles. This may or may not be an issue based on server load.

Second, some operating systems, frankly speaking, do not like to have a low-level process intercepting I/O calls. The more jealously that the OS guards its I/O, the more likely it is to treat I/O redirection as a virus or malicious software process and the more likely it is to use whatever means have been designed into it to abend the suspicious process.

In 2002, I received reports from several clients and others that a popular host-based virtualization software product was abending during volume resizing procedures. When the volume resizing process failed, apparently as a result of an operating system action, all data on the existing virtual volume was made inaccessible—not a good thing. Consultations with the vendor yielded only a flat denial that any problems existed in its software: "It never happens." However, chats with several analysts and integrators provided a contrary view: It happened as often as 60 percent of the time in the Windows environment, and nearly 40 percent of the time in various UNIX operating environments. Presumably, the resizing process was being treated as a violation of the OS kernel's processing domain.

In point of fact, as long as the virtualization software layer behaves in accordance with the rules governing applications in a given operating system, it should be treated simply as another application. That its function is to intercept I/O is irrelevant, provided that it issues its brokered I/O requests in an OS rules-friendly manner. But, this is not always guaranteed, especially with the ongoing litany of fixes, patches, and updates that emanate from major OS vendors, which system administrators must constantly apply to keep their environments secure and up-to-date.

A third potential problem with host-based virtualization is the conflict it can introduce in connection to other I/O processes, such as tape backup. This applies to all virtualization techniques, and not just to host-based approaches. As shown in Figure 7–4, if virtualization software and backup/restore software are not mutually aware—that is, if they do not provide accommodations for each other's operations—serious negative consequences can result.

Imagine a 1 terabyte data restore requiring over 100 hours to accomplish! Given that the rated speed of current automated libraries hovers around 2 TB per hour, such a delayed restore is unthinkable and potentially devastating in an actual disaster recovery situation. A client of mine

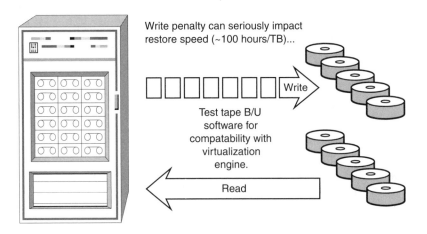

Figure 7–4   Tape restore issues and virtualization.

confronted just such a problem, which was traced to the fact that his backup/restore software was unaware of his host-based virtualization software. What was slowing down the restore process was the need to pass all streaming data from the tape through the "virtualization engine," where it was being reviewed and redirected to the appropriate physical disk targets. A severe case of the "write penalty," familiar to anyone who remembers early software based RAIDs, was accruing to the process. With no standards—open or *de facto*—for virtualization, such software incompatibilities may just be the tip of the iceberg.

Finally, host software-based virtualization has the potential drawback of being difficult and costly to maintain given large numbers of servers. Vendor efforts to resolve the hassle of software maintenance and upgrade management have usually entailed the implementation, at additional expense, of multihost software administration utilities. Software license fees for host-based approaches are also a potential drawback.

"IN-BAND" VIRTUALIZATION

Host-based virtualization, as noted above, is only one of at least four discernable variants in the SAN virtualization game. A second group of approaches are referred to collectively as "in-band" or "in-the-wire" virtualization by the trade press and analyst community. This description, while it has the advantage of convenience by capturing several product implementation philosophies under single moniker, also confuses the issue. All SAN virtualization techniques are, by their nature, located in the data path (see Figure 7–5).

In the case of virtualization software located on a host, the software layer is near the beginning of the I/O request, but still in the path. So-called in-band techniques are also in the path because they impact data traffic as it travels between the initiator of the I/O request and the target of that request, the storage platform. Current favorites for this type of virtualization are specialized "appliances"—single-purpose servers running virtualization software and installed in the wire—and "fat" switches—storage switches enhanced with new software functionality for performing virtualization.

The third approach, ostensibly called "out-of-band" virtualization, is effectively classified as "in-band" as well. A specialized server appliance sits outside the data path, where it monitors the condition of volumes and determines when capacity must be added. When necessary, it initiates a device driver update process and rewrites the parameters of the device

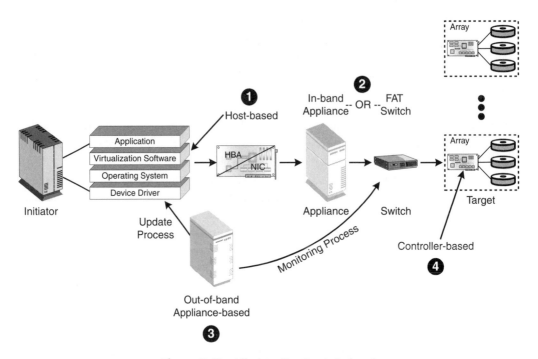

Figure 7–5   All virtualization is in-band.

driver on each host in order to change the size of the virtual volumes that applications are able to use. The device driver acted upon by the appliance is in-band.

The final approach, virtualization on the controller of an array, is also an in-band approach, since the access made to backend storage is through the "front door" of the controller's virtualization engine. From the perspective of the data path, the distinction between in and out of band is meaningless.

Having said that, what we are calling in-band virtualization—in the data path appliances and enhanced switch functionality—is currently the hot spot for virtualization engineering. In 2003, it seemed that nearly every storage hardware manufacturer, and many storage management software vendors, were either establishing alliances with in-band appliance vendors or teaming with leading Fibre Channel and IP switch vendors to migrate virtualization software to those platforms.

Conceptually, it makes more sense to reduce the complexity of virtualization by vesting the functionality in a single, more easily managed and administered location such as a switch or appliance, rather than on hosts or storage arrays individually. A number of vendors seized upon this model early on, using commodity server hardware and operating system extensions to build appliance products.

Concerns were immediately raised about the potential saturation of the commodity server bus by placing it in the line between an expanding number of initiators and an expanding pool of targets. Said one IT manager for a large insurance company, "Queuing theory alone suggests that you can't push traffic from 800-plus servers communicating with 180 TB of disk organized into storage array platforms through what is essentially a PC bus without introducing a significant chokepoint and significant latency."

One out-of-band storage appliance vendor used a hypothetical math problem to demonstrate the difficulties "inherent" in its competitors' in-band approaches:

> As an example, in a SAN with 50 application servers, the throughput required for each can reach 100 MB/sec. This value, 100 MB/sec * 50 servers = 5 GB/sec. While it is fairly easy to install multiple RAID subsystems with aggregated performance exceeding this requirement, a typical symmetric appliance based on a standard Pentium III processor with a 64/66 PCI bus can deliver no more than 520 MB/sec (that is 260 MB/sec sustained rate as data needs to enter and exit through the PCI bus on the appliance)—a far cry from the specified requirement. Needless to say, as the SAN becomes larger, this problem becomes more acute.
>
> The hardware cost to construct [an in-band] appliance that will support 20 servers with reasonable performance could reach $25,000 and more; this cost is at least doubled if a High Availability configuration is required.
>
> Some [in-band] designs are attempting to circumvent the performance problem through adding a cache facility to the appliance. This approach further loads the appliance's memory subsystem. For many reasons cache is much more effective when it is distributed (i.e., part of the RAID subsystem) rather than centralized (i.e., part of the storage management appliance).
>
> The use of caching also complicates High Availability (HA) configurations, which try to avoid single points of failure, as well as Scalable configurations, where additional appliances are added to respond to increased load. If caching is used with multiple appliances, some kind of cache coherency strategy is required. Experience with RAID controllers shows that this can be very complicated (and expensive).
>
> In order to achieve high performance on the server side, while using two (or more) HBAs, a software driver should be installed on each server. That feature is common to the [in-band and out-of-band]

solutions. Both need software to be installed on the server in order to create redundant and high performance (multiple paths) solutions for increasing throughput.[1]

Thus, consumer speculation, reinforced by vendor infighting, has created an impression of in-band virtualization inefficacy that has, in turn, proven the most difficult hurdle for vendors of in-band appliances to surmount. In fact, virtualization performance is determined by three factors: processor efficiency (how quickly data can be processed), parallelism (how many processes can be accomplished in parallel or at the same time), and data pathing (how optimized is the path used to move data to where it needs to go, among and between internal components such as cache memory and CPU, and through busses and networks). In the mainframe world, where vendors have enjoyed nearly complete control over the design of both equipment and operating systems, this control has been used to optimize system architecture specifically for virtualization, elevating virtualization in the process to the status of an architectural mainstay. In the realm of open systems, such single-vendor hegemony does not exist, and implementations have been uneven in terms of performance optimization.

Products like DataCore Software Corporation's SANsymphony, however, are maturing rapidly. This virtualization engine, which is part of the offerings of other vendors including Hitachi and Fujitsu SOFTEK, is designed to run on multiprocessor Storage Domain Servers (SDS), which do not have the interrupt processing requirements of general-purpose servers. According to the company,

> Multi-processing SDSs continuously poll I/O channels for new activity (read or write requests) using one or more very fast CPUs. I/O processing takes place uninterrupted using local memory as very high-speed disk block caches. At least one CPU in each SDS is set aside to handle interrupt-driven background management tasks that would otherwise interfere with I/O processing. Through these techniques, SANsymphony software overcomes I/O performance limits encountered by heavily interrupted hosts.
>
> A configuration that might cap at 15,000 I/Os as an interrupt-heavy host can deliver upwards of 200,000 I/Os as an SDS.[2]

DataCore claims that its caching technique actually reduces the disk I/O latency typically experienced by applications. The vendor attributes this to the fact that SDS caches are fast, yet lower cost and scalable across the network. It also cites its built-in data prefetching scheme and read request sorting as an accelerator, rather than a decelerator of I/O.

> Caching also hides some of the write delays experienced by applications storing data on slower devices. The caches acknowledge the write after quickly depositing the data in memory. In the background, software opportunistically coalesces several of these cached blocks destined for the same area of a disk into one physical I/O. Fewer and larger transfers replace multiple smaller I/Os to reduce the overhead on the back-end device and its channels.
>
> Some observers fear data loss or data corruption from write caching. Robust write caching techniques have been around for years and have been shipping in volume with every major disk array. As with all the successful write caching implementations, SANsymphony replicates the I/O in real-time to an independent location before acknowledging completion. The redundant data is maintained on an entirely separate SDS node. This ensures full data access to an alternate image if the primary cached contents are unreachable.[3]

In summary, DataCore makes salient observations about its platform intended to answer the many detractors of in-band virtualization in the analyst community, trade press and marketing departments of competitors.

- Storage Domain Servers are generally three to four generations ahead of the processors and busses assembled in array controllers.
- SANsymphony software effectively uses multiple independent PCI busses in each Storage Domain Server to match the bandwidth needs of the storage pool. For example, each SDS node cited earlier in the performance reports drove five separate PCI busses, three of which accounted for 1.6 GB/sec of storage networking bandwidth.
- Sheer horsepower and economics make it possible to front-end premium priced arrays with low-cost Storage Domain Servers at a fraction of the price.
- Storage Domain Servers field most of the repetitive read requests right out of their high-speed caches to effectively offload the arrays.
- At the time of this writing, just two modestly configured Storage Domain Servers can handle 2 to 10 times the peak transaction and throughput of the world's most powerful arrays.
- Increasing the I/O budget for [DataCore] storage pools is as simple as nonintrusively adding another low-cost Storage Domain Server.

That means more cache, more CPUs, more ports and more bandwidth can be quickly added to handle unpredictable demands. Basically, in-band sensing, end-to-end I/O path management and in-band caching have been shown to improve the behavior of a dynamic storage network. You can't offer the same benefits from the sidelines using an out-of-band appliance.[4]

OUT-OF-BAND VIRTUALIZATION

DataCore and other in-band virtualization appliance providers, such as StorageTek, have been fighting a two-front war for the past several years to offset the concerns raised by the placement of devices in the data path between initiators and targets in a switched fabric. On the one hand, such a strategy arguably usurps the functionality of array controllers themselves, mitigating in the process the value proposition that has supported the pricing of high-end arrays to more than 20 times that of simpler arrays. Brand name array manufacturers have been less than receptive to the notion of a "super-controller" place in front of their products that potentially reduces them to a JBOD.

In-band vendors have also fought with peer start-ups comprising an out-of-band virtualization camp, companies like StoreAge and pre-merger Compaq Computer Corporation. Compaq originally conceived of an out-of-band virtualization engine, which it branded as VersaStor, to fulfill the storage management and control functionality requirements described in its Enterprise Network Storage Architecture (ENSA) Whitepaper, considered to be a foundational document describing contemporary SAN architecture.

In effect, the VersaStor server sat on the sidelines of the SAN, evaluating application requirements and capacity utilization, and monitoring available storage resources connected to the SAN infrastructure. The VersaStor server was to accomplish the virtualization of the storage in the SAN by writing virtual volume descriptions to a proprietary chip on the host bus adapter installed in the application server.

The industry turned a cold shoulder to Compaq's proposal of a proprietary VersaStor chip, despite arguments from the vendor that writing the virtual volume descriptions to a proprietary chip would make them less vulnerable to hackers. An alternative that circumvented the proprietary chip issue by writing volume descriptions to application host systems was proposed by StoreAge and is now a fixture of the virtualization solution from that company.[5]

The out-of-band approach appeared to be leading the charge as the least intrusive strategy for open systems storage virtualization, but the outlook has dimmed since 2002 as a result of the 1) general economic downturn, which is stalling implementation plans for SANs generally, 2) the disillusionment over SAN management in many quarters, 3) the acquisition of its most well-known champion, Compaq, by Hewlett Packard Company and subsequent "reconsideration" of ENSA by that company, and 4) the recent and increasingly noisy dialogue between leading vendors of both host software-based virtualization products and high-end disk arrays, and switch vendors such as Cisco Systems, Andiamo Systems, and Brocade Communications Systems. As of this writing, virtually all eyes are on switch-makers as the future providers of virtualization services in a SAN.

ARRAY CONTROLLER-BASED VIRTUALIZATION

Array manufacturers may seem odd bedfellows with switch-makers, given their stake in virtualization as a function of controller design. After all, much of what is taken for storage virtualization architecture today is drawn from the designs of high-end array controllers.

The inefficacies of host software-based RAID in the late 1970s and early 1980s gave rise to the development of hardware-based implementations of RAID technology and led to the rise of a cadre of recognized storage centric vendors that today are household words in the industry. EMC Corporation and others dedicated substantial resources to adding value to their boxes of increasingly commodity disk drives by adding intelligence to controllers. Virtualization (a.k.a. LUN aggregation) arose from direct access storage device (DASD) development efforts at IBM, EMC, Hitachi Data Systems and elsewhere throughout the 1980s and 1990s.

In the process, each vendor developed proprietary approaches arguably intended not only to enhance value to their customers, but also to lock their customers into their products solely. Today, controller-based virtualization achieves its greatest level of sophistication and value if a customer uses only the arrays of a single vendor. By extension, and as a consequence of proprietary technology, Fibre Channel SANs work best only if the storage arrays that they interconnect to servers are homogeneous—all purchased from one vendor (or a certain cadre of vendors who have exchanged sufficient technology to work and play well together).

The openness of SANs is a myth for as long as proprietary array architecture precludes the virtualization of arrays across vendor boundaries. This is the essence of the teaching derived from a SAN vendor interview cited in Chapter One. The fellow posed the question, "Do you really believe that an open SAN will ever make its way to market? An open SAN would move intelligence from proprietary array controllers to the network itself—probably onto the switch. People would get the same performance from a JBOD as they would from a high-end array from EMC. They would realize very quickly that they had been paying way too much for storage. Do you think that EMC or any other large array manufacturer would ever let that happen?"[6]

ARE SWITCHES THE NEW VIRTUALIZATION PLATFORM?

Given the intrinsic truth in this observation, it may strike readers as quizzical that large array vendors now appear to be courting switch-makers and readily ceding some of their "secret sauce" functionality to them. The answer may have to do with the strategies of the array makers themselves.

In the case of EMC, a stated direction of the company for the past couple of years has been to pursue more aggressively a storage management software strategy. While the company has not backed away from its aggressive marketing of its own storage arrays, increased attention has been placed on its management software, which models itself on EMC's own array management philosophy and techniques.

For EMC, obtaining an early lead in storage area network management market by embedding its technology on the SAN switches of leading providers makes sense as a means of garnering greater market share. Competitor Veritas Software, a long-time advocate of host-based storage management and virtualization, is pursuing a similar course, based on statements made by CEO Gary Bloom at the Computer Measurement Group's annual conference in Reno, Nevada, in December 2002.[7]

Are switch platforms the ideal location for LUN aggregation? Increasingly, the industry appears to be giving the strategy its approval. This may be fostered in part by the increasing presence of Cisco Systems in the SAN space.

Already a leader in IP network switching, Cisco was a major proponent of IP-based SANs and a force, together with IBM, in the development of the SCSI over Internet (iSCSI) standard within the Internet Engineering Task Force's IP Storage Working Group. The company had been evangelizing IP-based storage networks throughout 1999 and trash-talking everything Fibre Channel until a widely publicized announcement by the company that it would work together with the dominant Fibre Channel switch vendor, Brocade Communications Systems, to develop a protocol for using IP to stitch together isolated Fibre Channel fabrics (so-called "SAN islands") in mid-2000.

As previously discussed, the announcement raised more than a few eyebrows until it was understood that the two companies had been compelled by some of their larger customers (shared in common) to "play nice" with each other to fix the problem of SAN bridging. The Fibre Channel Over IP (FCIP) tunneling protocol was the outcome of the union, which dissolved with all of the acrimony of a Hollywood divorce in April 2002, amidst off-the-record claims by Cisco that Brocade was endeavoring to coopt the open standard to work only with its own switch gear.

Cisco's involvement with storage networking accelerated from there. By 2001, the vendor had become a fixture in the ANSI T11 Committee, which handles the development of standards for Fibre Channel, often criticizing standards proposals for their lack of completeness.[8] Often rebuffed in its efforts to steer Fibre Channel standards within T11, accused by pure Fibre Channel-focused vendors of being a thinly-veiled IP storage bigot and playing the role of a standards obfuscator, Cisco acquired its own Fibre Channel SAN switch company, Andiamo Systems, in August 2002, establishing itself squarely in both the IP and the Fibre Channel storage space.

In June 2003, the two companies—Cisco and Andiamo—introduced a draft Request for Comment (a preliminary standards draft in IETF parlance) to the IP Storage Working Group to develop nine management information bases (MIBs) for managing Fibre Channel fabrics. Within the document are MIBs for managing Fibre Channel SAN processes and elements that have never been defined, much less approved, by ANSI's T11 Committee as components of the organization's FC standards family. The apparent end run around ANSI was at least in part motivated by a desire to have Cisco's switch-based SAN fabric (as opposed to disk) virtualization method recognized by some standards group, according to prominent members of the IP Storage Working Group.[9]

Called VSAN, or Virtual SAN, Cisco's technology is intended to help designers build larger consolidated Fibre Channel fabrics with the same or greater security and application isolation than what is currently possible with conventional FC switch zoning. VSAN offers the ability to create separate virtual fabrics on top of the same redundant physical infrastructure, according to the vendor, but only if fabrics are created using switches that support the technology—Cisco's own MDS 9000 Family of Multilayer directors and fabric switches, for now.[10]

With Cisco Systems becoming a more and more powerful force within the storage networking world, vendors with an eye on growing their market share in the storage virtualization software space are keen to do business with the networking giant. In April 2003, EMC and Cisco Systems jointly announced an agreement to work together to, among other things, create provide customers with intelligent switch technology for storage.

Not to be upstaged, Brocade Communications Systems has also been working to develop fatter switches through the integration of management software. In early 2002, the company was talking to analysts about its intentions to field a "V-switch" (a switch offering disk virtualization capabilities within the next 12 months). Whose technology would be integrated into the switch remained a mystery, given Brocade's partnerships with a wide range of virtualization technology vendors, including host software-based virtualization vendor, Veritas, in-band solution provider, DataCore, and out-of-band rival, StoreAge, until May 2003. At the Veritas Vision conference in Las Vegas, Nevada, the companies announced a co-development effort aimed at porting Veritas Volume Manager and Storage Resource Management software to the Brocade SilkWorm® Fabric Application Platform (SilkWorm Fabric AP). A prototype of the solution was demonstrated at the show.

BACK TO REALITY

Given the deals that are currently being struck between switch makers and virtualization vendors, one might have the erroneous impression that the virtualization issue is close to being resolved. This is far from true.

Technically, porting virtualization software to a certain vendor's switch platform is a nontrivial task. Doubtless that with sufficient resources vested in research and analysis, the ways and means could be found to equip a switch platform with the kind of LUN aggregation capability currently represented as virtualization. However, this alone will not solve the problem.

Standards do not exist for disk virtualization and vendors of both virtualization solutions and storage arrays are no closer today to closing ranks on a universal approach than they were two decades ago. As a result, storage architects within IT shops will still confront the same problems going forward. They will have to check to see which hardware they own (or are considering purchasing) will work with a given virtualization solution. Moreover, they will need to undertake substantial due diligence testing to determine whether the virtualization products that they are considering for their shop are compatible with software that they already use. In short, little, if anything, changes.

Many are still pondering the question of whether virtualization is worth the problems that it might introduce. Some vendors argue that you need to virtualize storage to simplify its management and to lower cost of ownership. Others say that virtualization is required to enable scaling and increase storage fault tolerance.

In fact, none of the arguments are true. The best that can be said of virtualization is that it is an enabling technology. If some sort of standards-based virtualization scheme appears (or one vendor's approach becomes dominant), it is possible that virtualization will set the stage for simplifying storage management and reducing the number of persons required to manage storage.

Similarly, with a standardized virtualization engine, it may be possible to add and subtract storage from virtual volumes in response to application storage capacity requirements, thus optimizing capacity allocation efficiency to some extent and reducing downtime for storage reallocation.

However, none of these benefits is a function of virtualization itself, but of additional layers of software that may be added atop a standardized virtualization layer. In the absence of standards that allow virtualization to be compatible with the broadest possible range of software tools, storage management software options are bound to be limited. In cases today where vendors offer virtualization platforms that include a suite of storage management software tools—a sort of "one-stop-shop"—consumers tend to shy away. Common complaints include that the suite includes inferior tools that they do not want or need.

The truth about storage virtualization is that it does not deliver fully on any of its value proposition. No virtualization technique enables cross-platform LUN aggregation that array vendors themselves do not permit.

Moreover, LUN aggregation addresses only part of the capacity allocation efficiency requirement. To achieve allocation efficiency, you need the ability to "carve" the unused portion of storage behind one application and "splice" it to the storage allocated to an application that is consistently running out of room. See Figure 7–6.

LUN carving and splicing technology is almost completely missing from current external virtualization solutions, though, arguably, it does exist inside arrays from certain vendors such as Xiotech, and in utilities provided in Microsoft Server 2000 for dealing with "basic disks." In its ab-

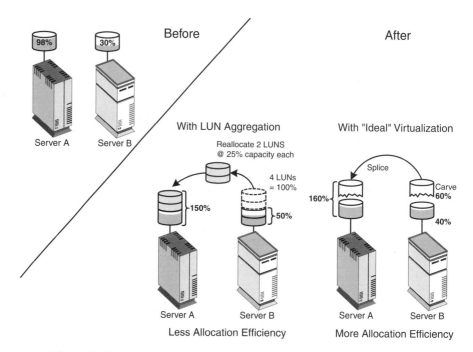

Figure 7–6   Storage is allocated inefficiently, but virtualization (LUN
aggregation) can't resolve the problem.

sence, according to industry insiders, disk capacity is only allocated to
about 40 percent of efficiency in UNIX and Microsoft environments, to
20 to 30 percent of efficiency in Linux environments, and to only about
60 percent of efficiency in the case of mainframe DASD.[11]

Using a blunt tool like LUN aggregation to deal with the capacity allocation problem confronting most shops today is only effective if all
LUNs are defined at the smallest possible size. That way, virtual volumes
can be assembled in very small increments (think "Leggo™ building
blocks"). Otherwise, a lot of disk capacity is going to go to waste.

While wasteful, capacity allocation inefficiency isn't as costly as its
evil twin, capacity utilization inefficiency. If we consider the amount of
space on expensive storage arrays occupied by junk files, duplicate files,
and rarely accessed data that could be stored on less expensive arrays or
archived to tape, the utilization efficiency of most storage infrastructures
today would be abysmally low: somewhere in the 30 percent range. Even
at $1.50 per GB for storage, that is a significant cost to your organization.
Given RAID mirrors and mirror-splits that seem to be appearing in nearly

every shop today as a data protection measure, the problem is multiplying geometrically.[12]

It is to this issue that we turn our attention next. For now, this dissertation on virtualization needs an ending.

Figure 7–7 provides a comparison of two images. The one at left shows the nine circles of hell as described in Dante's *Inferno* in the early 1300s. For each type of sinful behavior, according to the text, there is accorded a special place in the underworld.

The image at left shows a simplified view of virtualization from the perspective of the disk, building out to the array, then the FC SAN. There are many layers of virtualization, from the original mapping of bit domains on a disk surface, to the superimposition of a file system, to the creation of RAID sets, to the definition of LUNs, then to SAN Zones.

And at the bottom of the model, for those of us who have been very misbehaved in our lives and have much for which to atone, there is something we have come to call "virtualization."

Maybe Dante was a storage manager in another life.

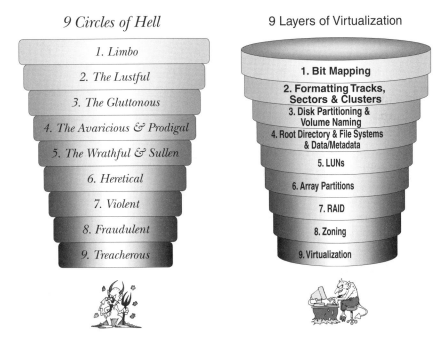

Figure 7–7 Dante was a storage manager.

ENDNOTES

1. From StoreAge Networking Technologies Ltd., "High-Performance Storage Virtualization Architecture: A StoreAge White Paper," 2002, StoreAge Networking Technologies, Ltd., One Technology Drive, Bldg. C-515, Irvine, CA 92618, *www.store-age.com.*

2. DataCore Software Corporation, "Enhancing I/O Performance and Availability through In-band Storage Virtualization: SANsymphony Software Design and Practices," 2002, DataCore Software Corporation, 6300 NW 5th Way, Fort Lauderdale, FL 33309, *www.datacore.com.*

3. Ibid.

4. Ibid.

5. Jon William Toigo, "Nice Neat Storage: The Reality," *Networking Computing,* May 27, 2002.

6. Jon William Toigo, "Will SANs be the Giant Slayers," *Solutions Integrator,* October 1998. An interesting sidebar: When I quoted this fellow again in an article written for Enterprise Systems Journal in 2002, his office called to ask to have his name removed from the quote. I asked why, given that it was one of the more prophetic and intelligent things anyone had ever said about SANs and received the response that, given the relationship that had been established between EMC and the fellow's company, "It is a career limiting observation." Out of deference to the speaker and sensitivity for his political situation, I have refrained from attributing the quote here.

7. Jon William Toigo, "As 2002 Goes Into the History Books, Sanity Rules," *Enterprise Systems Journal,* January 9, 2003.

8. Jon William Toigo, "Discerning Standards from Shinola," *Toigo's Takes on Storage,* SearchStorage.com, July 11, 2001 and "Wrong Time for an End Run," *Enterprise Systems Journal,* September 1, 2001, *www.esj.com.*

9. From a forthcoming report by Jon William Toigo for *Enterprise Storage Strategies,* June 27, 2003, *www.esj.com.*

10. For more information, see Dan Hersey and Tom Nosella, "Using VSANs and Zoning in the Cisco MDS 9000 Family of Multilayer Fibre Channel Switches," Cisco Systems, Inc., 170 West Tasman Dr., San Jose, CA 95134, *www.cisco.com.*

11. Comments of Randy Chalfant, from Jon William Toigo, "Allocation versus Utilization," Enterprise Storage Strategies, ESJ Online, January 23, 2003, *www.esj.com.*

12. Ibid.

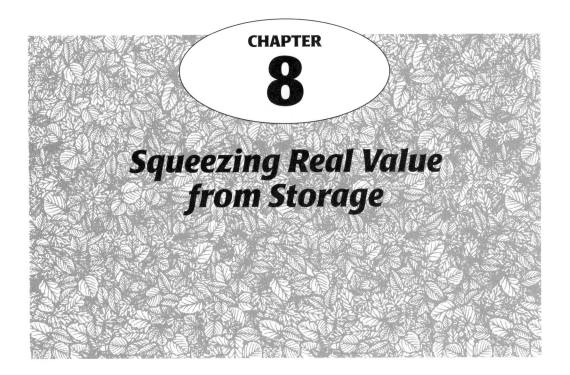

CHAPTER

8

Squeezing Real Value from Storage

The preceding chapter considered the state of virtualization technology and its potential role in simplifying data storage for ease of management, while at the same time advancing the cause of greater capacity allocation efficiency. We determined that, despite the momentum that is building behind switch- and appliance-based virtualization in Fibre Channel fabrics, the absence of standards for virtualization continued to limit the reliability of the business value claims of products. As a result, potential deployments of the technology would need to be tested and validated on a one-off basis for their actual ability to simplify storage architecture.

It was argued that capacity allocation efficiency cannot be achieved using current LUN aggregation-style virtualization techniques. While these tools could enable nondisruptive volume scaling (within limits fixed by proprietary array controller designs), the LUN aggregation strategy itself lacked the level of granularity—and the necessary LUN carving and splicing capabilities—to enable storage administrators to truly allocate storage capacity on an efficient basis.

From the perspective of capacity utilization efficiency, these virtualization tools offer virtually no value whatsoever. This chapter looks at the causes of storage utilization inefficiency and efforts to address it within the industry.

WHAT IS CAPACITY UTILIZATION EFFICIENCY?

Capacity utilization efficiency refers to the efficient usage of storage platforms based on a consideration of data access requirements and platform costs. At one level, it is an extraordinarily simple concept to grasp. Data, once written, has a discernable pattern of access. Once committed to disk, the accesses made to data tend to drop an average of 50 percent within three days. Within a month, the frequency of access attempts made to the same data may drop by as much as 90 percent or more. Given this "rule of thumb" in data access trends, you need to ask yourself how much of your infrequently accessed data is being stored on your most expensive high-end storage platforms? That question gets to the heart of capacity utilization efficiency.

It goes almost without saying that most organizations today are allocating storage capacity inefficiently. Provisioning storage to applications is one of the two "pain points" most frequently cited by storage administrators in survey after survey (the other being backup). Allocating, then reallocating, storage capacity to applications is a burdensome, time-consuming task that might be made somewhat less onerous through the application of techniques such as LUN aggregation. Randy Chalfant, Chief Technologist for StorageTek, offers the following illustration of the situation.[1]

> "The picture below (see Figure 8–1) shows the typical storage needs for a database using conventional disk. Some vendors advertise a very attractive price for raw storage capacity in their array products, but in

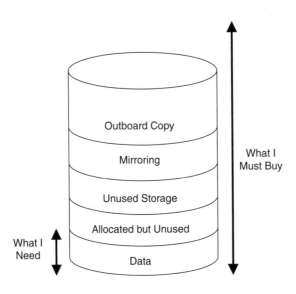

Figure 8–1 Storage allocation to a database.

reality mirroring and replication can cause storage efficiency to be low. It is always a good practice to purchase between 20% and 40% more than you expect to use when managing database storage. This growth factor is depicted in the figure as 'unused storage'."

"When setting up storage for a database, the Database Administrator or Systems/Storage Administrator (DBA/SA) must first determine how much space is required. Once this number is determined, the storage administrator will allocate (or reserve) a volume on the storage subsystem that equals the specified size. Since databases utilize tables, the allocated space initially represents only the table size but no actual data. This variance between the table size and the actual amount of stored data is what we define as 'allocated but unused' storage. If a storage system has many databases stored on it, this allocated but unused storage can add up quickly."

"In order to protect critical data while maintaining 24x7 availability, DBA/SAs may utilize an 'outboard copy' (data replication or 3rd copy). This allows backups to be carried out while the database remains available to the users."

"As this example shows, conventional disk proves to be very wasteful when the actual data needs can be as little as 20–30% of the total storage capacity. The bottom line is that for databases, conventional storage offers poor storage efficiency and high cost."

Chalfant agrees with the observation that, with few exceptions, even with the best virtualization tools and the most efficient capacity allocation program, capacity utilization inefficiency remains. He submits, however, that his company's Shared Virtual Array provides some alleviation of allocation inefficiency.

An implementation of a virtualization technique that StorageTek calls "Dynamic Mapping," Chalfant describes the Shared Virtual Array (SVA) as a "lynchpin to virtual architecture because pre-determined storage capacity, which he says "almost always far exceeds the actual amount of real data," can be presented to applications via the technology without actually being physically allocated. This "indirect mapping," he argues, is another (though less often discussed) benefit of virtualization. With such an approach, the "SVA is able to offer the allocated but unused space to other volumes, which in turn increases the overall storage efficiency."

Like most virtualization solutions, however, StorageTek's SVA is proprietary and offers platform support that is only as comprehensive as third-party array vendors will allow. Moreover, from the standpoint of capacity utilization, inefficiencies persist. That is mainly because mechanisms do not yet exist to automate the migration of data between platforms based on usage characteristics.

Hierarchical storage management (HSM), discussed in detail below, does not currently migrate data based on access frequency, but on the basis of last updates ("write date"). Most HSM packages assume that if a file or dataset has not been updated, overwritten by a new version, within a given timeframe, it should be moved from one part of the physical storage hierarchy to another. Just as current virtualization technology is inadequate to the task of achieving capacity allocation efficiency, current HSM technology is inadequate to the task of capacity utilization efficiency.

Ultimately, some sort of capacity utilization efficiency technology is needed, or else organizations will literally bankrupt themselves with amassing storage costs. Ideally, such a technology would provide automated intelligence for migrating data from more expensive to less expensive platforms "in the background" without operator intervention. For this to happen, significant changes are required in how data is named and characterized in the first place. Moreover, a stable, well-managed, and secure, networked storage infrastructure is prerequisite for automated data migration.

HIERARCHICAL STORAGE MANAGEMENT

Capacity management is at the heart of current thinking around storage management. This thinking has an historical precedent.

In 1979, surveys of IBM's GUIDE user group members revealed several startling facts. For one, storage administrators could only manage about 11 GB of storage effectively. Moreover, direct access storage devices (DASD) were being utilized only to about 35 percent of their capacity, while customers were reporting storage growth at a rate of between 30 and 40 percent per year.[2]

Those at IBM at the time were flabbergasted by these statistics. The issue for IBM was simple: If something wasn't done quickly to improve storage management, they would be hard-pressed to sell more DASD to their customers. Practical issues like available floor space and budgets for personnel and hardware would impose limits to growth on customers and limit the vendor's ability to sell more gear.

From this sanguine analysis, Systems Managed Storage (SMS) was born. IBM created a group to work on the problem of storage management. A fundamental assumption was that the logical requirements of data storage needed to be separated from the physical aspects of the disk platform itself. This involved the creation of a management approach with two distinct and separate constructs: "storage class," which enumerated the logical requirements pertaining to application data itself, and "storage group," which defined the physical attributes of the back end storage platforms.

The idea was to have IT managers define what the storage requirements were for the data produced by their various applications, then for an intelligent system of policies and rules to allocate storage of the right flavor and the right capacity automatically—simply by stating that this new data belonged required storage class X and storage pool Y.[3] (This sounds strikingly familiar to the way that SANs were supposed to work according to the early pioneers at Compaq who authored the Enterprise Network Storage Architecture (ENSA) white paper in 1997.)

SMS development, according to folks who were involved, was an enormous undertaking that started with about 11 people and grew to as many as 1,200 (not including the support from other groups within IBM responsible for S/390 OS development, hardware development, database development, etc.). Technical hurdles abounded, but they were minor compared to the effort involved in weaning IBM customers away from old practices and into the "new" way to manage storage that was being advanced by SMS.

IBM spent an enormous effort studying customers and helping them implement SMS. One of the co-patent-holders on SMS said that he had personally performed over 350 storage studies and visited 650 data centers in the Global 2000 customers in efforts to understand storage management requirements and to evangelize the SMS approach.[4]

SMS actually had three logical policies (Storage Class, Management Class, and Data Class) and one physical policy (Storage Group). The purpose of each is as follows:

- Data Class: Originally intended to simplify Job Control Language (JCL), developers hoped that it could be expanded later to address the properties of the data that might tag it to the proper management or application. IBM never made it that far.
- Management Class: This policy intended to provide lifecycle management and backup management at the file level, and included specifications for Hierarchical Storage Management (HSM) controls, deletion control, backup frequency, number of backups, lifetime of backups, etc. It was totally integrated into the workings of the Data

Facility Hierarchical Storage Management System (DFHSM) product of the SMS suite.

- Storage Class: This policy identified a level of service associated with the data to guide initial storage selection, as well as preferred access method. The latter correlated with facilities in S/390 that would allow data-in-memory or expanded storage (E-store) data loading. Storage Class would partly be responsible for selecting which data loading method was preferred based on data access requirements. Storage Class also controlled which application received priority whenever the cache in the subsystem was overloaded. In short, it provided much more sophistication than simply setting the proper location for initial data placement.

- Storage Group: The only physical policy in SMS, Storage Group identified a physical set of storage, real physical volumes that could be placed in a locked room, could have different allocation thresholds, had the same lease expiration, etc. One practical use of this feature was that it facilitated the phasing out of storage devices that were nearing their end of lease. Administrators could change the Storage Group policy to prevent new data from being allocated to those devices. In this way, the group of storage would "empty through atrophy." [5]

The effectiveness of SMS, released as DFSMS/MVS in 1988, was demonstrated in the storage capacity that it allowed an individual administrator to manage. SMS took storage management in the S/390 world from 11 GB per person to about 15 Terabytes per administrator. At the same time, in shops using SMS to its full potential, allocation efficiency climbed from 35 percent in 1979 to where it is today: about 60 percent.

One takeaway from this historical view is that capacity allocation and utilization efficiency cuts to the heart of storage costs. Only by effectively managing storage—at the level of data itself—can we address the underlying cost multiplier in storage cost of ownership: labor.

IBM SMS goes well beyond current storage management concepts and approaches popular in open systems environments today. Collectively speaking, Storage Resource Management (SRM) tools, which have been the focal point of a $10, $14, or $21 billion dollar storage management software industry (depending on the analyst you read), largely ignore the need for management based on access characteristics and platform attributes.

Arguably, this oversight is partly the fault of the hype around SANs, which were originally billed as utility storage infrastructure that would serve up the right kind of storage to whatever application needed it automatically. One might posit that the vendors have been drinking their own Kool-Aid™, adopting the view that the requisite intelligence for managing capacity allocation and utilization in a SAN would be provided by some "higher authority" vested the SAN fabric itself.

As a result, the philosophy of many, if not most, SRM products seems to be that the job of SRM is to monitor the operation of devices in the SAN to ensure that they are not overheating or exhibiting the onset of other operational errors or faults. Some mystical feature of SANs will do the rest.

A BRIEF OVERVIEW OF STORAGE MANAGEMENT ARCHITECTURE

Today, there are four storage management architectures, one still very much in development and three in fairly widespread use across IT shops, which can be defined and categorized based on two criteria: (1) the granularity of management they offer—how well they move you toward capacity utilization efficiency—and, (2) their cost from the standpoint of storage administration labor and time. Figure 8–2 depicts these architectures.

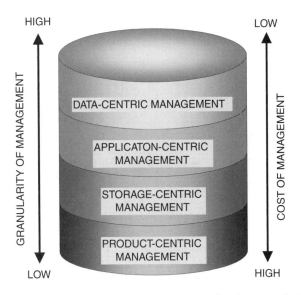

Figure 8–2 Storage management approaches by granularity.

PRODUCT-CENTRIC MANAGEMENT

A product-centric approach involves the use of a variety of point tools to manage different storage components. (See Figure 8–3.) In practice, this is probably the most common "architecture" for storage management today. IT professionals often use the platform-specific tools that came with their servers and storage arrays and augment them over time with a collection of single-purpose software that they have acquired, or written themselves, in response to the storage issues they confront on a day-to-day basis. This is sometimes referred to as the "quiver of arrows" approach.

The challenges posed by this approach include the requirement to evaluate and select multiple point products from different vendors and to keep each point product up to date with product release cycles and the storage and server platform changes.

Using multiple point products also makes it difficult and expensive to transfer the knowledge required for this management approach to new hires. Moreover, the need to use multiple product-specific tools will also impose a practical limit on how many GBs of storage an administrator could effectively manage in a single workday.

Despite these limitations, however, the "quiver of arrows" approach remains the most common management strategy employed today.

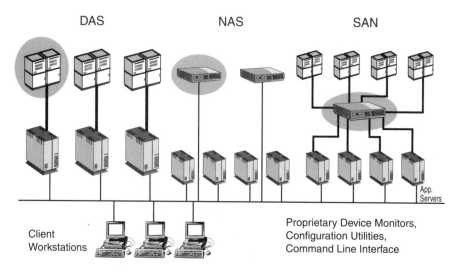

Figure 8–3   Product-centric management.

INFRASTRUCTURE-CENTRIC OR STORAGE RESOURCE MANAGEMENT (SRM)

Another storage management approach is the "horizontal" or infrastructure-centric approach, as depicted in Figure 8–4. About two years ago, there was a rush to this model for storage management, spurred on by hype around SANs and virtualization. (So pervasive was the marketecture that even prominent vendors, like Veritas Software, gave their products names with "SAN" in the title—as if to assert that SANs were quickly displacing all other topologies for storage.)

The underlying argument of this approach is that, if you just keep the components of a SAN in good repair, the SAN itself it will provision storage to whatever application needs it. Today, these tools are typically referred to as Storage Resource Managers (SRM).[6] They integrate multiple task-oriented products or modules into a single product suite in order to deliver a consistent user interface and to reduce the user learning curve.

However, unless your environment includes all of the storage topologies (direct-attached, NAS and Fibre Channel SAN) supported by the suite, the software may seem overly complex to use. More than one user has complained that the problem with multifunction software suites is that they perform no function particularly well. Even "brand-name" SRM suites produce disgruntled users who are angered by the need to li-

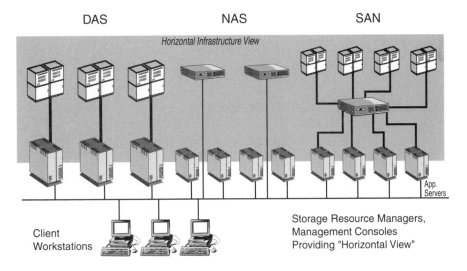

Figure 8–4   Infrastructure-centric management.

cense software components for which they have no use or that lack, in their estimate, the best-of-breed features of other products in the market.

The savviest vendors in this space, like Ken Barth, who is CEO of Dallas, Texas–based Tek-Tools, suggest that SRM is, at best, "a kind of software development tool set."

Barth correctly observes that it is left up to the consumer to identify and select the "best of breed" tools from among a group of about 250 vendors, then use them to cobble together a storage management system that works reasonably well for his or her shop. Tek-Tools own offering in this space doesn't claim to do everything for everybody, and Barth notes that he actively seeks out partner vendors to supplement his own offerings to better meet customer needs. In lieu of storage standards that ensure the interoperability of all storage management software, Barth's view encapsulates the best approach available today.

Generally speaking, what SRM products fail to do is to associate the storage resource with the application that uses it. The "magic" that was supposed to provide this all-important function was never successfully developed in a SAN, arguably because Fibre Channel, which lacked the services of a true network protocol, could not support such "upper-stack" functionality.

SRM is currently undergoing change as leading vendors seek to develop more comprehensive resource management functionality in their products. This was prompted to some degree by the increasing focus on virtualization as a foundation technology for SANs and by the success of BMC Software in gaining market traction with its Application-Centric Storage Management (ACSM) vision in the early 2000s.

APPLICATION-CENTRIC MANAGEMENT

BMC Software was among the first to note the deficit of the SRM approach to storage management and, in 2000, began pursuing an alternative strategy of application-centric storage management.[7] The idea was to segregate the horizontal view of the storage infrastructure on an application-by-application basis and to tie all storage management activity to application performance metrics (see Figure 8–5).

While this strategy would not have, by itself, provided a solution for storage utilization efficiency, application-centric management suggested an effective replacement for the intelligent automatic provisioning that SANs were supposed to deliver, but never did.

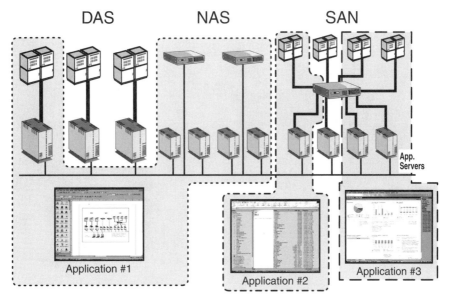

Application-centric management console displays all
resources associated with specified application.

Figure 8–5 Application-centric storage management.

BMC began to complement its Patrol Storage Manager product with a set of tools that would enable manual storage provisioning—with application performance providing a means to validate task completion. So practical and successful was this approach that other "800-pound gorillas" in the market, including Veritas and EMC, began chanting the BMC mantra, and IBM was both using BMC Software in its own facilities while proposing it in large storage deals in place of its own SRM tools from Tivoli.

BMC preached application-centrism for four years until their sudden and unexpected departure from the market in early 2003. Other vendors have sought to pick up the mantra, but the results have proven the truth of the old saw that there is a big difference between "talking the talk" and "walking the walk."

Many products can, after a fashion, emulate the application-centric presentation of the data storage infrastructure: a baseline functionality requirement for an application-centric management approach, as shown in Figure 8–6. However, few offered the tools that BMC provided to enable the administrator to intervene based on whatever hot spots or choke points were discovered.

For example, if a database index and data set are written to the same storage platter, application performance may actually suffer as the result

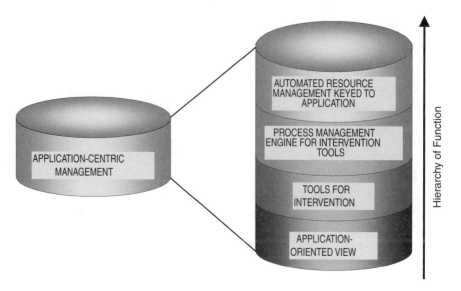

Figure 8–6   Hierarchy of functionality in application-centric storage management.

of contention for read/write heads. An effective application-centric management scheme provides both the means for visualizing this condition and also the tools to move stored data around between and among platters to aid in fixing such hot spots or choke points.

Going further up the hierarchy of application-centric storage management, such a product must also capture data on processes or procedures frequently undertaken to resolve common issues and provide an engine for automating responses to such conditions whenever they arise. BMC, through its relationship with Invio, was well on its way to achieving such functionality. As of this writing, none of the company's successors were as far along on this path.

The pinnacle of the application-centric storage management functional hierarchy consists of the ability to automatically allocate storage to an application and to manage that storage through the tools and policies located lower in the function stack. Such an approach requires a knowledge base containing typical data storage requirements for popular application software, tunable by customers to meet their specific needs, that would interface with a second knowledge base containing the specific details of the storage platforms deployed in the customer's shop. In operation, new applications would be provisioned with storage automatically, then reprovisioned per policy whenever resources neared a given threshold.

Figure 8–7 provides a model for such a system that is being pursued by several "name brand" SRM vendors today. The "storage management server" uses a virtualization (that is, LUN aggregation) layer to track storage resources and provide dynamic scaling in response to an automated response engine. SRM tools and an event monitoring function help to keep the storage platform in proper operating condition. Atop the stack is an ACSM-like policy engine that provides the functionality depicted in the application-centric storage management model.

Even had BMC's efforts been fully realized, it is doubtful that improved storage capacity utilization efficiency would have resulted from such a strategy. Application-centric storage management concerned itself pragmatically with the alleviation of the storage provisioning pain confronting IT professionals and less with optimizing capacity allocation and data migration within storage management infrastructure. It was very much a descendent of SMS from the IBM mainframe environment.

However, utilization efficiency requires the consideration of another dimension of storage management: data access patterns. It is difficult to see how an application-centric storage management approach could effectively improve storage utilization since it does not consider how data itself is used.

Figure 8–7   High level architecture of an ACSM-based storage management server.

DATA-CENTRIC STORAGE MANAGEMENT

The ultimate solution to capacity utilization efficiency, and to storage management more broadly, is not to manage devices, but to manage the data that uses the storage infrastructure. A few vendors today have begun to pay lip service to the concept of "data lifecycle management," though like so many grandiose terms, this is at present mostly a repackaging of traditional SRM products.

Not one vendor has articulated a core requirement for such a strategy: self-describing data.[8] If data could carry with it a simple description of its origin and contents that could include (or be cross-referenced to a data table to discern) instructions about its accessibility and storage requirements, the problem of intelligent storage provisioning might quickly become history.

Figure 8–8 provides a high-level view of how self-describing data would facilitate provisioning and management. An application creating the data initiates a write command. As part of this function, or as a separate function of low-level software, the data is intercepted and a small header containing descriptive bits is added. The write operation is completed and the data is written to the appropriate target device. Henceforth, processes responsible for life-cycle management utilize the

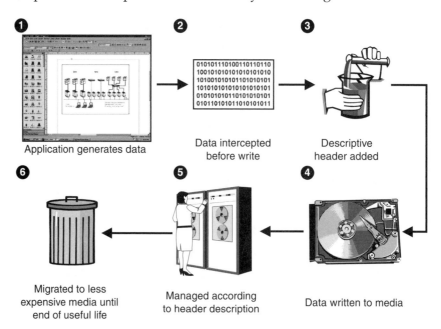

Figure 8–8 A simplified data naming scheme.

descriptive header to provision the data with the proper type and "flavor" of storage (and ancillary services such as inclusion in mirroring schemes or backups, etc.) until finally, in accordance with its associated data retention requirements, it is removed permanently from storage.

In this conception, the data header added to the application write provides a mechanism for

- Determining the origin of data: The data would be associated with specific applications and versions of applications and possibly also with end users who created it in order to 1) facilitate its use at some time in the future, 2) help define security requirements associated with the data, and 3) to permit its inclusion in data replication, migration or normalization schemes at a later date;
- Setting the criticality of the data: Data derives its criticality from association with applications and or business processes, either as a result of defined business continuity requirements or regulatory mandates on data retention and protection. Based on this information, the data might be selected for inclusion in various backup or mirroring schemes and tracked throughout its lifecycle to the specific physical platform on which it resides at any time;
- Providing data integrity checking: By including a message digest header, checksum, or some other metric for identifying the state of the data at time of creation, the descriptive header might help to ensure that data integrity is not compromised as it migrates from platform to platform during its lifecycle.
- Setting the end of useful life of the data: To facilitate its removal from the storage system, and the maintenance of storage capacity availability, the header might indicate the end of the data's useful life.

In effect, just about any criteria that might be useful in managing, moving or tracking data through the storage infrastructure over its useful life could be included in a simple 16- to 32-bit naming header. Perhaps the more flexible the criteria, the more innovative IT professionals could be in leveraging the header to meet their own needs.

Of course, such a scheme of data naming as proposed here would need to be non-intrusive, and compatible with all file systems and operating systems, databases and applications. It would need to be an open system, allowing storage managers (henceforth called "data managers") to apply a naming schema of their own choosing from a customized header object repository (see Figure 8–9). It would also need to append to data

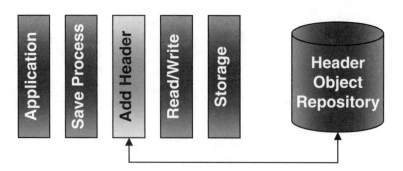

Figure 8–9   Data naming header attachment process.

without delay and without introducing latency into I/O processes, and would have to be compatible with all storage media and platforms and all storage transport protocols.

The openness of the strategy would facilitate its use by storage management software of all flavors, including data discovery engines, migration tools, replication tools, security engines, hierarchical storage managers, etc. In full flower, the header could even support the function of zero copy protocols that enable direct memory-to-memory exchanges across networks, without the need for slower stack- and cycle-intensive data copy operations.

Data naming would go a long way toward establishing the foundation for capacity allocation and utilization efficiency improvement. It would enable the allocation of storage resources on a much more granular scale than what is possible with even the most sophisticated of our current storage management tools.

Such a system would also need to support a flexible set of bits in its header, called reference and change bits,[9] to facilitate access frequency-based data migration: a kind of hierarchical storage management system on steroids. As sketched in Figure 8–10, when access is made to the data by any application- or user-initiated process, the change bit would switch on.

A secondary process would then poll data headers at regular intervals, identifying those files or datasets that have been accessed since the last time polled (e.g., those with their change bits turned on). A recently accessed file would have its bit reset to off by the process and would have a second reference bit, signifying access frequency, incremented, while those that have not been accessed would not have their access frequency bit incremented by the process. In this way, less frequently accessed data could be identified readily and marked for migration from expensive hardware platforms to less expensive platforms (or to archival storage).

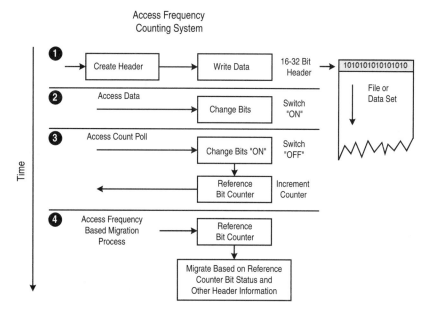

Figure 8–10   An access frequency-based data migration approach.

Migration based on (1) the frequency of data access and (2) other characteristics of the data as described in the header is the key to capacity utilization efficiency. Combined with a policy engine and knowledge base covering the kinds of storage platforms installed in a given shop (in order to define migration paths), a solution of this type would offer a compelling payback simply by assigning data to the most appropriate platform on a cost/access frequency basis. The more automated this migration process becomes, the more data could be managed effectively by fewer staff resources, saving the organization more money over time.

NOT SPECULATION

The scheme described above has historical precedents and mirrors the thinking in many development laboratories today. For example, EMC Corporation, in 2002, announced its Centera storage product that adds a "content address" data passing across its storage array controller. The purpose is to enable tracking of data through its migration between and among storage platforms over time—and also to ensure that data has non-repudiability (that is, that it can be demonstrated that the data has not changed bits over time or during transport).

The company's stated objective[10] was to create a storage solution for handling fixed content or reference data, particularly that data that must be retained online despite its low frequency of access, and with its integrity guaranteed, for regulatory reasons. University of California Berkley researchers determined in a study in 2000 (sponsored by EMC) that reference data was the fastest growing data segment in business organizations. While neither the vendor nor the university researchers had the prescience of forethought to anticipate corporate financial scandals a year or two later that brought forth a flood of new federal regulations pertaining to secure, long-term data retention, EMC has certainly profited with its Centera offering.

Centera technology is an interesting implementation of a kind of data naming scheme, but also an example of what might happen if naming schemes are not based upon open standards. To use content addressing from EMC, your storage platform must be equipped with Centera controllers, which as of this writing are only installed on EMC's own Centera storage arrays.

Data naming may not be the first objective of Microsoft Corporation, but the company has been making substantial effort to develop its brand of extended mark-up language (XML) as a data wrapper. XML is primarily viewed as a mechanism for facilitating cross-platform data exchange, replacing hard-coded electronic data interface (EDI) schemes for system-to-system data exchange. Some experimentation has been undertaken regarding the use of XML to describe objects such as files and other datasets that might be applicable to data naming going forward.

This is especially the case given Microsoft's stated direction in its next generation operating system, code named "Longhorn," to do away with file systems altogether, in favor of a SQL database and binary large objects (BLOBs).[11] Standardizing on a database for a file system is not a unique idea. It was proposed by Oracle Development Corporation in the late 1990s, and IBM was also talking for a while about using DB2 Open Edition and file structures as an effective file system replacement.

Going to such a database structure and replacing current file systems has the potential advantage of making implementation of a data naming scheme at the point of file creation much easier to accomplish. It also facilitates, as mentioned in a previous chapter, the reunification of storage platforms as block storage repositories, contributing to storage commoditization.

IN THE ABSENCE OF A DATA-CENTRIC STORAGE MANAGEMENT SOLUTION

The cursory description of a data-centric management scheme provided in the preceding pages is offered in the hopes that it will stimulate increased interest in and development of technology based on the concept of self-describing data. In and of itself, a data-naming scheme does not effect change in storage capacity utilization efficiency. If it is sufficiently open and compatible with existing operating systems, applications and storage platforms, it will enable the development of improved processes for managing data.

In the final analysis, a data-centric management approach makes sense. If we agree that storage is fast becoming its own infrastructure, whether as a result of increasingly networked topologies or as a consequence of the evolutionary deconstruction of the von Neumann machine, we must also agree that storage is no longer a repository, a place where data goes to rest. Thus management techniques focused on the maintenance of disk arrays is no longer valid.

Today, the entire storage infrastructure, including switches and cables, bridge/routers and array caches, disk and tape media, host bus adapters, and system caches, is better viewed as a dynamic system. Within this dynamic system, data is constantly in motion. We understand the more that we look at capacity utilization inefficiency, which has its roots in the mismatching of the frequency of access characteristics of data with the capabilities and expense of storage platforms. This inefficiency is expressed monetarily as the cost incurred by storing your least-often accessed data on your most expensive platforms—expensive because they are designed to provide the fastest data access.

References to "speed of access" imply motion, and references to "frequency of access" imply time. As these expressions creep more and more into our descriptions of the storage infrastructure within our shops, it should remind us that storage is not a static repository, but a dynamic system that requires a management philosophy and capability capable of coping with points, planes, objects, *and* time.

What should be done until self-describing data opens the door for capacity utilization efficiency improvements? That is a difficult question, like asking what should be done until the storage infrastructure becomes an intelligent utility.

Practically speaking, we must do what we have always done. Provision storage as efficiently as our wits and the blunt tools available for management allow.

Many storage management software vendors are working in earnest to devise a kind of SMS capability for open systems storage as this book goes to press. Most are leveraging virtualization technology, such as it is, to help define "Storage Groups." They are also leveraging policy engines such as those from CreekPath, together with SRM tools, and automated storage migration and replication technologies, to help define "Storage Classes." Their goal is to remove some of the manual effort that goes into provisioning capacity to applications.

The selection of which storage management architecture to select is a judgement call. Take care not to be swayed by vendor hype. The option always exists to purchase hardware only from a single vendor or vendor cadre. This approach offers ease of management since that vendor's point solution may be all you need to manage your environment.

This solution is generally less preferable in settings where an investment has been made in heterogeneous infrastructure. It also has the drawback of introducing dependency on a single vendor that may not be desirable for a number of valid reasons. For one, you are always vulnerable to sacrificing advantageous pricing or best-of-breed technology in favor of convenience.

Still, this approach can establish a stable platform—assuming the stability of the vendor—that offers certain management conveniences—not unlike the mainframe data center of old.

Another option is to purchase only the newest breed of hardware platforms from a growing number of vendors who have engineered "self-management" features into their hardware. Vendors ranging from Hewlett-Packard to IBM to EMC are preparing to address the problem of management burden by releasing to market hardware that is augmented with resident automated management utilities that "do it all so you don't have to."

This is essentially the SAN vision done another way: Instead of some SAN software providing application intelligent provisioning and self maintenance, the devices in the storage topology are themselves intelligent and deliver allocation efficiency to the applications that they serve. If the products live up to their claims, if they are truly "configure and forget" and will "phone home" to have themselves replaced at the first sign of trouble, they will certainly alleviate the burden upon (and the need for) storage managers.

The problem at this point is that vendor claims cannot be validated because products have not yet shipped. Moreover, there is no certainty whatsoever that products from different vendors will plug and play into the same infrastructure. Without further testing, it is impossible to tell whether these intelligent peripherals will provide any better efficiency than the proprietary boxes that they replace. You have only the vendor's assurances, which may be pretty difficult to believe given the existence of so much non-interoperable technology in the market today.

Option three is to manage storage capacity allocation and utilization the "old-fashioned way." Identify software products that seem to fix immediate problems—preferably ones with forward-looking roadmaps that give you confidence about the product (and the vendor's) longevity. Don't be afraid to consider products from newer vendors, many of whom have more innovative technology than name brand players (in part, because they have no ties to older approaches or an existing install base), especially when these products can deliver an immediate return on investment.

Needless to say, there is a lot of push back from many companies to this recommendation. Many IT managers have become conservative about the technology they are willing to try and believe there is a certain safety in buying products only from companies with three-letter acronyms for names (e.g., IBM, EMC, etc.) BMC Software demonstrated the fallacy inherent in this view in 2003. The vendor, a company with brand-name recognition and a sterling reputation, simply discontinued its application-centric storage management product and stranded 130 customers.[12]

There is really no reason not to be open to new technologies. The worst that could happen is that your storage will continue to be managed the same way that it is today: with all of the inefficiencies of a still-maturing technology segment. At best, you might actually develop a more cost-effective storage infrastructure.

Finally, if you find a software mix that works, make it a key determinant of the hardware you buy going forward. Tell your vendors that you won't buy their gear unless it supports the management approach you have determined to be the best for your shop. You would be surprised how quickly vendors can respond to requests for improved management support when confronted by enough customers who demand it.

Hardware selection also needs to be guided by a pragmatic assessment of application requirements and data access characteristics. Storage managers must identify these requirements proactively and realistically in order to make intelligent choices about storage platforms. Don't deploy a SAN when a NAS or direct-attached array with a scalable back-end delivers the same capability with less hardware to manage.

One last criterion in storage infrastructure hardware and software selection is data protection. Next to storage provisioning, data protection is the second most painful activity cited by storage management professionals. It is to this subject that we turn our attention in Chapter 9.

ENDNOTES

1. Interview with Randy Chalfant, Chief Technologist, StorageTek, Louisville, CO, June 2003.

2. Recounted by Nick Tabellion, Vice President of Development for Fujitsu Software Technology Corporation (SOFTEK) in Jon William Toigo, "Storage Management Issues Still Driving Us Crazy," *Storage Strategies Newsletter*, April 17, 2003, Enterprise Systems Journal Online, *www.esj.com*.

3. Ibid.

4. Interview with John Tyrrell, today an EMC Storage Architect, in Jon William Toigo, "SMS: From the Beginning," *Storage Strategies Newsletter*, May 29, 2003, Enterprise Systems Journal Online, *www.esj.com*.

5. Ibid. An additional note on the Data Facility Hierarchical Storage Manager (DFHSM): If you use DFHSM in the IBM mainframe world, you already know that it moves data to and from the storage automatically. DFHSM manages your DASD space efficiently by moving data sets that have not been used recently to alternate storage. It also makes your data available for recovery by automatically copying new or changed data sets to tape or DASD backup volumes. It can delete data sets, or move them to another device. Its operations occur daily, at a specified time, and allow for keeping a data set for a predetermined period before deleting or moving it. All DFHSM operatiosn can also be performed manually.

6. Generically speaking, SRM refers to any storage system that can be shared by multiple clients. The term "client" refers to a software program that runs on behalf of a user. Storage Resource Managers (SRMs) are described by some vendors as middleware software modules whose purpose is to manage in a dynamic fashion what should reside on the storage resource at any one time. There are several types of SRMs: Disk Resource Managers (DRMs), Tape resource Managers (TRMs), and Hierarchical Resource Managers (HRMs).

7. Barb Goldworm, "Vendor profile: BMC views enterprise management from an application perspective," *Voice of Experience,* SNW Online, June 3, 2002.

8. Jon William Toigo, "What's in a Name?" *Enterprise Systems Journal,* November 1, 2002.

9. This bit-based access frequency counter idea is a product of a discussion with Randy Chalfant, long-time industry insider, and currently Chief Technologist with StorageTek in Louisville, CO., and has its foundations in TBM Mainframe DASD Management.

10. Eric Hellweg, "EMC Sees a Quick Fix in Fixed Storage," *Business 2.0,* May 1, 2002, *www.business2.com*.

11. Peter Galli, "A 'Longhorn' View for Microsoft," *E Week,* May 12, 2003.

12. Alan Radding, "Is Storage Management Software Worth It?" *Storage Magazine*, April 2003.

CHAPTER 9

Final Word:
Tape is Dead . . . Maybe

The previous two chapters have discussed the provisioning of storage to applications: the most frequently cited source of pain in contemporary storage administration. Implicit in the discussion was a storage topology increasingly treated as a "given" in vendor marketing literature, but rarely fully explicated. As shown in Figure 9–1, this implicit storage architecture consists of at least three tiers of storage technology interconnected by a fabric or network.

Tier one consists of high-end arrays that offer superior access speed and internal intelligence and sophisticated data replication functionality: the expensive, state-of-the-art array one might purchase from a company with a three-letter acronym for a name. The second tier comprises less expensive, lower performance arrays—perhaps built with SAS and SATA drives by the time this book is published—or perhaps consisting of legacy tier-one products to push their useful service life out a few more years. These tier-two arrays provide high capacity for the reliable storage of less frequently accessed "reference" data. Finally, there is a tier of tape and optical disk primarily used for disaster recovery-focused data copy and/or archive.

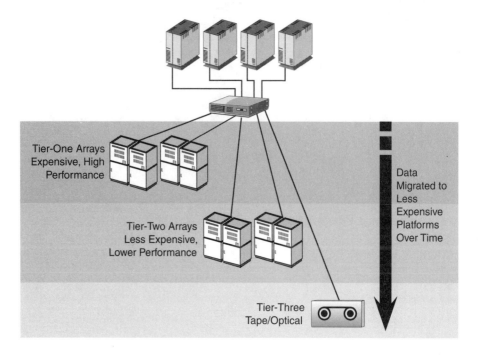

Figure 9–1   Multitiered storage architecture.

This three-tier model provides a platform that can be enhanced through software processes to support access frequency-based data migration, which was described in the previous chapter and whose operation is summarized in Figure 9–2. The purpose of such software processes is to facilitate enhanced capacity utilization efficiency in a manner that does not lock a consumer into a particular vendor's technology.

Such a technology reduces the cost of storage because it ensures that less frequently accessed data is not stored on the most expensive gear, and data that has outlived its useful life is purged from storage altogether. And, it does these things automatically and with minimal administrator intervention.

The key challenge inherent in such a system, if history is any indication, is the collection of information about business processes and applications that will form a knowledge base for use in data classification, retention policies, security requirements, and other definitions. This information is part of the "DNA" of a data description header and determines much of how data will be hosted and migrated throughout its useful life, as well as the method of protection that is best applied to the data.

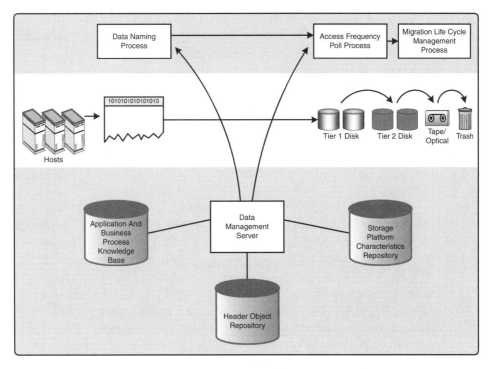

Figure 9–2   A data management system featuring access frequency-
based data migration.

The process of data collection on business processes and applications, and the determination of their criticality, has long been a challenge
for disaster recovery planners. It may entail a multi-month, sometimes a
multi-year, effort to track data back to its original application in order to
determine its importance to business continuity; to define its growth and
access characteristics; and, to identify any special regulatory or legal provisions affecting its retention. As a veteran of 60-plus plans, I can confi-
dently assert that the data collection and risk analysis processes are the
most difficult tasks in DR.

This view is echoed by those who worked to convert customers to
IBM's Systems Managed Storage approach to storage management
throughout the 1990s. The creation of Storage Classes in SMS required a
detailed understanding of the criticality of applications and of the requirements that the application imposed on its data in terms of retention, protection and accessibility. Only with such information could a policy be
developed that would target a certain class of data in a specified protective service such as mirroring or tape backup.

Today, the issue of application awareness is again coming to the fore as many organizations become interested in developing managed storage services for "sale" to internal "customers"—and as telcos and other organizations endeavor to become "second generation" Storage Service Providers (SSP). In both cases, the data access and storage requirements of applications need to be clearly understood in order to establish meaningful service level agreements (SLAs). While networked storage has not matured to a point to which performance and resiliency can be taken for granted, vendors (and former first-generation SSPs) like CreekPath Systems and Storability are creating what amount to workflow management software to facilitate storage services and accounting.

The industry has made some preliminary moves to build a storage infrastructure services quality model, called the 7-Layer Storage Management Model (an obvious homage to the OSI 7-Layer Network Model), to facilitate the use of a storage network to provide Managed Storage Utility. Authors of the model observe that separate, non-integrated, management tools exist for SAN disk subsystems, Fibre Channel fabrics and IP networks, NAS file heads, tape backup subsystems, SNMP-enabled remote management, OSS/BSS databases, etc. that must be combined into a common platform in order to manage a Service Provider storage network, and provision and bill for storage services. A desirable feature set for enabling storage utility from a storage network, writes one advocate of the model, includes disk virtualization, back-up automation, automatic storage provisioning, FC fabric/IP network integration, heuristic SLA management, and a customer management portal—all accessible through a web browser.[1] EMC Corporation was responsible for articulating layers 1 through 5 of the model (see Table 9–1), while CreekPath Systems is cited as the author of layers 6 and 7.

Table 9–1   The Storage Management Services Layer Model

Layer	Storage System Technology
7	Self-Healing Policy Driven Management
6	Automatic Provisioning
5	Remote Management and Portal Service
4	Interoperability and Sharing
3	Enabling Software for Data Management
2	Network Protocols
1	Storage Hardware

Ultimately, whether driven by the need to rationalize storage costs, or to deliver storage as a service, or to protect the most irreplaceable asset in any organization—its data—work must first be done to understand applications and their I/O.

DATA PROTECTION

As previously mentioned, understanding applications and their data protection requirements is a core requirement of contemporary disaster recovery planning. The nature of data—its volume, frequency of change, use by other critical business processes, its conformance to regulatory and legal mandates governing retention and nonrepudiation—sets the criteria for the selection of an appropriate data protection strategy.

The case could be made that the data protection strategy is the most important component of disaster recovery planning. Other strategies and logistics created in advance of an outage to cover the replacement of servers, networks, and end-user computing are meaningless if data cannot be recovered and restored to an accessible state. In the final analysis, systems and networks are useless without data.

More and more, organizations define disaster recovery requirements in terms of Time-to-Data, making data recovery synonymous with disaster recovery. Also underscoring the importance of data protection is the rule of thumb within the contingency planning field that, while all other resources and assets (save for personnel) of an organization avail themselves to protection strategies based either on redundancy or replacement, data protection can only be guaranteed through redundancy.

THE BACKUP VERSUS MIRROR DEBATE

Having determined that data protection is paramount to an effective disaster recovery plan, it is interesting to note that the industry has, up until very recently, advised that there were only two options for data protection: tape backup and disk mirroring. Tape backup solutions were traditionally aimed at organizations having a large volume of data to back up (capitalizing on the low media cost and high capacity of tape) and adequate "windows" in their processing schedules to allow tape backup operations to be completed. Rarely was there a discussion of restore speeds with tape, for reasons that we will explore later.

On the other hand, mirroring solutions were targeted at organizations that depended on real-time data and whose business processes manifested a high degree of vulnerability to even short duration outages. Often these organizations, which included most of the financial industry, had no available "window" in their operational schedule for performing traditional tape backup. And, for them, time-to-data—the amount of time to restore data to an accessible state—requirements were severely constrained.

Many of the arguments made over the past few years by vendors and various commentators for, or against, backup or mirroring are entirely specious. For example, the notion that tape is a dying or dead technology has resurfaced more often than this author can remember and has never been borne out by fact.

Most recently, tape was pronounced dead by vendors of Fibre Channel SANs, who apparently had overlooked the fact that the most frequently cited motivation for fielding a Fibre Channel fabric in survey after survey of customers was to share a tape library.

Others in the industry have announced the death of tape as a function of decreasing cost of disk media on a per GB basis. The argument that tape is being usurped by less expensive disk arrays is flawed in its premise. As Fred Moore, President of Horison Information Strategies, has done an excellent job of demonstrating, most arguments fail to include the system components required to operate tape and disk media, respectively.

According to Moore's analysis,[2] summarized in Figure 9–3, the cost per GB for tape decreased as the ratio of media to drives increased. Taken from the system perspective, disk continues to be 15 to 20 times more expensive than tape for data protection.

But Moore and others have also been quick to observe that systemic cost is not the only advantage of tape. The technology also supports an increasingly critical requirement in open systems storage: data portability.

With most mirroring software provided by vendors for use on their high-end disk arrays, only two arrays from the same vendor can be used to form a "mirror pair." "Multi-hop" mirroring, shown in Figure 9–4, is proffered as the ultimate solution for disaster recovery. Multi-hop configurations use a local mirror pair for symmetrical data replication and also establishes a remote connection with asymmetrical replication for geographic dispersal of the data asset. As with mirror pair configurations, all three arrays in a multi-hop mirror must typically be from the same vendor.

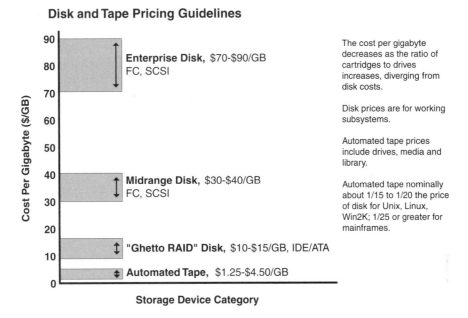

Figure 9–3 Disk and tape pricing guidelines. (*Source:* Horison Information Strategies, 100 Arapahoe Avenue, Suite 14, Boulder, CO 80302, *www.horison.com*.)

The important point is that most mirroring strategies are, at root, one-for-one hardware duplication strategies. Veterans of disaster recovery planning will tell you that one-for-one replacement is the priciest way to go in disaster recovery planning for any IT infrastructure component. Recovery on a consolidated platform makes significantly more financial sense.

By contrast to mirroring, tape enables cross-platform data restore (see Figure 9–5). This means that, in the recovery environment, data can be restored to different hardware platforms or storage topologies than those originally used to host data in the production environment. In 20-plus years of disaster recovery efforts, the record suggests that such flexibility is invaluable.

Tape is far from dead, and tape vendor roadmaps for their technologies, shown in Figure 9–6, suggest nothing if not a robust and aggressive effort to keep ahead of the capacity of disk media and to continue to provide value to users both as a data protection mechanism and as an archive media.

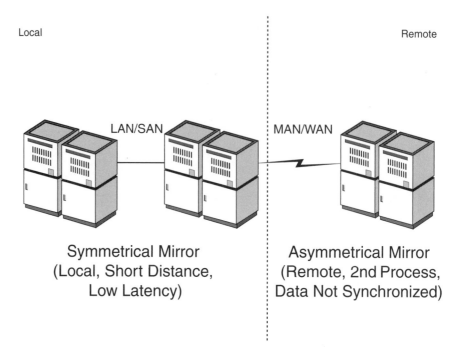

Figure 9–4   Multi-hop mirroring with identical arrays.

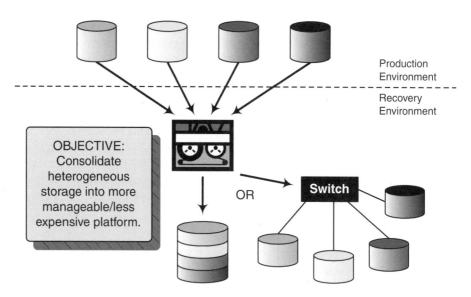

Figure 9–5   Tape enables cross-platform data restore.

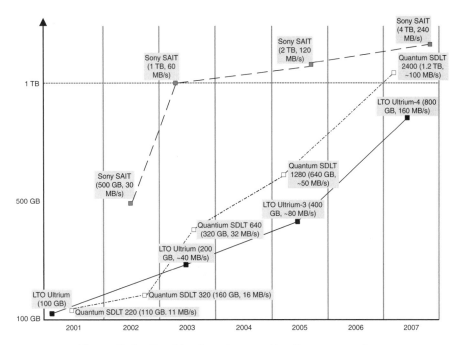

Figure 9-6 Combined roadmaps of leading tape products.

On the horizon, developments such as O-MaSS technology from Tandberg Data and Imation, and similar tape technology projects at Sony, are expected to boost both performance and capacity into the ranges required by the most demanding environments. Currently, O-MaSS technology is demonstrating capacities in the laboratory of 600 GB with 64 MB per second transfer rates. Plans currently provide for a 2.4 terabyte capacity media featuring 256 MB per second transfer (Generation 3), but the technology, which uses thin-film semiconductor array write heads and a unique optical read system, has the potential for producing media with 10 terabyte capacity and 1 GB per second transfer rates.[3]

Today, mainstream tape media and drives targeted at the midrange or open systems environment offer capacities of approximately 160 to 300 GB uncompressed and transfer rates of between 16 and 32 MB per second. With top-of-the-line automated libraries, tape can deliver a sustained transfer rate of approximately 2 terabytes per hour under optimal conditions.

The sufficiency of these capabilities to meeting the data protection requirements of a specific application must be decided on a case-by-case basis. There is no one-size-fits-all strategy for data protection.

TAPE IS NOT A PANACEA

The tape-centric approach to data protection has several potential drawbacks that prevent it from being a universal solution or panacea. These may include:

- The (comparatively) slow speed of data restore from tape to disk: Currently, tape-based restore speeds of about 1 to 2 TB per hour are possible using high-end automated tape libraries. This may become increasingly problematic for organizations whose data storage infrastructures are approaching petabytes of stored information. However, even in large shops, tape-based data restore speed is a problem with many fixes, however, including the pre-staging of the large percentage of non-changing data on the recovery platform in order to minimize the amount of data that must actually be recovered from tape.

- Unpredictablity in tape backup completion: Tape efficiency is a function of several factors that must work together to provide consistent and predictable performance. To enable 30-MB-per-second data streaming rates and to operate tape drives at top speeds, the right backup software and its careful tuning are required. Because of the nature of disk (the source of data to be streamed) and disk interface technology, and more specifically because of the processing stack that must be traversed to drive data from disk to memory then out through an HBA to an external tape library, it is necessary for backup software to initiate, not one, but as many as 16 parallel process threads in order to obtain the desired streaming throughput. Often these parallel threads provide the necessary performance at first, but over time, and as a function of the different containers sizes for disk-based data and their tendency to mitigate the balance and uniformity of threads, thread efficiency falls off and performance suffers. Moreover, as the data feeding each stream is exhausted, the number of threads that are streaming to tape begins to drop off, and backup performance also declines. A reduction in performance may also result from an increase in traffic across a network. *As networks get busy, and threads become elongated, streams become slower.* Whatever the root cause, storage administrators soon discover that only a portion of the number of backups that need to be made have actually been completed within the allowed timeframe. Solutions to this problem vary, but a promising approach is to create a virtual tape library consisting of a disk array that emulates a tape library subsystem. The benefit of this strategy, which is advanced by companies such as Alacritus Software, Veritas Software, StorageTek, and others, is that it capitalizes on the transfer rate of disk (about 80 MB per second), which is three to four times the transfer rate of tape drives at 16 to 30 MB per second, to enable more work to be done in less time. Using virtual tape (sometimes called tape-emulating disk or disk caching) expedites backups and enables, because of additional intelligence in virtual tape software that tunes performance to adjust for changes in data and network load, more backups to be performed more reliably within the same timeframe.

- The relative disparity in tape and disk drive media capacity: Until very recently, tape has lagged significantly behind disk in terms of storage capacity improvement, necessitating that more tape media be used to store data copied from a single disk drive. Since the beginning of the new millennium, this gap has been closed and tape technology appears to be keeping pace with disk drive capacity expansion.

- The growing problem of tracking and managing recorded media: The data explosion confronting many organizations has created an increasingly complex media management problem for organizations utilizing tape backup. Over time, and in certain organizations, labor costs for media management may increase the systemic cost of a tape solution to a point where it competes less effectively against the cost of disk to disk. Software is available or under development today to facilitate improved media management.

- The complexity of sharing and scheduling tape storage devices: The rise of n-tier client/server and other distributed computing models has seen the dispersal of data that needs to be included in a backup scheme. In turn, this has introduced two problems: (1) finding ways to share tape targets, and (2) finding ways to schedule the use by multiple initiators. These problems are being addressed through improved network and fabric attachment strategies for tape libraries to facilitate sharing, and improved tape virtualization techniques to front end tape with disk caches (to improve performance) and schedule management smarts. An example is StorageTek's SN6000.

- The logistical vulnerabilities of tape-based data recovery: in most cases, tape-based backup schemes involve manual, human-intensive, media gathering and transport requirements that are prone to error and expose data to potential loss before it reaches the recovery setting. As a portable medium, tape is, by design, exposed to more threats. There is no easy solution to this problem, only expedient ones, such as electronic vaulting (see below).

The above are some of the most commonly cited challenges confronting traditional tape-based data protection schemes. Some of the inherent time-to-data challenges of tape are exacerbated by the requirement to handle tape in and out of the primary facility to an off-site storage facility, and from the storage facility to a remote recovery center or hotsite, where data recovery actually occurs. As shown in Figures 9–7 and 9–8, these activities add to the time-to-data delays associated with tape-based data restoral.

However, some of this delay can be effectively addressed through the use of electronic vaulting and remote tape mirroring techniques that are becoming increasingly available from off-site storage and hotsite service providers (see Figure 9–9) .

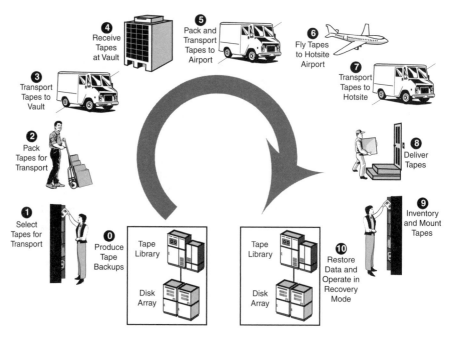

Figure 9–7   A traditional tape-based data protection strategy adds substantial time-to-data.

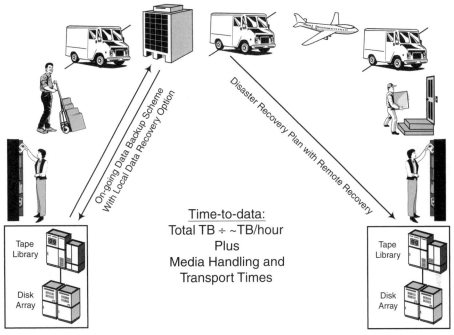

Figure 9–8   Tape-based restore is a function of media transfer rates plus handling and transportation times.

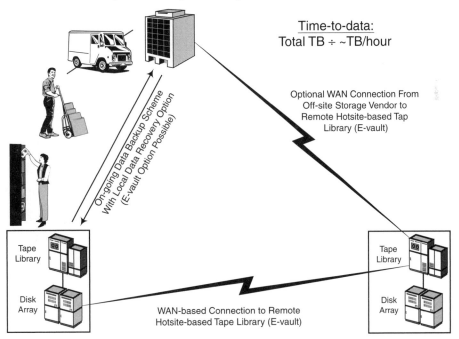

Figure 9–9   Electronic vaulting technology augments traditional tape to reduce time-to-data.

Bottom line: Tape backup confronts many challenges, but none that are insurmountable given the interest and budget to optimize the technology and the processes surrounding it. It must also be said that, while there are an increasing number of ways to optimize tape for data protection, the critical "time-to-data" sensitivities of some applications continue to drive many companies to the data mirroring option.

MIRRORING IS NOT A SILVER BULLET

Remote disk mirroring provides a mechanism for instantaneous data recovery, according to advocates. A simplistic configuration entails the use of two storage platforms connected by a wide area network link and placed at some geographical distance from each other. In operation, should disk platform A in the production environment become compromised, then applications and end-users "fail over" to a backup disk platform B at a remote location, which contains a current copy of the data in platform A. Information processing continues unabated.

Part of the high cost of mirroring is that it typically entails more than simply the deployment of two identical arrays. Within each array, or at least inside the primary array, most vendors recommend the use of "mirror-splitting,"[4] which, depending on how the strategy is implemented, can increase the price for an array by several times the price of the nonmirrored configuration.

Mirror-splits are created by synchronizing the data on one set of disk drives inside the array with another set inside the same array (that is, creating a synchronous or symmetrical mirror pair), then periodically removing the mirrored set from service (i.e., "breaking it off") and substituting a second synchronized mirror set in its place (see Figure 9–10).

It is important not to oversimplify this process, which requires a bit of magic to do properly. At the block-device level, data mirroring involves synchronously copying changes made at one storage volume (source) to another volume (target). From the host or application perspective, no write is considered complete until the changes have been applied to all of the mirrors as well as the original. Mirrors may be created within a single storage device or, if the application's architecture allows, between physically separate devices. When a mirror target device is broken away or 'split" from the original, the target device becomes a static, point-in-time (PIT) copy of the source.

This is where things get tricky. Depending on the steps taken to quiesce the application or file system at the moment before the mirror is split, the PIT copy will have a state of "coherency" relative to the application,

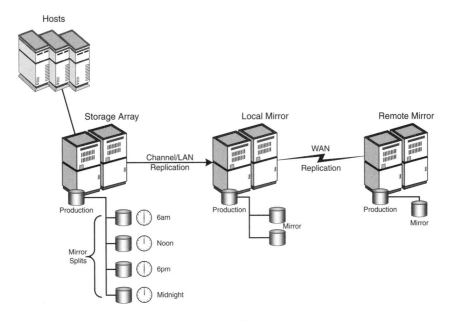

Figure 9–10   Mirror-splits and replication.

the file system, or the block device level. So, integration of the mirror-splitting process with the application is key to determining the level of data consistency found in the resulting PIT copy. States of coherency range from "transactionally consistent," meaning that the resulting copy represents a PIT copy of all user transactions completed up to the moment of the split, to "crash consistent," meaning that the copy looks pretty much like what would exist if someone had simply pulled the plug on the application server. With crash consistent PIT copies, some undetermined number of user transactions may be incomplete or lost.

Performed properly, this process provides a safeguard against certain types of internal array failures and delivers instant access to the last version of the data saved at the time of the split. This process is usually replicated to some degree on each external mirror array.

The intention of implementing multiple mirror-splits is to speed the recovery effort and minimize the amount of real-time data lost in the event of an outage. A disk-based data protection strategy, using mirror-splits and replication, provides considerable improvement over tapes in terms of recovery speed.

Such solutions may be intriguing from a risk reduction standpoint, but the costs are enormous because an extra full set of disks is needed for each mirror-split, and additional disks may be required for local and remote replication, as well. In this strategy, for every terabyte of storage that is used to support a host application, nine or more terabytes of additional disk capacity are required to support mirror-splits (assuming a replication interval of every six hours) and split replication on other arrays.

In addition to these high costs, mirror-split and replication solutions also have the following major limitations:

- Four mirror-splits taken six hours apart (see Figure 9–10) only provide 24 hours of online protection. Older data must still be retrieved from tape, which lengthens restore times.
- The data in the mirror-splits can be hours old. A corruption event at 11:00 A.M. requires going back to the 6 A.M. mirror-split, possibly resulting in five hours of lost data. The only way to reduce this time is to either reduce the amount of online protection (e.g., four mirror-splits, one hour apart), or to increase the total number of online mirror-splits, which rapidly increases storage capacity requirements and costs.
- Restoration can still require hours to accomplish. While the mirror-split is available instantly, it must first be copied to primary disk before it can be used because it is vital that this mirror-split not be damaged. Additionally, the physical mirror does not necessarily align with the logical layout of files or databases (see crash consistency above), so often it is necessary to piece together data elements to affect a recovery.
- If the chosen mirror-split contains data modified after a corruption event has occured, then additional time may be required to identify errors and test other sources of accurate data.
- Mirror-splitting technology typically locks the customer into a single vendor solution.

New approaches and products, such as Time Addressable Storage (TAS) from Revivio, are helping to reduce the need for multiple mirror-splits and to optimize mirroring hardware requirements (see the discussion of TAS later in this chapter). However, mirroring in general has some additional potential drawbacks that should be considered.

- Application Latency/Data Concurrency: All mirroring strategies introduce some latency into application operations, even when primary and mirror arrays are in close proximity to one another. Applications must be suspended (or their I/O cached and queued, which introduces another set of potential problems) while data is written to the primary, then the mirrored, array. This problem is exacerbated in typical disaster prevention mirroring topologies in which the mirror platform must be placed at a geographically remote location to prevent it from falling prey to the same disaster that impacts the local production array. Simple physics imposes a time delay on the transfer of data to the mirror array (signals cannot propagate faster than the speed of light as summarized in Table 9–2), and this delay will result in either a slowing of application performance while mirrored writes are being made, or a lack of concurrency between the data on the primary and on the mirror (called a "delta" in the industry). The size of the delta—the difference between data on the primary and mirror platforms—impacts the efficacy of mirroring as a data protection strategy. A number of hardware and software-based "multitargeting" products exist in the market today that might aid in offsetting latency introduced by mirroring, as discussed below.

• Expense: Cost has always been a gating factor in mirror strategy adoption. While bandwidth costs are said to be dropping because of plentiful bandwidth in and around most major metropolitan areas, placing a primary or mirrored array in a location where network bandwidth is not so plentiful or cheap (corporate data centers are often placed in off-the-beaten-path locales to protect against certain disaster potentials associated with urban centers) is a cost multiplier

Table 9–2 Signal Velocity and Propagation Delay through Various Transparent Media and Copper Wire

Material	Propagation velocity (fraction of speed of light in a vacuum)	Index of refraction	Velocity of Signal (km/s)
Optical fiber	.68	1.46	205,000
Flint glass	.58	1.71	175,000
Water	.75	1.33	226,000
Diamond	.41	2.45	122,000
Air	.99971	1.00029	299,890
Copper Wire (Cat 5 Cable)	.77	N/A	231,000

in mirror operations. Moreover, to surmount application latency issues, many vendors of mirroring solutions promote the idea of "multi-hop mirroring" (as discussed previously) in which they endeavor to address application latency through the use of a second data replication operation. While this approach may provide a wonderful way for vendors to sell multiple copies of hardware platforms, it has the effect of adding significant cost to the solution as well as introducing more data deltas (delta 1 is the discrepancy at any given time between data sets in the local primary and mirror, and delta 2 is the discrepancy between the local and the remote mirrors). Costs need to be considered within the context of outage potentials and their cost to the organization in terms of lost revenue, lost customer confidence, and potential legal or regulatory penalties and fines.

- Vendor lock-in: Software utilities provided by vendors of hardware arrays to support mirroring (e.g., SRDF from EMC, XRF from IBM, etc.) primarily support mirror operations only between two (or more) platforms from the same vendor. While third-party software-based mirrors have begun to appear in the market (i.e., various volume level mirroring products from "virtualization" vendors) that may support cross-platform mirrors, these solutions 1) may not be supported by all hardware vendors and expose consumers to hardware warranty issues, 2) may be resource intensive if installed on application servers, 3) may be difficult to administer and maintain, or 4) may require an investment in new storage topology (such as a Fibre Channel fabric) for which the IT manager may not be able develop a business justification.

It should be added that mirroring, like other data copying schemes, does not protect against all threats to data integrity. Erred data, whether created by a software glitch, user input error, virus program, or other source of data corruption, is replicated across mirrors with the same speed and alacrity as good data. In this regard, disk- and tape-based backup are both vulnerable, though one could argue that the selective restoral of tape insulates against some threats that mirroring does not.

Of course, as many successful recoveries enabled by mirroring solutions demonstrate, the disk-to-disk data protection strategy can be a powerful one. Properly applied and carefully implemented, such a strategy offers the capability for short "time-to-data" recovery of mission critical data access.

ENHANCED BACKUP OPTIONS EXIST

The key thing to keep in mind when developing a data protection strategy is that the range of options is broader than current debates over tape backup and disk mirroring might lead you to believe. In fact, new technologies are appearing (literally) almost daily that enable data protection to be tailored to specific application requirements.

Many new products are "bolt-ons" to existing tape or disk schemes. Others are self-described "disruptive technologies," which claim to replace tradition backup and mirroring approaches to data protection altogether. Careful analysis and due diligence testing is the order of the day to separate the kernels of truth from the chaff.

In 2002, an industry organization called the Enhanced Backup Solutions Initiative (EBSI) was formed to help do just that. Founders—Quantum Corporation, Network Appliance, Legato Systems, and Avamar Technologies—created EBSI with the expressed goal of exploring the options between backup and mirroring and establishing reference standards for deploying these solutions. (This author also sat on the Board of Directors as a "consumer ombudsman.")

The meetings of the group were amazingly cooperative and convivial. Each company was clearly pursuing its own backup or mirroring "hybrid" strategies in an effort to address customer-perceived deficits in its own technology and seeking to capitalize on new architectures enabled by low-cost disk arrays and new intellectual property. Still there was general agreement that there were "many roads to Rome" and that it was in the best interests of vendors collectively to assist their customers in protecting their data assets.

As testimony to the perceived importance of data protection, EBSI generated a groundswell of interest in the IT community. The organization's website attracted over 450 end-user registrations within days of going online, and most registrations were from consumers who were concerned about the efficacy of their current data protection strategy or seeking to define their first strategy in the wake of disasters such as the September 11th terrorist attacks or new regulatory and legal mandates such as the Health Insurance Portability and Accountability Act (HIPAA), Sarbanes-Oxley, and the Graham Leach Bliley Act.[5]

In my role as "consumer ombudsman" on the board of directors for EBSI, I found myself inventorying the technologies that were coming to market to "fix" backup without necessarily incurring the expense of "mirroring." Figure 9–11 captures the spectrum of solutions that emerged from this inventory.

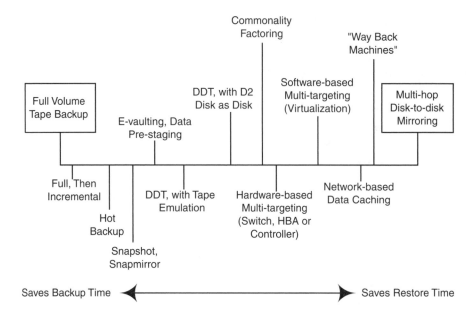

Figure 9–11   The ever-widening spectrum of data protection solutions.

From the diagram, you can readily see that some enhanced backup technologies are software-based, some are hardware-based, and others consist simply of topologies or secondary uses of other components. Many were "tin-wrapped software," an expression sometimes used around Silicon Valley to describe new software that has been wedded to a commodity server platform often running a Linux kernel to create a basic appliance. Such appliances are useful as a means for demonstrating the capabilities of software, though they may not necessarily be the vendor's platform or deployment strategy of choice.

In 2002, there were a lot of tin-wrapped software appliances floating around. Like B-movies of the 1950s, most were junk, a few were bound to be classics, but all sought to compete for the consumer's mental and network bandwidth.

ATTACKING BACKUP TIME

A subset of the new enhanced backup options sought to attack the problems associated with backup, while others looked at time-to-data or data restore. Some—like various software for performing backups only of change data ("full, then incremental, backups"), or for performing backups while applications were still active (so-called "hot backups"), or for capturing bare metal bit states and inodes in a "snapshot backups" or "snap mirrors"—had already been in the market for awhile.

These products sought to address network bandwidth constraints and shrinking backup windows by paring back the amount of data that needed to traverse the interconnect between tape and disk. In this way, vendors believed that tape could remain a viable medium for data protection well into the future.

E-vaulting also fits on the backup time savings side of the chart for the reasons described earlier in this chapter. Through a reliable e-vaulting service, in which backup data is transferred across a WAN or the Internet to an off-site location, preferably at or near the recovery center to which the organization intends relocate its IT operations in an emergency, a significant part of the time-to-data delay accrued to handling tapes in and out of storage and transporting them to the recovery center in an emergency can be eliminated. Iron Mountain has demonstrated this potential time and time again on behalf of customers of its PC Backup and electronic vaulting services.

DDT: NOT THE PESTICIDE, THE OTHER DDT

Toward the middle of the spectrum are two "flavors" of a topology for data protection nicknamed "DDT" for Disk-to-Disk-to-Tape. As shown in Figure 9–12, DDT describes a topology for data protection that builds upon the multi-tier architecture described at the outset of this chapter.

Depending on the vendor, this secondary tier of disk may serve any of several roles (see Figure 9–13):

- A "virtual tape" cache for a back-end library that enables tape media emulation, so that backup data can be aggregated and parsed to fill each tape media cartridge fully;
- A cache for low-latency data restoral on a local basis, with tape used as a medium for remote data recovery;
- A location for "scrubbing" backup datasets using correlation engines that prevent duplicate data from being recorded to backup media;
- A location for "cleaning data" using anti-virus software and exclusion engines that remove unwanted file types from the backup data set; and/or

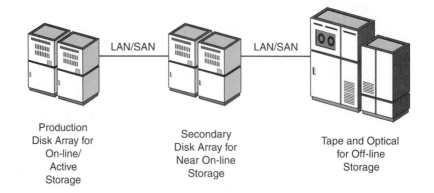

Production
Disk Array for
On-line/
Active
Storage

Secondary
Disk Array for
Near On-line
Storage

Tape and Optical
for Off-line
Storage

DDT or D²T: Disk-to-Disk-to-Tape

Figure 9–12   Disk-to-disk-to-tape.

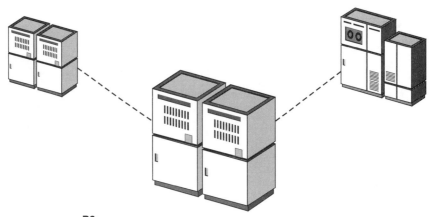

D2:
- Fewer Accesses = Less Expensive Media
- Platform for
    - Correlation Processing
    - Virus Scanning
    - Data Naming
    - Tape Media Imaging and Optimization
    - E-vaulting Via 3rd-Party Data Mover (NDMP)

Figure 9–13   Possible uses for second disk tier in DDT.

- A location for applying a data naming scheme such as the one discussed in the previous chapter. (While not specifically relevant to data protection, this is a potential solution for the problem of applying a naming scheme to the large quantities of data that may have been generated prior to the implementation of such a scheme.)

Vendors often augment the value proposition for this secondary disk storage tier by claiming that, in addition to reducing the risk of data loss in a disaster, the extra disk also saves the customer money. The basic argument is that secondary-tier storage can use inexpensive IDE/ATA or SATA drives, since access to this layer is expected to be less frequent and less demanding than access to primary storage arrays.

Some vendors hold that the secondary-tier array can be comprised of older storage platforms that the organization already possesses, thereby prolonging the life of existing storage investments. A few vendors offer that "D2" storage arrays can also serve as initiators of 3rd Party Data Mover processes such as Network Data Management Protocol (NDMP) that enable back-end transfers of data to tape without involving production servers (so-called "Server-less" backup).

DDT actually comes in two distinct "flavors": tape emulating and "disk as disk." In the first variation, tier-two disk is used as virtual tape, as described earlier in the chapter. The strategy, enabled by tape virtualization software, seeks to capitalize on the throughput of disk to shorten backup times. Traditional tape vendors have preferred this approach because it requires virtually no change in the backup software already installed in customer shops. The data streamed to the tape-emulating disk may be offloaded to actual tape as a secondary process in some configurations.

The other flavor of DDT treats disk as disk. Data is not streamed to the second disk tier, but is copied or mirrored. Advocates of this approach claim that disk-based replication enables fail-over in an emergency and highly granular file-by-file restores: advantages over tape for mission-critical applications. One of the best implementations of this approach is Avamar Technologies' Axion™ product.

Axion features "secret sauce" technology called commonality factoring that finds and eliminates redundant sequences of data as it creates copies of enterprise systems for regular data protection and archive. Intelligent client agents installed on enterprise systems identify replicated data sequences in files and across systems before sending data over networks, reducing strain on congested local or wide area networks. In actual customer environments, Axion sends and stores 100 times less data than conventional backup and restore solutions.[6]

Like EMC's Centera offering, Axion provides fault tolerance using a sophisticated Redundant Array of Independent Nodes (RAIN)[7] architecture. As shown in Figure 9–14, Axion RAIN distributes data and critical fault-tolerance information across storage nodes (compared to disks in a RAID array), allowing Axion to operate through and recover gracefully from node failures.

Axion supports RAIN-5,[8] a method for providing fault tolerance across nodes within a location at a fraction of the storage penalty required by solutions that support mirroring only. In addition to fault tolerance within a single location, Axion RAIN technology can also be configured to provide fault tolerance across geographical locations with Remote RAIN-1 (mirroring across two sites) or Remote RAIN-5 (efficient fault tolerance across three or more sites), protecting critical business assets from site disaster.

All RAIN implementations are active-active, which allows data to be stored and retrieved from all sites simultaneously. Axion RAIN eliminates all single points of failure in a properly configured and deployed system, ensuring high availability and system reliability. Finally, Axion can be configured to stream restores to external devices for environments that require offsite data archival on removable media.

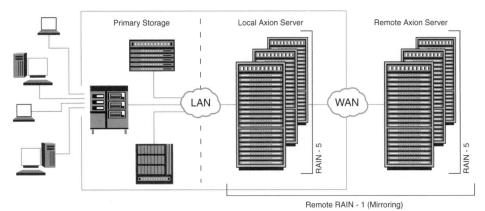

Fault-Tolerant RAIN Architecture
Axion RAIN architecture has been designed with no single points of failure and can be configured to provide recovery from site disaster. Axion Server replaces complex three-tiered tape architectures with a simple, easy-to-install network appliance.

Figure 9–14   Avamar Technologies' Axion Solution in a Rack-Mount RAIN® Configuration. (*Source:* Avamar Technologies, 1A Technology Drive, Irvine, CA 92618, *www.avamar.com.*)

Ultimately, technology like Avamar's Axion and EMC's Centera, both aim to reinvent disk storage by providing enhanced intelligence for data migration, fault-tolerant provisioning, and in the case of Axion, a sophisticated kind of data compression. Both solutions also, as of this writing, require the purchase of all storage components used in the solution solely from the vendor, though Avamar spokespersons claim that they will shortly announce compatibility of their technology with virtually any hardware array.

In addition to multi-tier or RAIN configurations, DDT could also be implemented as a network-attached storage "appliance" that enables it to be deployed wherever it makes sense within the organization's IT infrastructure. Figure 9–15 illustrates the concept: a network-attached storage (NAS) "head" (a thin server optimized for storage I/O and network attachment), with front-end or network-facing support for IP-based file system protocols such as Network File System or Common Internet File System (NFS/CIFS) and the burgeoning IP-based block storage protocol, Small Computer Systems Interface over Internet Protocol (iSCSI). The NAS head can be attached to a back-end switched Fibre Channel fabric or IP SAN comprising two (or more) tiers of disk, and also to a tape solution. Essentially, this is DDT in a box.

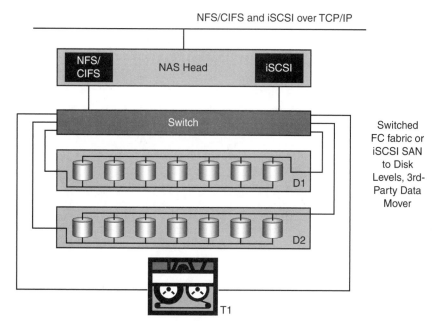

Figure 9–15 DDT in a box.

SAVING RESTORE TIME

Some DDT solutions, like electronic vaulting, seek not only to support time-savings in data backup operations, but also in data restore operations. Generally speaking, the tape backup software industry has always been more interested in talking about backup than it has about restore for a variety of reasons.

One reason is the focus of consumers on shrinking windows for backups, which has led vendors almost universally to emphasize performance in backup operations. While common sense dictates that backups are not performed for their own sake, but to provide insurance against unforeseen events that compromise the integrity of the primary copy of data, rarely has restore speed been a gating factor in the consumer mind. When it has been a serious consideration, vendors have rushed in to sell fail-over mirroring rather than tape.

Data restoral can be expedited in two main ways. First is to stream (or multistream) data directly from tape to the primary storage hardware from which the backup was taken—sort of server-less backup in reverse.

Such a strategy has merit, provided that the target platform to which data is being restored is configured identically (or nearly so) to the platform from which data was originally copied. This may not always be the case, especially if data is stored across many physical devices comprising a logical volume in a SAN. Ideally, such a strategy must also avoid passing data through a RAID controller or virtualization software engine that could introduces latency as it determines where to write each block of data being received. Such "bare metal" writes are available with some high-end RAID arrays today, but are not in widespread use.

The second way to speed data restore is to enable restore software itself to adjust dynamically to the environment in which it operates. An early leader in this space was BakBone Software, which uniquely touted its restore speed (about 80 percent of backup speeds in restore operations) as part of its earliest marketing campaign in the United States.

Most other products realize as high as 70 percent to as low as 20 percent of backup speed on restore operations. Vendors with low restore speeds almost universally blame operating systems, file systems, virtualization engines and RAID controllers for the difference between backup and restore timeframes. These all play a role in determining how quickly data can be written to target devices. However, the performance of leading applications in the face of similar impediments leads to the obvious differentiator: Some products are simply better engineered to adapt more quickly and restore faster than others.

A third set of alternatives for rapid data restore approached the problem from a variety of unique perspectives. Some vendors, for example, offered hardware-based multitargeting solutions based on switches, multiported controllers, multiported host bus adapters, intended to expedite data recovery from tape or disk platforms via multiple, parallel, data channels. This is roughly the same approach advanced by SAN virtualization vendors, who seek to use the capabilities of SAN switching, combined with their virtualization and data replication software, to expedite recovery through virtual volume fail-over within local or remote SANs. This is what DataCore Software illustrates in Figure 9–16.

Another approach offered by Tacit Networks and an increasing number of NAS platform providers is to implement a network of disk caching appliances throughout an IP network. These networked caches provide another data redundancy approach that can heal breakdowns either in the storage infrastructure or in the networks that provide access to it.

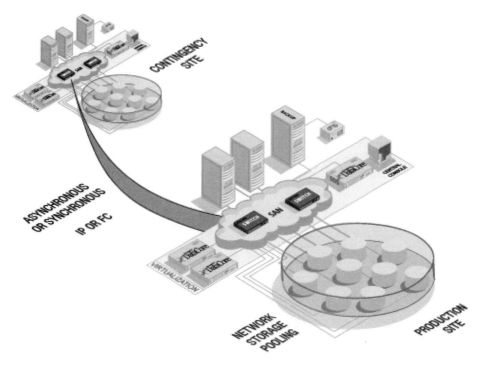

Figure 9–16   Virtualization-based data replication in a Fibre Channel fabric using DataCore Software SANSymphony. (*Source:* DataCore Software Corporation, Corporate Park, 6300 NW 5th Way, Ft. Lauderdale, FL 33309, *www.datacore.com.*)

In the case of Tacit's offering, caching appliances use the vendor's own protocol, called Storage Caching/Internet Protocol (SC/IP™), which translates standard network file system protocols such as NFS/CIFS into WAN-optimized protocols, to facilitate file cache coherency across wide geographical areas (see Figure 9–17). The approach differs from NAS appliances using remote snapshots and mirrors in that "Tacit's caching architecture solves the WAN latency issue." According to the vendor, optimizing copy operations via SC/IP obviates the need for expensive bandwidth connections.

Network-based file caching moves the enhanced backup solution set nearer to the traditional multi-hop mirroring end of the spectrum in Figure 9–11. Another set of solutions in that domain can be referred to collectively as "Way Back Machines." More than a homage to the "Bullwinkle" television cartoon series I enjoyed in my youth, this reference is to a specific concept in mirroring: the journaling of block-level changes to storage.

The following series of illustrations from Revivio, a leader in this particular technology, may help to articulate the concept.[9]

As of this writing, Revivio is bringing its technology to market as a fully fault-tolerant, block-level appliance that allows instant access to data

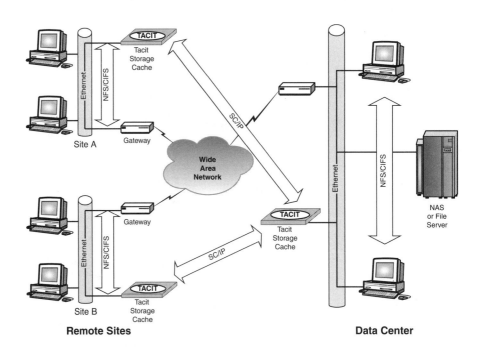

Figure 9–17 Tacit networks network-based file caching architecture. (*Source:* Tacit Networks, 4041M Hadley Road, South Plainfield, NJ 07080, *www.tacitnetworks.com.*)

as it existed at any point in time. Since the technology operates at the block level, it is able to protect applications that work on file systems, SQL or nonstandard databases, or even raw disk partitions.

In normal operation, depicted in Figure 9–18, the appliance presents itself as a standard set of disk drives (LUNS) called TimeSafe™ volumes. The platform imposes no performance or reliability hit on the live storage or applications using it.

If a data corruption event occurs at, say 3:55 P.M., the administrator can access the Revivio appliance and instruct it to "reflect" a TimeImage from a point in time before the corruption event. This point in time can be chosen arbitrarily after the event and does not require preplanning (as is the case with mirror-splits).

This reflected TimeImage is instantly presented as another complete set of volumes (disks) that contain the data from an earlier point in time (see Figure 9–19). These disks can be mounted on another host and validated for correctness.

If the chosen data set is defective (that is, the missing or corrupt data occurred prior to the chosen TimeImage target time), the appliance can be

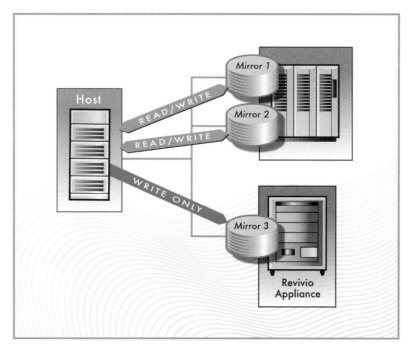

Figure 9–18 Revivio technology as write-only mirror during normal operation. (*Source:* Revivio, Inc., Lexington, MA. *www.revivio.com.*)

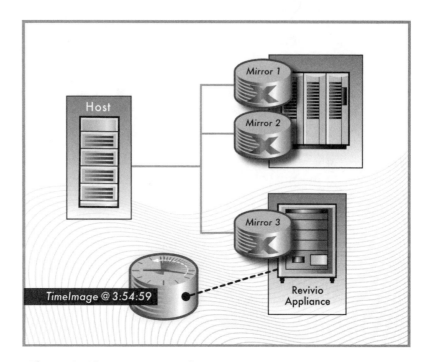

Figure 9–19   Presentation of TimeImage prior to corruption event. (*Source:* Revivio, Inc., Lexington, MA. *www.revivio.com.*)

instructed to provide another point-in-time image, which is also presented instantly.

Database experts understand that the act of recovering a database changes the underlying storage. This is why existing snapshot and mirror-split solutions require that data first be replicated in order to preserve the contents of the source snapshot or mirror-split. TimeImages are fully read/write capable, and changes made to a TimeImage do not change the primary storage. Revivio's inclusion of read/write and nondestructive testing capabilities dramatically shortens recovery time.

Once the image is verified, the appliance can instantly restore the validated point-in-time data onto the TimeSafe volumes, as shown in Figure 9–20. Again, this process happens without moving or copying data.

At this point, the TimeSafe volumes can stand in temporarily for the primary dataset. Database validation and application restart can immediately commence.

A background process resynchronizes the data, the TimeSafe volume, and the primary storage. Once this synchronization is complete, the host directs all read requests to the primary storage array, and the Revivio appliance returns to its normal status.

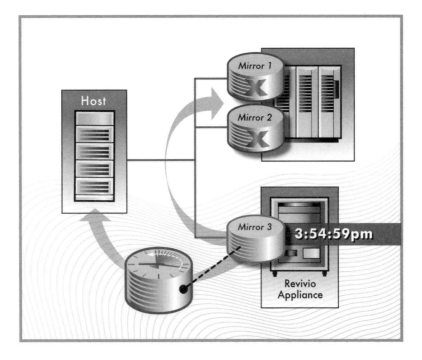

Figure 9–20 Rapid recovery with Revivio. (*Source:* Revivio, Inc., Lexington, MA. *www.revivio.com.*)

Revivio is yet another example of an innovative appliance-based solution for data protection that approaches the problems from the perspective of restore, rather than backup. Products of the "Way Back Machine" variety may find considerable interest in IT shops where mirror-splitting is currently used. Revivio, for example, boasts that deploying its product would effectively return up to 80 percent of array capacity to production use, assuming a traditional high-end array configuration with six separate local mirrored disk sets "for daily mirroring and point-in-time recovery."

THE BOTTOM LINE ABOUT BOLT-ONS

The bottom line is that enhanced backup technologies like those described in the preceding pages may help storage designers to consider new approaches for data protection, including many that might not receive much presence against the backdrop of a holy war over tape versus disk mirroring. To adapt these enhanced backup solutions to meet the specific data protection requirements of their business applications, planners must 1) know of their existence, 2) become familiar with product capabilities and limitations, and 3) undertake critical testing and analysis of the products themselves.

Every technology surveyed in this chapter delivers data protection through replication. The technologies vary based on their approach to delivering replication and in how rapidly they restore data to productive use. Some strategies entail hardware lock-ins or require a Fibre Channel SAN fabric, while others have predominantly open architectures that enable the use of any storage platform and any topology. Finally, all of the technologies exact a cost, some mainly in terms of acquisition and deployment expenses, others in terms of cultural change.

Understanding the demands already taking their toll on the storage professional's time, it may be difficult to track all of the new data protection strategies and products that seem to be appearing, literally, on a daily basis. However, to find the right technology or combination of technologies to meet the data protection requirements of your shop, you will need to find some way to keep yourself informed. It is becoming imperative for storage technology consumers to begin sharing their experience in specialized user groups, consumer-focused industry initiatives (like EBSI), and in the trade press.

A final word of advice on that subject of data protection: Despite what vendor brochures may seem to suggest, you don't need to commit to a single solution to protect all of the data in your shop. In fact, doing so might be a bad move.

Every application manifests its own I/O characteristics and criticality varies from one application to another. Thus, different data protection schemes may be better suited to different applications. If there is a core mistake in all of the debates around tape backup and disk mirroring it is the idea that a single approach is suitable for all data. This wasn't true in the mainframe world, and it isn't true in the open systems world.

ENDNOTES

1. See "Storage Management Layers: Value-Added Services for Storage Infrastructure," IntelliStorage website, *www.intellistorage.com*.
2. See Fred Moore, "Disk and Tape Pricing Guidelines," A Horison Information Strategies White Paper, 2002, Horison Information Strategies, 100 Arapahoe Avenue, Suite 14 Boulder, Colorado 80302, *www.horison.com*
3. Jack Robinson, Gregg Ormsbee, and Jorn Rasstad, "Breaking the Limits of Traditional Tape Technology," Tandberg Data White Paper, 2001, Tandberg Data ASA, Kjelsåsveien 161, PO Box 134 Kjelsås, 0411 Oslo, Norway,

www.tandberg.com. O-MaSS technology uses a matrix array write head, which Tandberg has been developing for seven years, that enables writing much-denser data and recording 32 tracks at a time. It uses an optical servo system and an optical read head. The intent is to use standard media that is available today that will be housed in a half-inch cartridge similar to that of present-day LTO and DLT, but the tape will be shorter and wider (2.5 to 3 inches) than today's media. O-MaSS uses a center-park, dual-reel design to provide fast access times, and the tape reels are oriented horizontally inside the cartridge. It is also unique in that the tape never leaves the cartridge and the recording head goes inside the cartridge during a read or write operation. With expected introduction in 4Q03, a first-generation implementation is projected to store up to 600GB of uncompressed data on a single O-MaSS data cartridge at data transfer rates up to 64 MB/sec. O-MaSS pricing is expected to be comparable to LTO Ultrium and Super DLTape at product introduction. The company also claims that the O-MaSS technology could be used by other tape technologies to boost their capacity and performance beyond those shown on their current road maps.

4. Discussed in Jon William Toigo, "Introducing Time Addressable Storage: A Common-Sense Approach To Data Protection," Toigo Partners International Business Technology Brief, May 28, 2003, Toigo Partners International LLC, 1538 Patricia Avenue, Dunedin, FL 34698, *www.it-sense.org.*

5. The attention garnered by the group also attracted the interest of the Storage Networking Industry Association (SNIA), which soon after formalized its own forum to look at data protection—after nearly five years of promising to do so. As of this writing, EBSI is contemplating a merger with SNIA.

6. See "Axion: Online Protection for the Enterprise," Avamar Technologies White Paper, October 2002, Avamar Technologies, 1A Technology Drive, Irvine, CA 92618, *www.avamar.com.*

7. According to Kevin Daly, CEO of Avamar Technologies, Redundant Array of Independent Nodes (RAIN) is a registered trademark of Avamar Technologies, but is widely used in the industry—albeit with slightly different interpretations and meanings. Unlike the case of Redundant Arrays of Independent Disk (RAID), a quasi standard first articulated during the 1988 annual meeting of the Association for Computing Machinery's Special Interest Group on Management of Data (ACM SIGMOD) in a presentation entitled "A Case for Redundant Arrays of Inexpensive Disks" by a team of University of California Berkeley researchers (Garth Gibson, Randy Katz and David Patterson), Daly concedes that there is no "definitive paper" describing what RAIN is or what RAIN "levels" mean. Interview conducted on July 1, 2003.

8. Ibid.

9. Op cit, Jon William Toigo, "Introducing Time Addressable Storage: A Common-Sense Approach To Data Protection," Toigo Partners International Business Technology Brief, May 28, 2003.

CHAPTER
10

The Cone of Silence

The previous chapter looked at data protection from the disaster recovery perspective: how to ensure that mission critical data could be returned to an accessible state rapidly in the wake of an unplanned interruption. We looked at many products, topologies and solutions for ensuring the timely replication of data and its timely restoration to productive use following a disaster event.

We saw how many emerging technologies for enhancing data protection capitalize on multi-tier storage architectures that, in turn, take advantage of new storage interconnects such as switched fabrics (Fibre Channel) and true storage networking (iSCSI) protocols. This same infrastructure is enabling the implementation of new management paradigms like access frequency-based data migration that promise to improve the ways that we provision storage to applications.

What was left out of the previous discussion was the other aspect of disaster recovery, which is disaster avoidance. Disaster recovery planning seeks to eliminate those potential causes of unplanned data access interruption that can be eliminated and to minimize the impact of interruption potentials that cannot be eliminated.

Within the Disaster Recovery Planning context, disaster avoidance helps to minimize or eliminate risks that may lead to disasters. In many cases, it amounts to little more than the application of common sense practices such as the following:

- Identify and eliminate known disaster potentials by looking at facility physical security, sources of potential electrical or combustion hazards, airborne particulate counts (which can cause equipment damage and fire), water hazards, and so forth. Simple steps can make the workplace a safer environment.
- Prepare a detailed inventory of all equipment especially computer and communications components and make sure you keep it up-to-date. The inventory should cover all hardware, software, communications equipment, peripherals, backup media, and power conditioning equipment. The inventory should include the following information:
  - Model & Serial Numbers
  - Firmware revision levels
  - Quantity
  - Vendor/Supplier
  - Alternate Vendor/Supplier
  - Availability
- Examine network and storage interconnects for potential single points of failure and rectify these as needed. Redundant ports, redundant lines, redundant power supplies, etc. are all options that might have been ignored at the time of initial design and deployment and may be able to be added at minimal cost to reduce risk.
- Negotiate a standby agreement with a local dealer, reseller or integrator for priority replacement of hardware and other LAN components in case of an emergency or disaster.
- Evaluate your current backup strategy to determine its consistency with changes in business processes and applications.
- Test your backup media on a regular basis to ensure that you are able to recover your systems and databases from backup media.

This last point is especially important. Unfortunately, many computer users have a naive faith in computer storage media. Examples are replete of users entrusting their only copy of a critical file to single floppy disk or CD-ROM.

The simple fact is that all forms of magnetic (and optical) media degrade over time and will ultimately fail. There is far less certainty than is widely assumed as to when a tape, disk, or CD media will fail. Recent studies of CD recording media, for example, revealed that many brand name products did not live up to the resiliency claims of their manufacturers in accelerated aging tests.

In any event, the advice remains the same: Save your copies of your work REGULARLY and NOT to the same storage device that stores originals. Backup frequency will depend upon how much data you have and how regularly it changes. As a guideline, if you couldn't bear to lose something, make a copy. Choosing an alternative backup location is eminently sensible or your backup will suffer the same demise as the original.

In addition to disaster prevention through effective data replication, it is increasingly important to look at data disaster prevention from the perspective of security. This is a "new frontier" in storage technology, and one that is thrust upon us as a result of burgeoning networked storage techniques and architectures. This chapter will focus on the role of data security in a networked storage world.

A SECURITY CAPABILITY FOR STORAGE

While the popular discussion of security requirements for storage is a relatively new phenomenon,[1] driven in part by concerns over the increased accessibility of storage arrays across a shared interconnect, fabric, or network, and the vulnerability this introduces to data from internal and external sources, information security itself is not new. Information security technology has undergone significant development over the past 20 years, especially in the areas of application hosting and networking, as a response to the growing realization of the increased dependency of business processes upon increasingly internetworked systems and applications.

Study after study has revealed that the same technologies that are making business processes more efficient are also increasing their vulnerability. Widespread deployment of standardized applications and operating systems, for example, and the omnipresence of the Internet, have not only increased the accessibility and ease of use of information systems, they have also facilitated the efforts of those who seek to access IT resources for the purposes of misuse, vandalism, or sabotage.

According to the most recent study released by the Computer Security Institute and Federal Bureau of Investigation, computer crime continues to be a significant fact of life in corporate America, with incidents costing the 250 or so companies who reported them a total of $201 million in 2003.[2] The study also yielded the following data points:[3]

- As in prior years, theft of proprietary information caused the greatest financial loss ($70,195,900 was lost, with the average reported loss being approximately $2.7 million).
- In a shift from previous years, the second most expensive computer crime among survey respondents was denial of service, with a cost of $65,643,300.
- Losses reported for financial fraud were drastically lower, at $10,186,400. This compares to nearly $116 million reported last year.
- As in previous years, virus incidents (82 percent) and insider abuse of network access (80 percent) were the most cited forms of attack or abuse.

Of course, almost weekly reports of new virus programs and intense media coverage of financial accounting scandals involving the manipulation and misreporting of corporate data have contributed to a more widespread perception of risks to electronic information access and integrity. This perception, in turn, is driving an increasing number of companies to take an active interest in protecting their infrastructure by developing a homegrown security capability.

For those who are new to information security, it is best described as a broad and multifaceted discipline with nearly as many methodologies as there are security consultants—rather like networked storage, one could argue. Surveying the literature of the field, it is easy to conclude that security is some sort of mystical or Byzantine practice best left to a small and secretive cadre of skilled practitioners.

The truth is that, while efforts to form a security capability for your organization might benefit from the guidance of a professional security consultant, security planning itself is a relatively straightforward application of common sense. Building an effective security capability involves an ongoing and iterative process of vulnerability assessment and solution implementation.

Organizations that have already experienced the devastation of an email virus, or realized a financial loss from a denial-of-service attack or deliberate data corruption by a disgruntled employee may already perceive the points of vulnerability in their systems or networks. However, it is a generally preferred practice to conduct a vulnerability assessment before a security incident occurs. That way, you can identify gaps in existing information technology infrastructure that might be exploited to disrupt operations, to gain access to confidential information, or to compromise the integrity of data, and take proactive steps to close them.

With the results of a vulnerability assessment, you will inevitably find that gaps exist and you have some work to do in order to build a security capability. A security capability is nothing more than a combination of policies, procedures, and security technologies that, together, mitigate certain risks and provide mechanisms for coping with the unavoidable.

Policies and procedures define security objectives and goals. They are intended to describe and control certain behaviors (primarily of organization staff) in a manner that advances or supports those goals.

Security technologies are best selected and implemented only after policies and procedures have been defined, to support them by "hardening" the behavioral limits established by policy. There is no single technology to solve all security problems. Rather, a combination of technologies is generally needed to meet the special requirements of applications and business processes within any given organization.

There are, however, three generic goals or objectives that should guide any effort to build a security capability, regardless of the type of organization involved. These are:

1. Protect information and infrastructure.
2. Provide authentication-based access with cost-effective administration.
3. Enable information nonrepudiation.

As you develop a security capability to meet these three generic goals of security planning—as well as any particularized objectives appropriate to your business setting—the key requirement to keep in mind is "balance." In most organizations, a balance must be struck between the steps that are taken to secure applications and data, and the impact of those steps on application performance and ease of use from the user perspective.

It is possible with current security products to lock down data, systems, and even networks in an extremely secure way—to impose a veritable "cone of silence" over your environment. However, a side effect of all this security may be reduced application performance or a significant increase in user inconvenience.

Planners need to find the appropriate balance between the level of security required to protect the organization and the level of performance reduction or user inconvenience that the organization can tolerate. To some extent the toleration for inconvenience is linked to corporate culture. For example, in organizations such as government intelligence or defense agencies, airtight security is an absolute requirement and user convenience is not an issue.

However, in most organizations, including most civilian government agencies and departments, businesses, and educational institutions, the culture of the organization is quite different. In these settings, the success of a security strategy is directly related to its "transparency" to the end-user.

If a security provision slows the performance of an application perceptively or creates other inconveniences for end-users, such as the need to remember several passwords, it will more than likely be rejected by end-users. Rejection may take the form of an ongoing stream of complaints about the security system or the use of "workarounds" (for example, attaching notes containing passwords directly to workstation monitors) that defeat the purpose of the security measure itself, or other, more direct action.

Balance also refers to cost of ownership. In addition to its acquisition price, security technology (like all information technology) has an extended cost of ownership that accrues over its entire useful life. As with storage technology, the bulk of security technology's cost of ownership is a function of labor expense. Reducing this expense requires better automation. The more automated the administration and management of the technology, the fewer monks you need to hire to operate it.

A balanced security strategy considers the cost to protect information and the cost to own the capability you create. Fear, uncertainty, and doubt is not the best premise for selling security to management: As with all technology acquisitions, you need balanced and compelling business cases that include not only risk reduction, but also cost-savings and business enablement value.

The bottom line is that balance must be considered at each step of security planning. Doing so will help you select security approaches that fit with the culture of the organization whose storage assets you are working to protect.

THE THREE A's OF SECURITY

To accomplish the first objective of information security—that is, to protect data and infrastructure—you must develop a cost-effective strategy for restricting access to data and infrastructure to authorized users only.

The ingredients of such a strategy consist of the "three A's": access control, authorization, and administration.

There are many types of authorization and access controls. They range in type and function from simple user identification (ID) and password systems, implemented directly in the program code of an application program, operating system boot-up or network login process, to more complex encrypted key systems that run outside of the application itself. ID and Password safeguards may be supplemented through the use of hardware IDs for client machines and/or biometric identification methods that use fingerprints, retina artery patterns, hand geometry, or other physical attributes to establish the identity of the user seeking access.

Generally speaking, the purposes of such controls are to (1) verify the identity of a person requesting access to protected data assets and infrastructure based on something he or she possesses (key), knows (password), or is (retina scan), and (2) to grant the kind of access to the user that is consistent with his/her predefined privileges or permissions.

The third "A"—administration—refers to how information used for authorization and access is gathered, managed, and maintained. Most application security administration approaches require the registration or "enrollment" of a user, often using a security administration application or database, prior to enabling access to any data or infrastructure components. Once the user is enrolled, he/she may be assigned access privileges to certain data assets and not to others, to certain applications and not to others, or to certain infrastructure elements (servers, storage devices, or networks) and not to others. In addition, administration approaches may set access periods that limit a user's access to certain days of the week or hours of the day.

The administration of authorization methods and access controls (see Figure 10–1) is often the most expensive aspect of data and infrastructure security because it tends to be the most labor-intensive. Administration tasks involve:

- Collecting and verifying identification information;
- Associating authenticated identities with applications and/or infrastructure elements;
- Configuring applications and/or infrastructure elements with authenticated identity information and setting permissions;
- Issuing and tracking passwords, encryption keys, or other authentication tokens; and/or
- Maintaining all of the above against a backdrop of constant change.

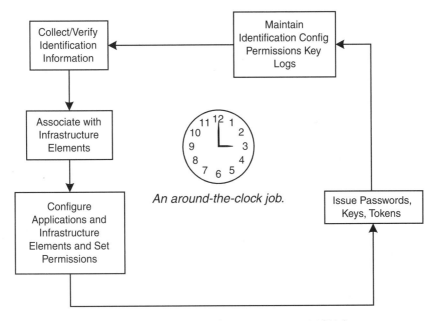

Figure 10-1   Security administration is a 24/7 job.

Given the amount of work typically involved in administering security, it is not surprising that it frequently comes up as a pain point in surveys of server administrators. With the current attention to storage security, security administration is likely to rise to the top of the pain charts in storage administration as well.

Paying close attention to administration requirements as you evaluate potential technologies for use protecting storage infrastructure is another facet of the quest for a balanced approach. Technologies that impose complex administrative burdens tend not to be implemented. Take, for example, the case of IPsec.

The Internet Engineering Task Force IP Security (IPsec) standard (the current version of the RFC dates to 1998) was intended to provide a security architecture for communications across the Internet.[4] It consists of a collection of protocols including:

- Authentication Header (AH): AH provides an authenticity guarantee for packets by attaching strong cryptography checksums to packets. AH supports a key exchange approach to authentication (see below), provides a checksum to assure the recipient that a packet was generated by the expected sender and not by an impostor, and reassures the recipient that the packet arrived intact, and was not modified in transit.

- Encapsulating Security Payload (ESP): ESP provides a confidentiality guarantee for packets by encrypting packets with encryption algorithms. If you receive a packet with ESP and successfully decrypt it using a unique key that only you and the sender possess, you can be sure that no one could have eavesdropped upon or wiretapped the packet in transit.

- IP payload compression (IPcomp): ESP provides services for encrypting packets. However, encryption tends to conflict with efforts to compress data traversing a network, so IPcomp provides a way to compress packet before its encryption by ESP.

- Internet Key Exchange (IKE): As noted above, AH and ESP needs shared secret key between peers. IKE provides a means to share keys secretly so they can be used to encrypt data before it traverses a secure Virtual Private Network "tunnel" established between two secure end points.

The Internet Key Exchange (IKE) approach embedded in IPsec, and illustrated in Figure 10–2, tracks its origins in part to PKI, short for Public Key Infrastructure. PKI is an implementation of public key encryption

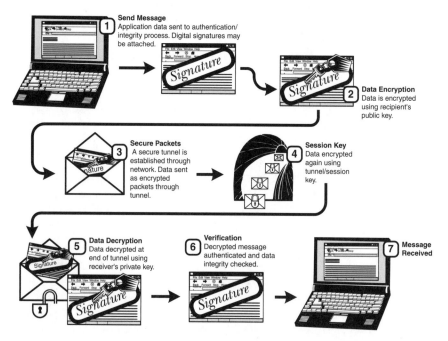

Figure 10–2   Internet Engineering Task Force IP Security (IPSEC) standard.

techniques intended to ensure the confidentiality of data communicated between two parties. PKI, as the name implies, involves using two software keys—one public, the other private—to encode a message or file so that the file cannot be read by anyone other than the authorized recipient.

The owner of the public/private key pair provides a copy of his or her public key to those with whom he or she routinely communicates. The public key is usually stored in a Digital Certificate or digital passport, which is essentially an "attachment" to an electronic message that conforms to the X.509 certificate standard recommendation under development at the International Telecommunication Union (ITU). Recipients of public keys can store them in a key repository for use in encrypting any message or file sent to the key owner.

Once encrypted using the public key, a message or file cannot be decrypted by anyone other than the owner of the public/private key pair. The recipient decrypts the message or file using a private key that is different from, but mathematically related to, his or her public key.

This method of secure file encryption was deemed so robust that, in the late 1990s, the U.S. government (together with the governments of other countries) sought a strategy for ensuring access to the contents of files and messages encrypted using the technique. In the United States, a system of Certificate Authorities was set up to 1) control the issuance of public/private key pairs, 2) verify the identity of the key pair recipient and issue a digital certificate containing the public key, and 3) maintain a copy of the public/private key pair in escrow should the government, under power of a court-issued warrant, ever need to decrypt encrypted traffic of the key pair holder.

PKI has been touted as the best approach to facilitate secure communications in decentralized computing environments, particularly the Internet, where centralized security administration is difficult or impossible to implement. And, as stated earlier, it is at the core of IPsec.

However, implementation of IPsec—and of IKE in particular—has been hampered by the complexity and management burden imposed by the key exchange system itself and by other issues including:

- Enrollment difficulties: Distributing digital certificates from and to all parties involved can be difficult, and maintaining the list and identifying revoked certificates can be labor intensive.
- Competing standards for digital certificate formats: There are two formal standards and several informal ones.

- Security concerns: The cryptographic algorithms used to decode traffic have been successfully broken by kids with standard PC processors.

- No trust in the gatekeepers: Certificate Authorities are widely perceived as the weak link in the trust-based system based on publicized incidents involving misuse or mistaken issuance of certificates by Certificate Authorities.

By 2001, IETF participants were calling for a moratorium on new features in IKE because, while the technology was sound from an engineering point of view, enhancements were only contributing to the complexity problems that had already stalled IPsec adoption by end-users.[5] Guidance from one open source development group held that "the configuration of IPsec is NOT EASY. There are way too many knobs to play with, and debugging is very hard due to wiretap-resistant nature of IPsec. Basically, we can't guess what is going on from packet trace. Try reading some books and standard documents/RFCs, hire consultants or whatever, before you try to configure it."[6]

The point is that complexity can inhibit the implementation and use of even the best security technologies. It is also worth noting that the issues surrounding the efficacy of IPsec promise to reassert themselves as IP-based storage protocols come into greater use.

WHICH IS MORE SECURE: IP OR FIBRE CHANNEL?

Arguments in the current holy war between advocates of Fibre Channel fabrics and champions of burgeoning IP protocol-based solutions such as iSCSI frequently include a debate over security. FC SAN companies routinely argue that, because of the relative mystery surrounding the Fibre Channel Protocol and the "closed" nature of Fibre Channel "networks" (that is, that they are not connected to LANs), FC SAN topology is inherently more secure than IP storage solutions.

This argument has some merit. The reason that servers on IP networks are so frequently targeted by hackers and virus programs is that they are "open" systems. LANs tend to be interconnected with other networks in order to enable the greatest possible reach and access for applications the broadest possible accessibility to applications and end-users.

Moreover, IP networking protocols are standardized, and information about them are readily available and widely disseminated. This, in turn, facilitates the development of a body of techniques for breaking into IP networking gear.

Some experts estimate that less than 10 minutes will elapse before the first hacker or hacking program visits a server newly deployed to the Internet. The know-how and the tools are available to anyone who wants them—from systems and network administrators to hackers and script kiddies.

Intuitively, all of the above lend credence to the argument of the FC camp that their "SANs" are more secure than IP LANs. However, objectively, what the FC camp fails to note is that their preferred SAN variant typically lacks the necessary services to support security whether as a function of vendor implementations of the FC protocol on their products, or because of outright deficits in the FC protocol itself.

It is typical for those deploying FC fabrics to also deploy an IP network, making a second connection to every device in the fabric, in order to provide out-of-band management and security functions. The management of devices such as storage arrays and FC switches is accomplished across this IP network using either proprietary management frameworks or Simple Network Management Protocol (SNMP) and SNMP Management Information Bases (MIBs).

SNMP, which is another Internet Engineering Task Force[7] standard, has come under attack recently as a source of vulnerability to hackers. In February 2002, an advisory issued by the Computer Emergency Response Team (CERT®)/Coordination Center at Carnegie-Mellon University reported that certain SNMP message handling implementations contained vulnerabilities that could allow unauthorized privileged access, denial-of-service conditions, or unstable behavior.[8] So important is the issue, CERT/CC currently maintains on their website a list of network product vendors annotated to reflect the vulnerability of their products to SNMP problems!

Of course, SNMP vulnerability is only an issue for a FC fabric if the IP network used to manage the FC fabric is "open"—that is, interconnected with other networks or accessible through clients other than the SNMP management console. If it is closed and physical access to the management console is protected, then the potential exposure is effectively mitigated. The same may be said of SNMP used in an IP storage network.

It should be added that many FC switches provide accessibility to their configuration management interfaces via the TELNET protocol, another IP protocol. As of this writing, only a few vendors have provided on-board security on their FC products that is capable of preventing casual users or deliberate hackers from using TELNET to access configuration controls and change setup parameters. Were this to happen, the disruption of the storage infrastructure could be severe. This again is an exposure that is seldom discussed in the FC versus IP debate.

IP-related vulnerabilities aside, FC SAN advocates typically refer to "zoning" as a guarantor of security. The basic premise of zoning is to control who can access what in a SAN.

Zoning is part of a multi-layer scheme of access management in the view of FC advocates that includes server, storage, switch, and software layers. At the top of this stack is the server, which provides a doorway to the SAN infrastructure.

On any server, there are mechanisms to control what devices an application can see and whether or not the application can talk to another device. At the lowest level, an HBA's firmware and/or driver provide a "masking capability" that determines what devices the server can see. In addition, most server operating systems can be configured to control which devices are mounted as storage volumes. Storage volume management, virtualization, and even file systems provide an extra layer of access control.

If the server is connected to a FC fabric, an additional layer of access control is arguably provided by zoning—another form of selective presentation of storage assets. The zoning process in a FC SAN switch uses the list of available LUNs on SAN-attached arrays and cross references this information to switch ports. This cross-referencing scheme establishes connections between server nodes and storage nodes that are used to control and shape traffic across the fabric. Simply put, security is provided through zoning by simply ignoring or rejecting access requests from server nodes that do not have permission to access nodes on a given storage node list.

Most, if not all, Fibre Channel switches support some form of zoning to control which devices on which ports can access other devices via other ports. Virtualization may enhance this access control, according to FC SAN advocates.

How exactly does zoning work? In very simple terms, when a node device is attached to the SAN and powered up, it performs a fabric logon and obtains its source address or destination address (SID or DID) from the switch. The device already has its own unique World Wide Name (WWN) as a function of a hardware-based identifier.

When each device logs on to the name server service in the SAN switch and registers itself, the switch builds up a database of all the devices in the fabric—a process that uses a mapping of the node and port WWNs to a 24-bit address. The login process completes when the server node asks the name server process to send back a list of what other FCP devices it can see in the fabric. This is where zoning policies are applied. The name server only returns a list of those FCP devices that are in the same zone (or a common zone) as the requesting node. In other words, the server only "learns" about the availability of those nodes that it actually is permitted to use.

The server, thus armed with a list of the addresses of all the devices it is supposed to be able to see, then typically performs a port logon to each device in order to discover what kind of FCP/SCSI device it is—a process that is quite similar to conventional SCSI bus queries. When the process is complete, presumably a secure zone has been established that controls device access in the SAN.

An important distinction to understand, however, is the difference between "hard" and "soft" zoning. Soft zoning refers to the security afforded by "not being told what you don't need to know." One often hears a metaphor for soft zoning used at conferences and elsewhere. Soft zoning is described as the equivalent of having an unlisted phone number. While your telephone number is not published, someone could still dial your number at random or by mistake, and your phone would still ring. The difficulty with this type of zoning from a security standpoint is that it leaves storage assets exposed to random access by unauthorized devices. Any device connecting to a soft zoned FC fabric could use an "unzoned name server query" to discover devices to which access has not been formally provided.

By contrast, hard zoning prevents unauthorized access. Metaphorically, it is like having a call block set up on your phone so that even if someone guesses your phone number, your phone does not ring. Hard zoning is a more secure approach. However, while many switch vendors claim to support it, the actual level of support provided varies greatly from vendor to vendor. Some switches implement hard zoning through a proprietary scheme of naming (i.e., via a specific port-ID syntax) that only works with switches of the same type or from the same manufacturer. Confusion arises when the term "hard zoning" is used interchangeably for SAN zone naming schemes based on node and port IDs—which is not the same thing.

Understanding hard zoning is important to understanding evolving FC SAN technology, like Cisco Systems' Virtual SAN (VSAN). VSAN addresses a key security and resiliency issue in FC fabrics with a new approach supported currently only on Cisco/Andiamo switches. The issue has to do with the recommended design strategy of running two, separate fabrics with each node connected to both fabrics. This design presumably affords fault tolerance by insulating devices from a discrete link failure or port failure affecting one of the fabrics.

However, even such dual fabric designs are subject to a single point of failure: the name server service in a switch. There is a small possibility that a misbehaved device could disrupt the name service to the extent that all devices on the fabric, not just those in the same zone, would be impacted. This would obviate the resiliency value of the dual wiring topology.

VSAN is proposed as a higher-level construct than the name server with a totally separate name server database, rather than one common to all zones. It may even run as a totally separate service within the switch, so the possibility of cross contamination is lower and problems are more localized. Affording some enhanced security, VSANs show promise. Of course, if a device is connected to two separate VSANs and misbehaves, then it can potentially bring down both VSANs.

As of this writing, VSAN has not been standardized. Cisco and Andiamo are actively seeking backers both at ANSI and at IETF. When and if VSAN is adopted, significant changes will need to be made to the manner in which node discovery is performed (unzoned name query, for example) across an FC SAN organized into VSANs. Implications for security remain to be fully explored, but advocates claim that they may provide more secure fabrics in much the same manner that VLANs augmented the security of messaging networks.

Not to be upstaged by Fibre Channel competitors, IP storage advocates make the inverse claim that iSCSI-based SANs are more secure than their FC counterparts because they can leverage existing standards-based, in-band security protocols, like IPsec. For the obvious reason that IPsec is complex and difficult to administer, which has limited its adoption and deployment in the real world, this claim is difficult to justify.

Efforts to develop IP SAN-specific security standards (or storage security standards generally) are in their infancy. If Cisco Systems' Virtual SAN (VSAN) effort is any indication, quasi-security-related technologies like Virtual Private Network (VPN) will find their way into storage networks shortly.

In the world of LANs, a VPN establishes a secure or "private" network within a public network by encrypting traffic between two communicating end points. Some VPNs also use "tunneling" technology for greater security. Tunneling, as the name implies, establishes a special low-level connection between the communicating devices and a reserves and exclusive path between the devices for use during the entire period of the communications session. The Internet Engineering Task Force (IETF) recommends a combination of tunneling and encryption as part of its IP Security (IPsec) standard, though considerable debate exists around the need for tunneling in non-IP networks such as ATM that already provide secure virtual circuits.

A tunneling protocol for moving Fibre Channel–transported storage I/O across an IP link (FCIP) has already been developed by the IETF. Co-developed by Cisco Systems and Brocade Communications Systems, the protocol was intended to facilitate the interconnection of isolated Fibre Channel fabrics (so-called "island SANs") across existing, lower-cost, IP backbone networks within companies or IP Wide Area Networks connecting geographically remote locations. The one potential drawback of FCIP is that it creates from all of the island SANs a single fabric, so incompatibilities in switch gear, node naming schemes, and zoning schemes must be considered carefully before joining two or more FC SAN islands together via this method.

Fibre Channel has also been mapped to IP directly with the Fibre Channel over Internet (iFCP) protocol. Unlike FCIP, iFCP operates Fibre Channel Protocol as an application across an IP network. This provides the ability to use IP to connect various FC fabrics, but also enables each connected fabric to retain its own unique naming and zoning conventions because the unique identity of each island fabric is preserved.

When FCIP or iFCP are deployed, the security issues that the FC community argue are the bane of IP come back to haunt them. At present, the truth about the security of any of the current manifestations of networked storage is best summarized in an observation once made by a former National Security Agency manager: "The only way to keep information secure in a network is not to put it there."

BURGEONING TECHNOLOGIES

As more data is entrusted to more highly accessible topologies such as FC fabrics or IP SANs, it is inevitable that the vulnerability of the data that they host and transport will increase. A question that is being asked more often these days is whether the existing safeguards in LANs, which interconnect servers to their back-end storage topologies, and in server operating systems themselves, are sufficiently robust to fend off an earnest hacker.

As shown in Figure 10–3, contemporary LANs and servers provide the bulk of the security capabilities that organizations have come to depend upon to insulate business processes from malicious outsiders—and

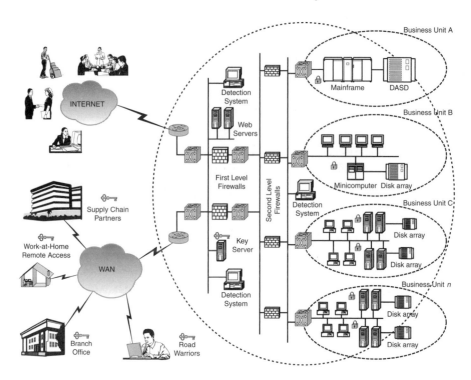

Figure 10–3   Typical security provisioning in a LAN.

to some extent from insiders. In the case of internal threats, most experts believe that there is much more work to do.

In 2002, a study of 146 companies by Activis, a security company based in Reading, England, determined that 81 percent of security breaches originated internally, another 13 percent came from ex-employees and 6 percent from external hackers.[9] While this did not jibe with the findings of the U.S.-focused 2003 CSI/FBI Computer Crime and Security Survey, which saw a slight-but-perceptible decline in internally originated (as opposed to externally originated) attacks, it does underscore the point that trusted personnel inside the organization can do as much or more harm to data than all the nameless malcontents who hack web servers.[10]

There continues to be serious doubt over the adequacy of security provided in existing networks and servers in coping with internal threats—especially since this exposure often comes from inside the demilitarized zone created by firewalls and other protection schemes and perpetrators often have authorization to access applications and their hosting platforms. Beyond establishing hard-line policies that threaten employees with prosecution, there seems to be little more that can be done in commercial organizations that will not impair system performance or generate user push-back. Many organizations have determined that multiple logins, login time-outs, and similar strategies are simply too costly or too difficult to administer, relegating the issue to the "too hard" file for now.

In the case of storage security, this is unacceptable. As storage becomes more and more networked, the actions of a single individual could cause significant and unrecoverable corruption of the primary asset of a company: data. One partial solution to this conundrum is transparent encryption.

STORAGE ENCRYPTION

As with message encryption in LANs, data encryption in storage is a straightforward method of ensuring that data is not subject to eavesdropping or to disclosure to unauthorized parties. The inherent problem with a key encryption scheme for storage encryption, however, is the number of nodes that are communicating at any given time.

How should encryption be provided so that it does not require user enrollment or inhibit I/O performance—that is, how can it be provided transparently? Asking this question results in a by now familiar set of responses.

- Encrypt at the switch: One solution is to implement encryption (as well as management and virtualization) on switches. Presumably, grouping nodes into zones, then establishing a trusted system of zone communications (essentially, which nodes are permitted to communicate) provides the basis for determining who sees unencrypted data. Switch vendors have begun to provide strong switch-to-switch authentication and there is some movement in the storage industry to support SAN node authentication (e.g., that a device connecting to the fabric is authentic and allowed). However, a switch-based approach does not protect the stored data while they are in transit or when they reach the subsystem or library. Implementing data encryption at the switch or even at the subsystem level will require additional performance, some sort of key exchange methodology, a measure of interoperability that vendors have yet to demonstrate and some sort of consolidated security management capability that has been the holy grail of security in the LAN space for many years.

- Encrypt on the host: Some vendors seek to add I/O encrypt/decrypt functionality to applications, to the operating systems of server hosts, or to installed network interface cards/host bus adapters (NIC/HBA). Application-based encryption is an obvious location for introducing encryption, and some applications offer this function now in connection with sending documents as attachments across the Internet. Such functions do introduce performance hits on application hosts, however, and are likely to be used, as they are today, strictly on a one-off basis: when a user feels the delay is merited by the nature of the data. In short, application-level encryption may not be used even when it is available. And, if it is used, it is only as secure as the server hosting the application.

  Encryption as a function of host operating system software is a perpetuation of host-based management or virtualization architectures. It has the potential drawback of adding substantial processing cycles to the workloads of servers by adding another process to an already inefficient stack process.

  The NIC/HBA strategy has the potential merit of offloading encrypt/decrypt processing, but only if the industry can agree on a common NIC/HBA authentication protocol that would authorize only NIC/HBAs to decrypt traffic from certain nodes. Substantial work is being done in this area, by the way, and some report that the outlook is promising.[11]

- Encrypt on the array controller: A few array vendors provide encryption functions on array controllers. Such a strategy is worthwhile, but only as a function of a larger system on node authentication and key exchange. One value of encrypting at the storage platform is only tangentially related to the broader issue of storage security and has more to do with warranty replacement of hard disks. In 1993, a healthcare service provider experienced failures in several array-based disk drives that were covered under a replacement warranty. However, he learned that the Health Insurance Portability and Accountability Act (HIPAA) of 1996 prohibited him from sending the drives to the vendor for replacement because they might contain private patient data. There was no way to disable the drives to guarantee that their data could not be read without physically destroying them, an action that would invalidate warranty replacement provisions. Any action short of physical destruction would need to be validated in terms of its success before the drives shipped (that is, the nonfunctioning drive would need to be operated to demonstrate that data erasure had occurred). This "Mobius Loop" in HIPAA regulations could be avoided if data was encrypted on the drive. The possibility of disclosure would have been a nonissue.

- Encrypt via an in-band appliance: Newcomers, including Decru and NeoScale Systems, are pursuing an appliance-based approach to encrypt/decrypt. In their view, the implementation of an in-the-wire, on-the-fly, encryption capability obviates the problems in other schemes by providing a proprietary scheme for authentication and key exchange (between appliances) that can be easily deployed and operates in a totally transparent manner. In the NeoScale approach (see Figure 10–4), a storage security appliance operates in-line and can be transparent to the application, to the storage subsystem, and can even be transparent to the switch or router. An appliance can be deployed according to an organization's security requirements such as: (1) between application-attached storage servers and the fabric, (2) within the fabric, (3) before or after gateway connections, (4) in-front of storage subsystems and (5) in front of virtualization systems.[12] According to the vendor, once stored data reaches the appliance, the data payload can be encrypted and sent forward or through a secure tunnel (in which the appliance or another device is the terminating point). If tunneling functionality is employed, the appliance will require awareness of switches or routers.

This flexible deployment can effectively complement security provisions such as port zoning. For example, the appliance can be associated with zoned ports that carry application-specific or sensitive storage data. Such a deployment can also adapt to current and evolving network storage topologies and business functions.

NeoScale argues that a storage security appliance has the advantage of high-performance, centralized, policy-based management and transparent operation. The appliance analyzes stored data traffic, dynamically applying appropriate encryption and forwarding the encrypted payload to the storage subsystem without impacting the surrounding storage operations. By placing the encryption functionality and processing in a built-for-purpose device, servers and application storage processing remain dedicated to the purposes for which they were intended.

Storage security appliance advocates speculate that data encryption within a storage appliance can be implemented in several ways. According to NeoScale, the first method is "broad application using a single or reduced key set."[13] In other words, a single set of encryption keys would

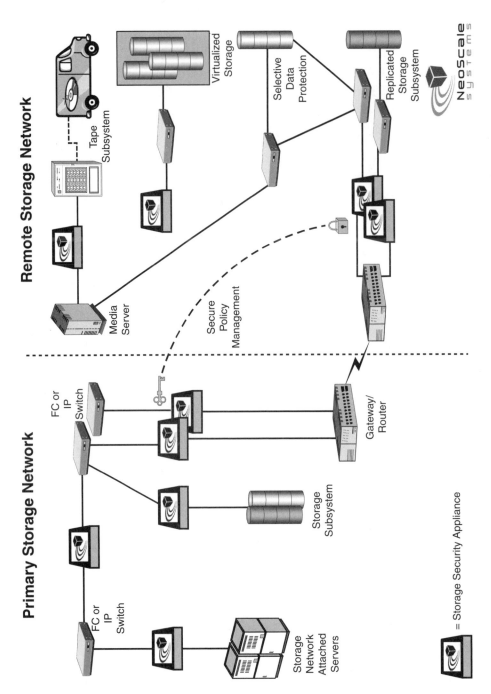

Figure 10–4 One deployment plan for NeoScale storage security appliances. (*Source:* NeoScale Systems, Inc., 1500 McCandless Drive, Milpitas, CA 95035, *www.neoscale.com.*)

be used to encrypt all data entering the appliance. This would minimize key management issues but will still require key escrow and some means to associate an encryption key to a block range, partition, tape, object, etc.

The vendor concedes that this approach "does not take into account unique applications or protecting different sensitive data with different keys."[14] Many companies would prefer to selectively encrypt sensitive stored data and leave nonconfidential unencrypted. Associating unique keys with unique data storage applications (e.g., by department, subsidiary, customer, data type, or application type) would effectively prevent any individual with access to a single key from having universal data access.

Another method is to provide dynamic and automated data storage encryption based on user-defined rules. This approach allows data encryption to be applied in response to different business requirements.

Rules would be created by the user and maintained by the appliance. Each rule would comprise data storage protection parameters based on selectable data elements (shades of the data naming scheme articulated in Chapter Eight) that would be available as part of the knowledge base of the storage security appliance. This approach has the merit of flexibility with respect to how organizations protect different application or functional data storage.

Appliance-based storage security simplify some of the burdens of key management and administration with respect to storage encryption, and it obviates some of the performance issues associated with other encryption techniques by offloading the function from servers, switches, and array controllers. Until (and if ever) new protocols and services are introduced that are optimized for storage I/O encryption, technologies like those offered by Decru and NeoScale Systems may be the best approach for keeping data secret.

ADAPTING OTHER SECURITY CONCEPTS TO STORAGE

Truth be told, security has not changed much since the Middle Ages when kings erected walls and dug moats around their castles and used book codes and other techniques to encrypt messages to their peers and field generals. In the modern LAN, technologies such as firewalls and Virtual Private Networks (VPNs) provide the walls and moats, and key encryption provides the codes. Organizations deploy these technologies to secure data assets, first, by protecting the perimeter of the network and, second, by preventing the misuse or disclosure of data if perimeter defenses fail.

Another data protection technique associated with data protection in medieval times was the signet ring. A message written and encoded was closed with a drop of candle wax into which was impressed the image of the face of the royal signet. This stamp authenticated the contents of the message providing nonrepudiation.

Nonrepudiability is also important in contemporary data storage, particularly to comply with requirements established by HIPAA and other laws. Recently, a large medical services company with tens of terabytes of digital records tried an experiment. It copied a subset of its electronic records, which included MRI scans and X-rays, from expensive disk arrays to tape, then restored the files from tape back to disk.

Unfortunately, a lot of bits were lost in the transfer. The company discovered that a 10 percent variance existed between the restored data and the original data.

The difference was disconcerting. While a small amount of data loss might not represent a serious problem for certain types of applications, it is different with medical records, which might be used later as a reference for ongoing treatment or as evidence in a malpractice court case. Even a slight change in data—one that could manifest itself, say, as a shadow on a lung—could have significant repercussions for doctors and patients.

The issue of data integrity and nonrepudiation is a growing problem for data storage managers. Several efforts are afoot within standards-making bodies, such as the Internet Engineering Task Force (IETF) and the World Wide Web Consortium (W3C), to come up with a fix. At the same time, work is proceeding behind the scenes within many storage vendor shops to develop proprietary solutions. Just keeping up with the terminology can be a challenge.

For example, many of the efforts involve using Message Digest Version 5 (MD5). Message Digest Version 5 (MD5) is an algorithm submitted to the IETF in 1992 to provide a means for authenticating data by creating a 128-bit fingerprint or message digest from a much longer string of bits. The algorithm, or hash, was intended to authenticate the contents of a dataset, since each fingerprint created with the hash would be different from all others.

While similar in concept to the checksum commonly used in storage, MD5 is described by some as "human proof."[15] While it is possible to change data and still arrive at the same checksum, you cannot change the data and still produce the same MD5 hash.

MD5 hashing, in addition to its applications for data integrity testing, could also be used to support a scheme of "content networking" or hierarchical storage management. Just as addressing is used to map contents to a memory location or disk sector in day-to-day computing, content addressing and HSM take a similar approach to data stored across a large storage platform or network. An effective content addressing scheme allows you to retrieve an entire object by looking up a portion of its contents, while an HSM system typically locates data that has been migrated to near-line or off-line storage using a reference stub.

Since MD5 hashing takes a large amount of data and condenses it to a small message header, experts say that it might become the basis for content networking in a next-generation storage system. The inclusion of an MD5 hash in a data naming scheme such as the one described earlier in this book could provide both a nonrepudiation function for the named data and a mechanism for tracking the data through its useful life.

CONCLUSION

The goal of protecting storage translates to the following general objectives in the storage world:

- Protecting the integrity of data against corruption or loss both while it "at rest" in data repositories (stored on hard disk drives, tape or optical media awaiting use) and while it is "in motion" (being processed by servers, accessed by users, or being transported across networks);
- Ensuring the confidentiality and privacy of data and protecting against its unauthorized disclosure and potential misuse;
- Protecting the applications that are used to manage data against alteration, corruption, or misuse;
- Protecting interconnects, fabrics and networks used to transport data against disruption or misuse.

This chapter has surveyed many of the components of a storage security capability and identified burgeoning technologies for access control, authentication and administration that are still very much in development as of this writing. Figure 10–5 is offered as a summary of vulnerabilities, some of which have yet to be addressed.

The targets for security in this illustration follow the data path from host device driver and host-based virtualization software "volume descriptions," to HBAs and NICs, to interconnects between servers, storage devices and networking or fabric devices, to switches and their configura-

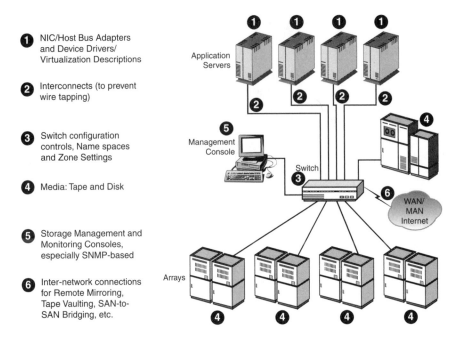

1 NIC/Host Bus Adapters and Device Drivers/ Virtualization Descriptions

2 Interconnects (to prevent wire tapping)

3 Switch configuration controls, Name spaces and Zone Settings

4 Media: Tape and Disk

5 Storage Management and Monitoring Consoles, especially SNMP-based

6 Inter-network connections for Remote Mirroring, Tape Vaulting, SAN-to-SAN Bridging, etc.

Figure 10–5   Security targets in storage.

tion controls, to media, and even storage management consoles (especially those based on SNMP).

Security must also be a component of disaster recovery provisions articulated in storage architecture. Remote mirrors and tape vaults, and SAN-to-SAN bridges across WANs, are all logical targets for security. They must be covered in whatever storage security strategy designers develop for their organizations.

This discussion also underscores a more subtle change that will be required for those seeking to build an intelligent networked storage architecture for their organizations. It is a change in the views we currently hold about storage and the skills set required to effectively plan storage infrastructure.

As the above suggests, it is no longer sufficient to content ourselves with a knowledge of bit domains, transfer rates, areal densities, disk interfaces, and LUNs as the knowledge and skills required for storage management. If storage is to become a utility infrastructure unto itself, we will need a set of new hybrid set of skills and knowledge to cope. We will need to develop broader expertise not only in the bits and bytes of storage technology, but also in networking, object-oriented programming, disaster recovery planning, and security planning.

Change always carries with it new burdens and new responsibilities. The ultimate risk to data is the current gap in the requisite knowledge and skills for its management.

ENDNOTES

1. Data security, even on storage platforms, has long been a concern of government entities concerned with intelligence gathering and defense planning. Certain businesses that are dependent upon intellectual property and trade secrets have also been applying security concepts to storage for many years. It is only been since the rise of the Internet and of networked storage that the subject has resonated with the general population and with businesses in all industry segments.

2. Robert Richardson, "Eighth Annual CSI/FBI Computer Crime and Security Study, 2003," Computer Security Institute, *www.gocsi.com*.

3. Ibid.

4. See S. Kent and R. Atkinson, "Security Architecture for the Internet Protocol," Request for Comments 2401, Network Working Group, Internet Engineering Task Force, November 1998, *www.ietf.cnri.reston.va.us/rfc/rfc2401.txt*.

5. See the IETF Multicast Security (MSEC) archive, August 2001, at *www.pairlist .net/pipermail/msec/*.

6. See "NetBSD Documentation: NetBSD IPsec" at *www.netbsd.org*.

7. See J. Case, M. Fedor, M. Schoffstall, and J. Davin, "A Simple Network Management Protocol (SNMP)," Request for Comments 1157, Network Working Group, Internet Engineering Task Force, May 1990, *www.ietf.cnri.reston.va.us/rfc/rfc1157.txt*.

8. See Ian A. Finlay, "Vulnerability Note VU#854306, Multiple Vulnerabilities in SNMPv1 Request Handling," February 12, 2002, CERT Coordination Center, Carnegie-Mellon University, *www.cert.org/advisories/CA-2002-03.html*.

9. Drew Robb, "Internal Security Breaches More Costly," CIO Update, July 19, 2002, *www.cioupdate.com*.

10. Robert Richardson, CSI/FBI Survey, op cit.

11. See "Data Storage Protection Risks & Returns," A NeoScale White Paper, October 2002, NeoScale Systems, Inc., 1500 McCandless Drive, Milpitas, CA 95035, *www.neoscale.com*.

12. Ibid.

13. Ibid.

14. Ibid.

15. Jon William Toigo, "Patent Pending: Times Change, Some Data Shouldn't," *Washington Technology*, April 15, 2002, *www.washingtontechnology.com*.

Conclusion: Joining the Quest for the Holy Grail

As this conclusion is being written, a news article has just come to my desk from somewhere out in the World Wide Web. The headline announces the discovery of an alien solar system with a planetary structure similar to ours. The lede to the article asks the always-provocative question of whether there may be a world like ours, populated with people like us, orbiting that distant star.

My take: If there is another Earth out there, I hope it has a few data managers. If so, we might be able to make an exchange of some sort, obtaining in the process some best practices and standards-based solutions that we need so desperately here on our planet.

At the beginning of this book, I noted that data storage is the most expensive line item in most corporate IT budgets, and it continues to grow irrespective of the condition of the general economy. There are several contributing causes to this phenomenon, including the apparent propensity of storage vendors to release non-interoperable and half-baked technology to market in order to get the jump on competition, and the prevalence of poor storage management tools that provide insufficient capabilities to enable us to manage burgeoning data with greater efficiency.

Ultimately, however, it is the absence of real data managers that best explains the phenomenon. Consumers are really to blame.

Today, most organizations entrust the design, management, and administration of their most prized and irreplaceable asset, data, to personnel who have none of the necessary prerequisites to do the job. Storage management is typically an afterthought: a set of tasks lumped onto the shoulders of IT technicians and systems administrators who 1) don't particularly care about data storage or data management, and 2) generally possess no specific skills or knowledge for performing those tasks. This isn't always the case, but more often than not those who manage storage for a living have zero training to do their jobs.

Under the circumstances, it should come as no surprise that storage today is so expensive, or that our storage platforms are oversubscribed and underutilized, or that contemporary data management is such a mess.

To be honest, with only a few exceptions, the field of data management doesn't exactly attract the best and brightest minds. Architecturally, storage may have been one of the three fundamental components of the original design of the von Neumann machine, the modern computer—the other two being CPU and memory. Historically, however, it was almost always been viewed as the weak sister of the three.

Slow and ugly and cumbersome, disk and tape storage has about as much "sex appeal" as a garbage truck. Historically, in mainframe culture, we put at least two layers of random access memory between the processor and the magnetic disk and spent far more time trying to figure out how to optimize these dynamic RAM caches than we ever did pondering the most efficient way to manage data dumped onto magnetic media platters. If DASD was the proverbial dump truck, central or expanded store RAM were Formula One racecars. Ask any computer engineering undergrad which one he or she would rather drive. You can probably guess the answer.

Just as storage technology is not the most sought-after degree program in technical colleges and universities, it is also a discipline with enormous responsibilities and few perks in the "real world" of work. In most contemporary IT organizations, if you are unfortunate enough to be tapped with storage management duties (doubtless because you were the slowest person to duck into your cubicle when they were handing out the assignment), you live a relatively thankless life. Users become aggravated with you whenever an application stops because of inadequate disk space, but relatively few dedicate any time to thinking about the consequences of all the email they refuse to purge or archive.

If you are tasked with storage planning, administration, and management, you probably have permanent footprints on your back from all the vendors of large-scale storage arrays or Fibre Channel SANs who, after you carefully and diligently reviewed their offerings and rejected them for your application requirements, decided to climb over your objections and make their case directly to the CFO. And, instead of being commended for looking out for the company's money and serving its needs for reliable storage, your efforts are rewarded by two guys who show up at your data center door with dollies asking where they should put several big storage arrays that you didn't order. The purchase order is signed by a senior business manager who, to paraphrase the old saw, doesn't know storage from Shinola.

In general, storage folk labor in isolation and obscurity. Until very recently, there have been no storage-specific user groups, and mentioning that you managed storage at a meeting of a computer user group was likely to get you a blank stare.

"You're a database administrator?" asks one polite attendee, probably someone's spouse. "No," you reply, "I manage storage. You know: tape, disk drives, like that." You probably aren't very popular on date night.

To paraphrase Rodney Dangerfield, storage management earns you little respect. There are no formal job titles in most organizations for what you do. You don't have any professional identity within the IT field. There is no clear career path for you except that you must eventually subject yourself to human cloning in order to manage more and more storage capacity.

Your isolation works to the advantage of the vendors. When something doesn't work, they can tell you with impunity that the fault was all yours. In the absence of a group of peers with whom to compare notes, you have no way to question the validity of their claims.

It must make you angry when you hear a vendor at a storage conference refer to the many focus groups and customer surveys they have conducted that led them to add this or that feature to their latest product—features for which you have no use. It must make you doubly angry when a vendor representative in a panel discussion says that the reason that a certain capability is not part of their product is because no one ever asked for it—but you have been telling your account representative that you needed the capability in question for no less than 10 years.

If things are as bad as I am suggesting, some readers may ask, why are there storage folk out in the trenches who are actually wandering around with big smiles on their faces? Don't their backups fail? Aren't they also being overcharged for disk arrays that they are basically just a few shelves of commodity disk drives inside a tin shell? Haven't they been sold brain-dead fabrics that didn't do any of the things promised by the SAN visionaries? Aren't they also confronting 40 percent allocation efficiency (and substantially less utilization efficiency) even on a good day?

Sure they are. Though some are in what the psychologists call a "state of denial." John Tyrrell, one of the patent holders on Systems Managed Storage, once remarked that he participated in the first 100 studies around SMS done with customers.[1]

"When we added up the people time to 'manage' storage, we not only counted the IT people but we interviewed application groups and asked them how they did their job with respect to storage. They said, 'We don't do storage management.' But after interviewing them, we found they spent lots of time cleaning up space, correcting job failures, resubmitting, looking for space on volumes, changing JCL and resubmitting, backing up their own data, and so on. When we added up the real cost of managing, we found that 80 percent of the management cost was in the application areas, not the data center. The real cost of managing lots of islands of storage is astronomical. We finally stopped keeping track of it. If you think about the time you spend managing your own little laptop island, this will make sense to you."

Distributed computing has made everyone—and no one—a data manager. No one much wants the job, which involves in roughly equal parts,

- Doing the manual maintenance chores that no one else wants to do with tools that trace their origins to some pre-computer era;
- Coming up with workarounds and fixes to product shortcomings so that the storage configuration bears at least some resemblance to the brochure;
- Sorting through the trade press for any information that goes beyond reprinted vendor press releases in the hopes of gaining a clue about what panacea technology the industry is preparing to spring on you next;
- Adjusting management expectations about the performance they thought they would see out of all the shiny new hardware they bought against your advice;
- Trying to avoid technologies with built-in obsolescence so that the next fork-lift upgrade won't involve your cubicle; and
- Trying to figure out strategies for working in a bit of healthful REM sleep between all of the pager messages from your systems advising you that something has broken down or been broken into.

The continuing story of open systems storage is, for all intents and purposes, a quest to find ways to recover the management discipline and tools that were thrown out with the proverbial bathwater when centralized computing gave way to distributed computing models. The current drive to "utility storage infrastructure" is just the latest chapter in this story: an effort to go back to some earlier time when storage was centralized and virtualized and simplified—and managed by folks who were professionally trained to do the job.

The problem is, however, that the storage industry, for all of its platitudes and industry associations, doesn't really seem to want a disciplined, well-managed, "storage utility"—not if it means that a vendor will have to share floor space with a competitor's gear. To paraphrase the old reggae song, Everyone wants to go to heaven, but no one wants to die to get there.

THE SOLUTION IS OUT THERE

We could go on and on about the many ways that vendors have taken advantage of the deconstruction of centralized computing. While they can wrap themselves in the flag and claim that open computing broke the domination of all computing by a single vendor (IBM), vendors must also concede that this also ushered in an anarchical era in storage technology. In the world of contemporary open systems storage, one in which vendors manifest the Hobbesian ideal of self-interested opportunism, and life for storage consumers is nasty and brutish, if not altogether short.

At the time that the first *Holy Grail* book was being developed, the late 1990s, consumers didn't pay very much attention to burgeoning issues like storage management. For as long as the economy was robust and storage devices kept dropping in price, consumers were content to simply buy more, with little or no attention paid to the ultimate price that unmanaged storage would exact.

Today, we are at last feeling the "two towers" of storage pain: the need for cost-effective capacity provisioning in a "do more with less" world using inadequate tools, and the need for a data protection strategy that will endure in the face of an unmanaged infrastructure and threats that seem to be growing daily.

From a technical perspective, most of the problems of provisioning could be effectively addressed today by a combination of true, standards-based, cross-platform LUN carving-and-splicing technology (true virtualization), a robust global namespace for file storage, and a more effective management strategy based upon an open, standards-based scheme of self-describing data and access frequency-based data migration.

In terms of finding space to store all of that exploding data, there are, on the horizon, a number of additional technologies that promise to expand the areal density limits of magnetic storage dramatically. These include

- Atomic Force Resolution: A number of vendors are working to provide a thumbnail-size device with storage densities greater than one terabit (1,000 gigabits) per square inch. The technology builds on advances in atomic probe microscopy, in which a probe tip as small as a single atom scans the surface of a material to produce images accurate within a few nanometers. Probe storage technology would employ an array of atom-size probe tips to read and write data to spots on the storage medium. A micro-mover would position the medium relative to the tips.

  The technology confronts four primary challenges.[2] First is the storage medium: Researchers are looking for a cost-effective and durable phase-change medium for recording bits (basically by heating data spots to change them from one phase to the other). Second is the probe tip, which must emit a directed beam of electrons when voltage is applied. A strong beam flowing from the tip to the medium heats a data spot as needed to write or erase a bit. A weak beam can be used to read data by detecting a certain spot's resistance (or other phase-dependent electrical property) with which the tip is in contact or almost in contact. Third is the actuator or micro-mover that positions the media for reading and writing at the nanometer level. Fourth is packaging to enable the device to be integrated into other devices. Complicating this is the requirement that the components currently require a near vacuum to reduce the scattering of electrons from the read-write beam and to reduce the flow of heat between data spots.

- Holographic Storage: For nearly four decades, holographic memory has been the great white whale of technology research. Despite enormous expenditures, a complete, general-purpose system that could be sold commercially continues to elude industrial and academic researchers. Theoretical projections suggest that it will eventually be possible to use holographic techniques to store trillions of bytes—an amount of information corresponding to the contents of millions of books—in a piece of crystalline material the size of a sugar cube or a standard CD platter. Moreover, holographic technologies permit retrieval of stored data at speeds not possible with magnetic methods. In short, no other storage technology under development can match holography's capacity and speed potential.

These facts have attracted name-brand players, including IBM, Rockwell, Lucent Technologies and Bayer Corporation. Working both independently and in some cases as part of research consortia organized and co-funded by the U.S. Defense Advanced Research Projects Agency (DARPA), the companies are striving to produce a practical commercial holographic storage system within a decade.[3]

1999 was a watershed year in which tests were performed of prototype systems, which differed substantially in design and approach. They did share certain fundamental aspects in common, however. An important one is the storage and retrieval of entire pages of data at one time, each containing thousands or even millions of bits and stored in the form of an optical-interference pattern within a photosensitive crystal or polymer material. The pages are written into the material, one after another, using two laser beams. One beam, known as the object or signal beam, is imprinted with the page of data to be stored when it shines through a liquid-crystal-like screen known as a spatial-light modulator. The screen displays the page of data as a pattern of clear and opaque squares that resembles a crossword puzzle.

A hologram of that page is created when the object beam meets the second beam, known as the reference beam, and the two beams interfere with each other inside the photosensitive recording material. Depending on what the recording material is made of, the optical-interference pattern is imprinted as the result of physical or chemical changes in the material. The pattern is imprinted throughout the material as variations in the refractive index, the light absorption properties or the thickness of the photosensitive material.

When this stored interference pattern is illuminated with either of the two original beams, it diffracts the light so as to reconstruct the other beam used to produce the pattern originally. Thus, illuminating the material with the reference beam re-creates the object beam, with its imprinted page of data. It is then a relatively simple matter to detect the data pattern with a solid-state camera chip, similar to those used in modern digital video cameras. The data from the chip are interpreted and forwarded to the computer as a stream of digital information.

Practical impediments to the productization of the technology include the discovery of a durable media and the creation of beam alignment technology that does not require a staff of guys in lab coats to adjust.

- Patterned Media: One simple solution to the problem of supermagnetism is to segregate the individual bits by erecting barriers between them. This approach, called patterned media, has been an ongoing area of research at most laboratories doing advanced work in storage technology.[4]

  One technique showing promise is to create media with mesas and valleys. Bits are kept from conflicting with each other's magnetic fields by segregating each bit in its own mesa. The difficulty is in making the mesas small enough: they would have to be around eight nanometers across or smaller in order to achieve the kind of densities that developers are seeking. IBM has been able to build such structures with feature sizes as small as 0.1 and 0.2 micron (inset), or 100 and 200 nanometers.

  To fabricate media with such mesas and valleys, companies have been investigating photolithographic processes used by the chip industry. Electron beams or lasers would be needed to etch the pattern onto the storage medium. Mesas would then need to be grown on a substrate layer, one bit in diameter. But this technique needs much refinement. One estimate is that the current lithographic processes can at best make mesas that are about 80 nanometers in diameter—an order of magnitude too large for what is needed.

  Another challenge is to develop an entirely new technology for reading weak signals produced by such small bits. A radical departure from current magnetic disk would be required.

- Optical-Assisted Recording: One strategy for extending the life span of the workhorse magnetic-disk drive is to supplement it with optical technology. Such a hybrid approach could push storage densities to well beyond the current range of 10 to 30 gigabits per square inch. Industry insiders claim[5] that capacities could eventually top 200 gigabits per square inch, surpassing the anticipated limit imposed by the superparamagnetic effect.

  In operation, a laser heats a tiny spot on a disk, which permits the flying head to alter the magnetic properties of the spot so that it stores a binary 1 or 0. Two lenses focus the beam to an extremely fine point, enabling the bits to be written onto the disk at very high density. An objective lens concentrates the beam on a solid-immersion lens—the cornerstone of the system—which, in turn, focuses the light to a spot smaller than a micron across.

The point of this brief survey is that new technology that scales well beyond the limits of magnetic disk is only a few years away. While it might sometimes seem appealing to do as little as possible to solve our current storage problems in anticipation of limitless storage space on a sugar cube, practical necessity dictates otherwise. Many organizations are already at a crisis point when it comes to unmanaged storage costs, and they need solutions now—hence their willingness to try half-baked technologies like FC SANs.

However, the promise of new technologies should not be allowed to enable a whole new generation of IT folks to unlearn the hard lessons about storage management that are being foisted upon organizations today. While higher density, faster access storage might forestall some of the issues around data provisioning, this technology does not address the second tower of storage pain: data protection.

Today, an obscene amount of mission-critical data remains at risk. Despite numerous events that have pressed data vulnerability into the forefront of business and IT thought, very little has actually been done to rectify the situation.

Case in point, within the past year, I had the opportunity to chat with a storage manager for a U.S. federal government agency responsible for printing all of the checks for civilian agencies and departments. The fellow noted that not one of his hundreds of servers had ever been successfully backed up. This was particularly disconcerting because of the close proximity of his data center to the Pentagon, which was targeted by terrorists in the infamous September 11th attacks. Said the manager, had the plane diverted its course only a few degrees and flown a few more miles to where his data center was located, the U.S. government's abilities to pay employees, service providers, and others would have ceased to exist.[6]

For its own part, the federal government has produced only a weak mandate in the area of data protection (as opposed to data security and long term retention, as discussed below). In response to the attacks on the World Trade Center, several financial agencies did convene a panel to look into the efficacy of mirroring arrangements as a disaster protection measure. They discovered that those organizations that had established storage mirrors across the Hudson River certainly fared the attacks better than those that didn't, but they were rightfully concerned that the location of mirrored data centers—within a 30-mile radius of a "target rich" environment like New York City—left them susceptible to the geographic reach of other types of attack scenarios. Just when it appeared that the Office of the Comptroller of the Currency, the Security & Exchange Commission, and other agencies involved in the panel were going to impose some significant distance requirements on backup facilities—thereby placing a burden on storage vendors to develop some real data protection strategies—they backed off the issue completely, stating that they did not have the authority to proscribe distance requirements.[7]

While the legal mandate for data protection in the context of disaster recovery continues to be weak, this is not the case with data protection from the standpoint of security and privacy. Regulations and laws, borne out of financial scandals and concerns about healthcare patient privacy, are today exacting a toll on organizations from the standpoint of storage security provisioning.

Dealing with storage security, as discussed in this book, will require the adaptation of medieval security techniques to an entirely new threat paradigm: one in which the bad guys may not be interested in the contents of the castle, but only in the pleasure of vandalizing the castle itself. In the new millennium, you no longer need a motive to do bad things. For many computer criminals, the answer to the question of their motivation is simply, "Why not?"

The latest developments in the fast-moving world of network security—developments that may find their way into the realm of storage security as well—are technologies like Invicta Networks' Variable Cyber Coordinates.[8] This technology, patented by a former KGB major and cryptography expert who defected to the United States in 1980, is simple in concept. Basically, it provides security for a network connection by making it "invisible" to would-be eavesdroppers. This is done by rapidly changing the logical network addresses of the communicating end stations.

The core of the technology is an algorithm (which is also claimed by BBN Technologies) deployed at each of the communicating endpoints that changes addressing information at the rate of many times per second. Currently, implementation of the algorithm is in the form of a proprietary system that includes a secure network card that must be installed in each communicating system, a secure gateway that must be installed in each LAN, and a security control unit that is used to implement and manage the algorithm-based protection itself.

The approach sidesteps notions such as secure operating systems, firewalls and payload encryption—techniques that have seen billions of dollars in research and development investment but produced little meaningful return in light of increasing incidents of computer crime. Even skeptics seem to be warming to the idea because of its simplicity and the fact that it eliminates the difficulties associated with firewall customization and key management.

It remains to be seen whether innovations such as VCC will make a difference in how we secure the data assets of our organizations going forward. For now, the key issues confronting storage security are less about technology than about training—and the cultivation of data management as its own profession.

PROFESSIONALISM, PRAGMATISM, AND CONSUMERISM

As has been suggested throughout this book, there is no "secret sauce" technology that can deliver an intelligent storage infrastructure today. The intelligence in any storage infrastructure is a function of effective design and pragmatic technology choices.

The basic building blocks of storage, especially disk drives, are becoming more and more commoditized. It is intellectual property—primarily in the form of software and firmware—that is increasingly used by vendors to differentiate products from one another.

Intellectual property is the true wellspring from which new ideas flow from the drawing board to the research and development laboratory and ultimately manifest themselves in products themselves. Vendors have a legitimate argument to make when they want to be compensated for their product IP. It is not the argument of this book that all storage is commodity storage. Storage products can be differentiated by their added-value features and functions, and the market has its own way of deciding the worth of innovation.

Problems begin to arise when products are represented as so different from one another that any comparisons between them are viewed as fundamentally invalid. The claim of many large-scale array vendors is basically that "When God created my product, he broke the mold."

This is not true, and the vendors know it. However, with substantial marketing budgets to shape consumer perceptions, with storage managers themselves effectively isolated and atomized, and with analysts and media feeding from the troth of vendor marketing and advertising budgets, who is going to question the vendor line?

The situation becomes worse when you realize that vendors are the primary participants in standards development organizations. On the one hand, it makes a great deal of sense for the best and brightest technicians to help develop baseline standards for technology. However, the flip side is that standards development is too often held hostage to the marketing objectives of the vendors themselves.

In the most severe case, this takes the form of a declaration by the chairman of the IP Storage Working Group at IETF that his company already holds a general patent on all IP-based storage networking and that the work of the group will eventually need to pass through his company for licensing before it is implemented in anyone else's gear.[9] Another case of excessive vendor control is seen when a large networking company leverages its market presence to obtain adoption of its proprietary SAN technology—just so it can claim to be standards-based.[10] In still other cases, vendors water down standards so there is enough "wiggle room" that even their most proprietary and noninteroperable products can claim to be standards compliant.[11]

One could respond that the market will shake loose all pretenders in time, as it did in the case of TCP/IP and Ethernet protocol-based products over a 20-year period. Consumers will ultimately vote with their wallets.

However, this assumes that consumers have 20 years to wait. Moreover, it takes for granted that consumers are informed about products, their capabilities, and limitations, and about alternatives. That is assuming a lot.

Surveying the literature of the storage industry, one finds precious little in the way of product performance test data. Vendors have in some cases set up roadblocks to prevent the dissemination of unsanctioned test results. One major array vendor goes so far as to invalidate its warranty if a customer discusses publicly the performance received from its product.

As for due diligence testing by consumers themselves, this is less and less frequently done for reasons of time, lack of facilities, and lack of knowledge. As mentioned at the outset of this book, test labs appear to be among the first targets of corporate cost-cutting in lean economic times. Without them, it is difficult to do your own evaluation.

It should come as no surprise that an increasing number of consumers outsource their product decision making altogether to resellers and solutions integrators who often serve suppliers with greater enthusiasm than they do their customers. During the course of the development of this book, I had to turn down a lucrative speaking opportunity from a top value-added reseller. The company wanted me to tell their reseller/integrator clients that Fibre Channel SANs were a tremendous opportunity to cash in and that they would be doing their customers— and their own bank accounts—a favor by recommending Fibre Channel for all storage requirements. That the customer didn't really need a SAN in every case was beside the point: the objective was to fire up attendees (resellers) about Fibre Channel SANs so they would help move a large inventory of product before "legacy" Fibre Channel was replaced by IP storage.

While there are doubtless some trustworthy resellers and integrators, outsourcing storage decision making is generally unwise. As a matter of best practice, resellers can be tasked to test solutions and to offer other advice, but never should they be allowed to assume the role of technology decision-maker for a company. This practice makes about as much sense as the practice of buying products on the basis of vendor reputation and tenure alone.

In the current economic client, it is common to see big storage consumers pass on the purchase of technology from any vendor whose name is not three letters long (e.g., IBM, HDS, EMC, etc.). Their rationale is typically one of fear: They are afraid that the smaller vendor will disappear and they will be left with an unsupported product.

However, given the short payback interval large companies expect from their storage acquisitions (that is, the abbreviated period of time in which cost-savings realized from the product are expected to offset acquisition costs), this philosophy really makes no sense. Typically, in larger companies, a technology acquisition is expected to return its acquisition expense within about 13 months. Moreover, a replacement for a product is already being sought within a year of product implementation. So, the total exposure that a company faces to an unsuccessful product acquisition is about one year or less. By contrast, many technologies offered by both long-tenured vendors and relative newcomers return their investment within days, weeks, or months of implementation.

Established vendors have been quick to capitalize on consumer conservatism and to raise the spectre of doubt about start-ups with innovative ideas. At about the time of this writing, a brand-name vendor took the opportunity as a keynote speaker at an industry tradeshow to announce the results of the testing that his internal lab had performed of the disk-to-disk backup products of several start-up companies. The speaker used the results, which were arrived at through undisclosed methodology, to dismiss the products of burgeoning competitors outright. Doubtless, a negative impression of the new products was left with all of the consumers in attendance, coming from such a reputable source.

These shenanigans are not confined to established players. In 2001, a newcomer in the NAS space pronounced that its product was a hundred times faster than industry leading products from established players. The vendor presented internal test data and compared it with published speeds and feeds data taken from competitors' websites to make his case. Later, it was revealed that the tests measured only how quickly data could be retrieved from the memory cache of the newcomer's storage appliance, while competitive statistics reflected the amount of time required to retrieve data from the back-end disk subsystems of the competitors' arrays—in short, an unfair comparison.

What's worse: Employees of the same newcomer vendor later misrepresented themselves on a web-based bulletin board frequented by investors interested in a competitor vendor's stock. The perpetrators claimed to be customers of the competitor's storage products and went to great pains to criticize the architecture, performance, and service delivered around the vendor's products. Asked whether management was aware of the employee behavior, the response from a company spokesperson was that management had been aware of "one or two instances" and had since instructed staff "not to engage in such actions in the future." In any other industry, such behavior would have been grounds for dismissal.

While vendors engage in such campaigns against each other, the consumer is victimized by poor information. In the worst case, they are held in outright disdain by vendors. During one exchange over standards version numbering conventions for the iSCSI protocol, a participant on the IP Storage Working Group, representing a prominent storage technology company, stated unabashedly that it didn't matter which numbering scheme was used to identify the version of the protocol. He noted that his customers didn't know how to use a protocol analyzer anyway, so they couldn't look at the version number and determine if their equipment supported the final standard or some prestandard variant. Veracity of the statement aside, it underscored the concern of this author that vendors do not answer to the consumer anymore.

WHAT IS TO BE DONE?

What is needed to correct this situation—and to harness the tremendous engine of the free market to help solve practical storage problems—is an informed storage consumer. More specifically,

- To understand and properly assess the business value of technology, the storage consumer needs education.
- To give his or her recommendations about storage architecture and acquisitions credibility and sway with nontechnical business managers, the storage consumer needs status.

- And, to shape technology innovations within the industry so that they favor a more interoperable and robust storage infrastructure model, the storage consumer needs numbers.

How these requirements will be met remains to be seen. One approach is to form a storage user group that can branch out into many chapters across the United States and around the world. The only impediment to such a strategy is the time and effort required on the part of participant members: Storage managers are notorious for having unpredictable schedules and very little time for activities outside of work.

An alternative is to create an on-line community or institute that will facilitate consumers with convenient access to their peers, to trustworthy platform test data, to skills training, professional development and certification programs, and to reference standards on technology and best practices that have been derived from, and proven to work in, the trenches of actual IT shops. There, storage practitioners can realize that they are part of a larger group of Data Managers and can develop a professional identity and discipline that will earn them respect and recognition among their peers, within IT, and among business management.

A second goal of such a group is to enable the formation of a powerful, collective, and consumer-oriented voice within the storage field. With such a collective voice, storage consumers can demand the kinds of storage technologies that deliver real and measurable business value. And the industry will have no alternative but to listen.

The Data Management Institute, which I have recently founded, is intended to provide just such a community for storage practitioners and consumers. By the time that this book is published, the Institute should have a full suite of training and certification programs and should be well along its path toward collecting and disseminating vendor-agnostic, actionable information for storage technology consumers. Visit the Data Management Institute at *www.datainstitute.org* for more information.

I thank you for reading this book and hope you will join us in the next evolution: the Holy Grail of *Data* Management.

ENDNOTES

1. Interviewed in Jon William Toigo, "From the Beginning: Giving Credit Where It is Due," Storage Strategies, *Enterprise Systems Journal*, May 29, 2003, *www.esj.com*.

2. See Jon William Toigo, "A Decade Away: Atomic Resolution Storage," *Scientific American*, May 17, 2000.

3. See Jon William Toigo, "On the Horizon: Holographic," *Scientific American*, May 17, 2000.

4. See Jon William Toigo, "Patterns of Bits," *Scientific American*, May 17, 2000.

5. See Jon William Toigo, "Adding Optical to Magnetic," *Scientific American*, May 17, 2000.

6. Jon William Toigo, "Homeland Defense: Are We Walking the Talk? What's really happened to the security of information technology since Sept. 11?" *Enterprise Systems Journal*, May 1, 2002, *www.esj.com*, and Jon William Toigo, "From the Trenches: DR planning war stories," *Toigo's Take on Storage*, SearchStorage.com, November 5, 2002, *www.searchstorage.com*.

7. Jon William Toigo, "No Legal Mandates for Data Mirroring Today," *Toigo's Takes on Storage*, May 6, 2003, SearchStorage.com, *www.searchstorage.com*.

8. See Jon William Toigo, "Patent Pending: Good Thing this KGB Guy's on Our Side Now," *Washington Technology*, January 7, 2002, *www.Washingtontechnology.com*.

9. Jon William Toigo, "EMC: A Checkered Past in Storage Openness," Enterprise Storage, *Enterprise Systems Journal*, January 1, 2002, *www.esj.com*.

10. Jon William Toigo, "What You Missed in Chicago, Phoenix and Las Vegas," *User Advocate*, SNW Online, May 19, 2003, *www.snwonline.com*.

11. See Jon William Toigo, "Wrong Time for an End Run," Enterprise Storage, September 1, 2001, *Enterprise Systems Journal*, *www.esj.com*.

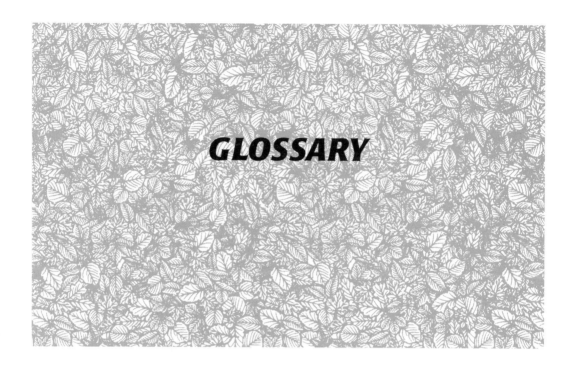

GLOSSARY

ACCESS TIME: Of a hard disk, the combined time for seek, head switch, and rotational latency in a read/write operation. Of an optical disk, the time it takes to access a data track and begin transferring data. In an optical jukebox, it's the time it takes to locate a specific disk, insert it in an optical drive, and begin transferring data to the host system. If the disk is already in the drive, then access time is determined by seek time. Otherwise, it's determined by disk swap time, spin-up time, and seek time.

ACCESS: Refers to the process of obtaining data from, or placing data into a disk storage device, register, or RAM. (i.e., accessing a memory location).

ACCESS FREQUENCY BASED DATA MIGRATION: A strategy for migrating data between storage platforms based on frequency of access rather than by the date that the data was last modified. This strategy is superior to HIERARCHICAL STORAGE MANAGEMENT (HSM) from a storage capacity optimization perspective.

ACTUATOR ARM: A mechanical device used to carry all read/write heads in a multi-platter disk drive.

ACTUATOR: An electro-mechanical device that moves an object, such as the robotic arm that moves an optical disk within the jukebox, or the device that controls the read/write head on a disk drive.

ADAPTIVE CACHING: Technology that allows the drive to tune the cache (number of segments and segment size) to best suit the system's needs.

ADDRESS MARK: Two byte address at the beginning of both the ID field and the data field of the track format. The first byte is the "A1" data pattern, the second byte is used to specify either an ID field or a data field.

ADDRESS: (physical) A specific location in memory where a unit record, or sector, of data is stored. To return to the same area on the disk, each area is given a unique address consisting of three components: cylinder, sector, and head. *CYLINDER ADDRESSING* is accomplished by assigning numbers to the disk's surface concentric circles (cylinders). The cylinder number specifies the radial address component of the data area. *SECTOR ADDRESSING* is accomplished by numbering the data records (sectors) from an index that defines the reference angular position of the disks. Index records are then counted by reading their *ADDRESS MARKS*. Finally, *HEAD ADDRESSING* is accomplished by vertically numbering the disk surfaces, usually starting with the bottom-most disk data surface. For example, the controller might send the binary equivalent of the decimal number 610150 to instruct the drive to access data at cylinder 610, sector 15, and head 0.

ADJUSTABLE INTERLEAVE: Interleaving permits access to more than one memory module, e.g., if one memory module contains odd-numbered address and another even-numbered address, they can both be accessed simultaneously for storage. If the interleave is adjustable, the user may select which ranges or areas are to be accessed each time.

ADVANCED INTELLIGENT TAPE (AIT): A helical scan technology developed by Sony for tape backup/archive of networks and servers, specifically addressing midrange to high-end backup requirements.

AFC (Anti-Ferromagnetic-Coupled) MEDIA: See *PIXIE DUST*.

ALLOCATION UNIT: A group of sectors on the disk reserved for specified information. On hard drives for small computer systems, the allocation unit is usually in the form of a block, cluster, or sector. (*See also BLOCK, CLUSTER*, and *SECTOR*.)

ALLOCATION: The process of assigning particular areas of the disk to specific data or instructions. (*See also ALLOCATION UNIT*.)

AMERICAN NATIONAL STANDARDS INSTITUTE (ANSI): A standard-setting, independent organization that develops and publishes manufacturing and design standards for the United States.

AMERICAN STANDARD FOR CODED INFORMATION INTERCHANGE: ASCII.

ANSI: *See AMERICAN NATIONAL STANDARDS INSTITUTE.*

APPLICATION PROGRAM: A sequence of programmed instructions that tell the computer how to perform an end use task (i.e., accounting, word processing, or other work for the computer system user). To use a program, it must first be loaded into *MAIN MEMORY* from some *AUXILIARY MEMORY* such as a floppy diskette or hard disk.

ARCHIVAL MANAGEMENT: A storage management solution for cataloging files and moving them to long-term storage, where they can be stored and accessed inexpensively.

ARCHIVE: A copy of reference data or document images that are stored on optical disks, floppies, tape, paper, or microfiche. Typically refers to long-term storage of data for later possible access.

AREAL DENSITY: Bit density (bits per inch, or BPI) multiplied by track density (tracks per inch, or TPI), or bits per square inch of the disk surface. Bit density is measured around a track (circumferential on the disk), and track density is radially measured.

ARRAY: A group of disk drives which have been combined into a common array and appear as a single LSU (Logical Storage Unit). (*See also DISK ARRAY.*)

ASCII: *See AMERICAN STANDARD FOR CODED INFORMATION INTERCHANGE.*

ASYNCHRONOUS DATA: Data sent usually in parallel mode without a clock pulse. Time intervals between transmitted bits may be of unequal lengths.

ATA (AT Attachment): This term defines the signal and logical protocol described in X3.221 for IDE (Integrated Drive Electronics) peripherals. (*See also INTERFACE.*)

ATAPI: *See AT ATTACHMENT PACKET INTERFACE.*

AT ATTACHMENT PACKET INTERFACE (ATAPI): A command protocol used for accessing ATA (IDE) peripheral devices. Widely used on CD-ROM and Tape Backup units attached to ATA bus.

AT BUS: An acronym representing Advanced Technology bus. The standard PC compatable peripheral bus to which video cards, I/O cards, internal modem cards, and sound cards are added. Also called the ISA bus, it runs at a maximum of 8.33 MHz and has a 16-bit wide data path.

ATOMIC RESOLUTION STORAGE: A technology derived from atomic probe microscopy in which a storage medium moves along under tiny probe tips that emit lasers no wider than one atom. To read already-recorded patches of medium, the probe tips produce a weaker, even more sensitive, laser.

AUTOLOADER: A single-drive, tape-based backup device that houses a number of tape cartridges. An autoloader is designed to support routine, automatic backup procedures, using a mechanical arm to sequentially load a new tape for daily backup.

AUXILIARY MEMORY: Memory other than main memory; generally a mass storage subsystem, it can include disk drives, backup tape drives, controllers, and buffer memory. Typically, *AUXILIARY MEMORY* is non-volatile.

AUXILIARY STORAGE DEVICE: Devices, generally magnetic tape and magnetic disk, on which data can be stored for use by computer programs. Also known as secondary (in a two tier storage configuration) or tertiary (in a three tier storage configuration) storage.

AVERAGE ACCESS TIME: The average track access time, calculated from the end of the *CONTROLLER* commands to access a drive, to drive "seek complete" time averaged over all possible track locations at the start of ACCESS, and over all possible data track *ADDRESSES*.

AVERAGE LATENCY: The average time required for any byte of data stored on a disk to rotate under the disk drive's read/write head. Equal to one half the time required for a single rotation of the platter.

AVERAGE SEEK TIME: The average time it takes for the read/write head to move to a specific location. Calculated by dividing the time it takes to complete a large number of random seeks by the number of seeks performed.

BACKUP DEVICE: Disk or tape drive used with a fixed Winchester disk drive to make copies of files or other data for off line storage, distribution, or protection against accidental data deletion from the Winchester drive, or against drive failure.

BACKUP FILE: File copies made on another removable media device (disk, tape, or sometimes a remote hard disk system) and kept to ensure recovery of data lost due to equipment failure, human errors, updates, and disasters.

BACKUP: 1. A duplicate copy of a program, disk, or data files. 2. A procedure for duplicating key data files, often automatically, and storing them in a safe place for the purpose of file recovery.

BACKWARD COMPATIBILITY: A design standard that assures that new software, hardware, devices, and media will be compatible with earlier versions.

BAD BLOCK: A block (usually the size of a sector) that cannot reliably hold data due to a physical flaw or damaged format markings.

BAD TRACK TABLE: A list affixed to the casing of a hard disk drive that states which tracks are flawed and cannot hold data. This list of bad tracks is entered into the low-level formatting program when the drive is formatted at the factory.

BANDWIDTH: The amount of data that can be transmitted via a given communications channel (e.g., between a hard drive and the host PC) in a given unit of time.

BASE CASTING: The rigid structure which holds the mechanical sub-assemblies of a hard disk drive. Together with the top cover, creates an airtight, extremely clean enclosure.

BI-DIRECTIONAL BUS: A bus that may carry information in either direction but not in both simultaneously.

BINARY: A number system like the decimal numbers, but using 2 as its base and having only the two digits 0 (zero) and 1 (one). It is used in computers because digital logic can only determine one of two states—"OFF" and "ON." Digital data is equivalent to a binary number.

BIOS (BASIC INPUT OUTPUT SYSTEM): A program permanently stored in the memory of the computer and is available without an operating system disk. For example, it performs the internal self test of the computer and searches for the operating system on the disk drive.

BIT CELL LENGTH: Physical dimension of the bit cell in direction of recording along the disk circumference of a track.

BIT CELL TIME: The time required to pass one bit of information between the controller and the drive. Cell time is the inverse of the drive's data rate.

BIT DENSITY: Expressed as "BPI" (for bits per inch), bit density defines how many bits can be written onto one inch of a track on a disk surface. It is usually specified for "worst case," which is the inner track. Data is the densest in the inner tracks where track circumferences are the smallest.

BIT JITTER: The time difference between the leading edge of read and the center of the data window.

BIT SHIFT: A data recording effect, which results when adjacent 1's written on magnetic disks repel each other. The "worst case" is at the inner cylinder where bits are closest together. *BIT SHIFT* is also called pulse crowding.

BIT: An abbreviation for a binary digit which can be either 0 or 1. A bit is the basic data unit of all digital computers. It is usually part of a data byte or word, but bits may be used singly to control or read logic ON/OFF functions. A bit is a single digit in a binary number. Bits are the basic unit of information capacity or a computer storage device. Eight bits equal one byte.

BIT: The smallest unit of data. Consists of a single binary digit that can take the value of 0 or 1.

BLOCK: A group of BYTES handled, stored, and accessed as a logical data unit, such as an individual file record. Typically, one block of data is stored as one physical sector of data on a disk drive. In UNIX workstation environments, the smallest contiguous area that can be allocated for the storage of data. UNIX blocks are generally 8 KB (16 sectors) in size. In DOS environments, the block is referred to as a cluster. (Note: This usage of the term block at the operating system level is different from its meaning in relation to the physical configuration of the hard drive.) (*See also CLUSTER* and *SECTOR.*)

BLOCK ERROR RATE: The average number of errors that occur (or can occur) while writing or transmitting a block of data.

BOOT: Short for bootstrap. Transfer of a disk operating system program from storage on diskette or hard disk drive to computer's working memory.

BPI (Bits per inch): A measure of how densely information is packed on a storage medium. (*See also FCI.*)

BPSI (Bits per square inch): A measure of areal density calculated by multiplying bits per inch (BPI) by tracks per inch (TPI).

BUFFER: A temporary data storage area that compensates for a difference in data transfer rates and/or data processing rates between sender and receiver.

BURST MODE: A temporary, high-speed data transfer mode that can transfer data at significantly higher rates than would normally be achieved with non-burst technology; the maximum throughput a device is capable of transferring data.

BUS: A length of parallel conductors that forms a major interconnection route between the computer system CPU and its peripheral subsystems. Depending on its design, a bus may carry data to and from peripheral's addresses, power, and other related signals.

BUS MASTERING: A method of data transfer which allows data to be moved between a peripheral controller and system memory without interaction with the host CPU or a third party DMA controller. This technique allows the peripheral controller to take control of the system bus, and in the case of EISA, to move data at up to 33MB/s.

BYTE: A sequence of adjacent BINARY digits or BITS considered as a unit, 8 bits in length. One byte is sufficient to define all the alphanumeric characters. There are 8 BITS in 1 BYTE. The storage capacity of a disk drive is commonly measured in MEGABYTES, which is the total number of bits storable, divided by eight million.

CACHE: A temporary storage location, usually Random Access Memory (RAM), for data. In input/output operations, the organization of the cache is important because it enables time-saving functions such as read-ahead.

CACHE HIT: This occurs when the data requested is already in the cache. A cache hit saves the time of getting the data from the rotating disk; the seek, latency, and read times.

CACHE MEMORY: A portion of RAM allocated for storing frequently accessed information from a storage device.

CAPACITY: Amount of memory (measured in megabytes) that can be stored in a disk drive. Usually given as formatted capacity (*see FORMAT OPERATION* and *FORMATTED CAPACITY*).

CAPACITY ALLOCATION EFFICIENCY: The automated provisioning of storage capacity to applications based on thresholds and policies.

CAPACITY UTILIZATION EFFICIENCY: The automated provisioning of data to storage platforms based on data access and retention characteristics and platform cost.

CARRIAGE ASSEMBLY: Assembly in a hard disk drive which holds read/write heads and roller bearings. It is used to position the heads radially by the actuator, in order to access a track of data.

CD-ROM (Compact Disk Read Only Memory): A read only storage device which retrieves up to 660 Mbytes of information from a removable laser disk similar to an audio compact disk.

CENTRAL PROCESSOR UNIT (CPU): The heart of the computer system that executes programmed instructions. It includes the arithmetic logic unit (ALU) for performing all math and logic operations, a control section for interpreting and executing instructions, fast main memory for temporary (VOLATILE) storage of an application program and its data.

CHANNEL: In regard to disk drives, a channel is an electrical path for the transfer of data and control information between a disk and a disk controller. The Primary and Secondary Hard Drive Port Addresses are an example to two channels.

CHARACTER: An information symbol used to denote a number, letter, symbol or punctuation mark stored by a computer. In a computer a character can be represented in one (1) byte or eight (8) bits of data. There are 256 different one-byte binary numbers, sufficient for 26 lower case alphas, 26 upper case alphas, 10 decimal digits, control codes, and error checks.

CHIP: An integrated circuit fabricated on a chip of silicon or other semiconductor material, e.g., a CHIP is an integrated circuit, a microprocessor, memory device, or a digital logic device.

CIFS: *See COMMON INTERNET FILE SYSTEM.*

CLIENT: Typically, a desktop computer hooked up to a network, and designed to work with a more powerful server that runs applications and stores data.

CLIENT/SERVER: An environment that allows interactions between "clients" (typically desktop computers) and "servers" (computers that store data and run software programs). In client-server environments, data may be stored on a remote server rather than a computer's hard disk; applications may be stored on a server and delivered to individual desktop computers as needed. The server acts as a gateway to the network, running administrative software controls, and providing access to the network and its resources.

CLOCK RATE: The rate at which bits or words are transferred between internal elements of a computer or to another computer.

CLOSED LOOP: A control system consisting of one or more feedback control loops in which functions of the controlled signals are combined with functions of the command to maintain prescribed relationships between the commands and the controlled signals. This control technique allows the head actuator system to detect and correct off-track errors. The actual head position is monitored and compared to the ideal track position, by reference information either recorded on a dedicated servo surface, or embedded in the inter-sector gaps. A position error is used to produce a correction signal (FEEDBACK) to the actuator to correct the error. (*See TRACK FOLLOWING SERVO.*)

CLUSTER SIZE: Purely an operating system function or term describing the number of sectors that the operating system allocates each time disk space is needed. In DOS environments, the smallest contiguous area that can be allocated for the storage of data. DOS clusters are usually 2 KB (4 sectors) in size.

CLUSTERED SERVERS: The concept of combining multiple host computers together through a private communication line, such as Ethernet backbone, to form a ring of host computers; this ring of host computers act as a single entity, capable of performing multiple complex instructions by distributing the workload across all members of the ring.

CLUSTERED STORAGE: The concept of combining multiple storage servers or intelligent storage devices together to form a redundant ring of storage devices; clustered storage systems typically perform multiple read and write requests through parallel access lines to the requesting computer.

CODE: A set of unambiguous rules specifying the way which digital data is represented physically, as magnetized bits, on a disk drive. One of the objectives of coding is to add timing data for use in data reading. (*See DATA SEPARATOR, MFM,* and *RLL.*)

COERCIVITY: A measurement in units of orsteads of the amount of magnetic energy to switch or "coerce" the flux change (di-pole) in the magnetic recording media.

COMMAND: (1) An instruction sent by the central processor unit (CPU) to a controller for execution. (2) English-like commands entered by users to select computer programs or functions. (3) A CPU command, which is a single instruction such as "add two binary numbers" or "output a byte to the display screen."

COMMAND DESCRIPTOR BLOCK (CDB): SCSI commands are issued from an initiator by transferring a Command Descriptor Block to the target device. For some commands, a parameter list sent during a Data Out phase accompanies the request. A CDB contains an opcode, logical unit number, set of command parameters, and control byte.

COMMAND OVERHEAD: *See OVERHEAD*.

COMMON ACCESS METHOD (CAM): Defines a set of software and hardware interfaces which attempt to standardize an operating system's access to peripheral devices.

COMMON INTERNET FILE SYSTEM (CIFS): A proposed standard protocol that lets programs make requests for files and services on remote computers on the Internet or across any TCP/IP network. CIFS uses the client/server programming model. A client program makes a request of a server program (usually in another computer) for access to a file or to pass a message to a program that runs in the server computer. The server takes the requested action and returns a response. CIFS is a public or open variation of the Server Message Block (SMB) protocol developed and used by Microsoft. The SMB protocol is widely used in today's local area networks for server file access and printing.

COMPACT DISK-READ ONLY MEMORY (CD-ROM): An optical disk recording format in which the optical disk carries pre-recorded data, music or software. Users cannot add or delete data to a CD-ROM.

COMPACT DISK-RECORDABLE (CD-R): An optical disk recording format that allows data to be written to optical disks. The disks can be recorded just once, but played virtually without limit.

COMPACT DISK-REWRITABLE (CD-RW): An optical disk recording format that allows disks to be recorded and re-recorded, much like floppy disks or audio tapes. The disks can be rewritten up to 10,000 times and played virtually without limit.

COMPUTER OUTPUT TO LASER DISK (COLD): An optical storage technology for transferring computer-based information to an optical disk for near-online storage. Typically used as an alternative to paper or microfiche-based storage of computer-generated reports.

CONSOLE (also called CRT or Terminal): A device from which a computer can be operated; often includes a monitor and keyboard.

CONTROLLER: A controller is a printed circuit board required to interpret data access commands from host computer (via a BUS), and send track seeking, read/write, and other control signals to a disk drive. The computer is free to perform other tasks until the controller signals DATA READY for transfer via the CPU BUS.

COST OF OWNERSHIP: The purchase price of equipment plus the cost of operating this equipment over its projected life span.

CPU: *See CENTRAL PROCESSOR UNIT.*

CRASH: A malfunction in the computer hardware or software, usually causing loss of data. (*See HEAD CRASH.*)

CRC: *See CYCLIC-REDUNDANCY-CHECK.*

CYCLIC-REDUNDANCY-CHECK (CRC): Used to verify data block integrity. In a typical scheme, 2 CRC bytes are added to each user data block. The 2 bytes are computed from the user data, by digital logical chips. The mathematical model is polynomials with binary coefficients. When reading back data, the CRC bytes are read and compared to new CRC bytes computed from the read back block to detect a read error. The read back error check process is mathematically equivalent to dividing the read block, including its CRC, by a binomial polynomial. If the division remainder is zero, the data is error free.

CYLINDER: The cylindrical surface formed by identical track numbers on vertically stacked disks. At any location of the head positioning arm, all tracks under all heads are the cylinder. Cylinder number is one of the three address components required to find a specific *ADDRESS*, the other two being head number and sector number.

DAFS: *See DIRECT ACCESS FILE SYSTEM.*

DAISY CHAIN: A way of connecting multiple drives to one controller. The controller drive select signal is routed serially through the drives, and is intercepted by the drive whose number matches.

DAT: *See DIGITAL AUDIO TAPE.*

DATA: Information processed by a computer, stored in memory, or fed into a computer.

DATA ACCESS TIME: *See ACCESS TIME.*

DATA ACCESS: When the controller has specified all three components of the sector address to the drive, the ID field of the sector brought under the head by the drive is read and compared with the address of the target sector. A match enables access to the data field of the sector.

DATA ADDRESS: To return to the same area on the disk, each area is given a unique address consisting of the three components: cylinder, head, and sector. *HORIZONTAL:* accomplished by assigning numbers to the concentric circles (cylinders) mapped out by the heads as the positioning arm is stepped radially across the surface, starting with 0 for the outermost circle. By specifying the cylinder number the controller specifies a horizontal or radial address component of the data area. *ROTATIONAL:* once a head and cylinder have been addressed, the desired sector around the selected track of the selected surface is found by counting address marks from the index pulse of the track. Remember that each track starts with an index pulse and each sector starts with an address mark. *VERTICAL:* assume a disk pack with six surfaces, each with its own read/write head, vertical addressing is accomplished by assigning the numbers 00 through XX to the heads, in consecutive order. By specifying the head number, the controller specifies the vertical address component of the data area.

DATA BASE MANAGEMENT SYSTEM (DBMS): Application program used to manage, access, and update files in a data base.

DATA COMPRESSION: An automatic utility that reduces the size of a data file by removing redundant bits of information. An algorithm built into the hardware, firmware, or software handles compression and decompression.

DATA ENCODING: To use a code such as GCR, MFM, RLL, NZR, etc. to represent characters for memory storage.

DATA FIELD: The portion of a sector used to store the user's DIGITAL data. Other fields in each sector include ID, SYNC, and CRC, which are used to locate the correct data field.

DATA MIGRATION: *See HIERARCHICAL STORAGE MANAGEMENT (HSM).*

DATA SEPARATOR: The circuit that extracts data from timing information on drives that store a combined data and clock signal.

DATA TRACK: Any of the circular tracks magnetized by the recording head during data storage.

DATA TRANSFER: The movement of data from one point to another within a computer system, for example, from an optical disk to a computer's hard disk.

DATA TRANSFER RATE (DTR): Speed at which bits are sent: In a disk storage system, the communication is between CPU and controller, plus controller and the disk drive. Typical units are bits per second (BPS), or bytes per second. I/O transfer rate is the data rate between the drive and the CPU. Internal transfer rate is the rate data is written to/from the disk. (*See TRANSFER RATE.*)

DATA WAREHOUSE: A large centralized database designed to hold and manage a company's information over a long period of time. Data warehouses are often used to mine key data for reference, for example, to detect trends, spot new market opportunities, and monitor business results.

DECREASE THE FLYING HEIGHT: A method for increasing areal density. Since the head core is closer to the media surface, the lines of flux magnetize a smaller area. Thus, more bits can be recorded in a given distance, and higher BPI (bits per inch) is achievable.

DEFAULT: A particular value of a variable that is used by a computer unless specifically changed, usually via an entry made through a software program.

DENSITY: Generally, bit recording density. (*See AREAL, BIT,* and *STORAGE DENSITY.*)

DFHSM (Data Facility Hierarchical Storage Manager): IBM's hierarchical storage management system, part of DFSMS.

DFSMS (Data Facility Storage Management System): Data management, backup, and HSM software from IBM for MVS and OS/390 mainframes. Introduced in 1993, it combines separate backup, copy, HSM, and device driver routines into one package, which provides all the I/O management for the operating system.

DIGITAL: Any system that processes digital binary signals having only the values of a 1 or 0. An example of a non-digital signal is an analog signal which continuously varies, e.g., TV or audio.

DIGITAL AUDIO TAPE (DAT): A storage technology that uses 4mm tape to record data. DAT is similar to an audio tape, but instead of recording data linearly along the length of the tape, data is recorded at an angle. This recording format, called DDS, is the industry standard for all DAT devices.

DIGITAL DATA STORAGE (DDS): A recording format used by all major DAT drive and media manufacturers, and the only recognized industry standard for DAT systems. A number frequently follows the DDS designation to indicate the generation of the standard: for example, DDS-3 represents a third-generation product.

DIGITAL LINEAR TAPE (DLT): A serpentine technology first introduced by Digital Equipment Corporation and later developed by Quantum for tape backup/archive of networks and servers; DLT technology addresses midrange to high-end tape backup requirements.

DIGITAL VIDEO DISK (DVD): A disk that closely resembles a standard CD in size, color, and physical format, but holds about seven times as much data. A typical CD holds about 650 MB of data, whereas today's DVDs hold 4.7 GB, with a targe capacity of about 17 GB in the future. A two-hour feature-length movie can fit on a DVD, making it an attractive medium for the entertainment industry as well as PC makers. The current state of DVD technology, allowing play-back but not recording on DVDs. Multiple DVD-RAM and DVD-Rewritable standards exist to support both play-back and recording on DVDs. At this time, no standards have been adopted industry-wide for recordable/rewritable DVD.

DIRECT ACCESS: Generally refers to an *AUXILIARY MEMORY* device, having all data on-line. A tape drive without a tape mounted is not direct access, but a *WINCHESTER DRIVE* is direct access device.

DIRECT ACCESS FILE SYSTEM (DAFS): A high-performance file sharing protocol based on the VI memory-to-memory architecture. DAFS provides bulk data transfer directly between the application buffers of two machines without having to packetize the data. It also allows applications to access hardware without operating system intervention.

DIRECTORY: A special disk storage area (usually cylinder zero) that is read by a computer operating system to determine the *ADDRESSES* of the data records that form a *DISK FILE*.

DIRECT MEMORY ACCESS (DMA): A means of data transfer between peripheral and host memory without processor intervention. DMA improves speed and efficiency by allowing the system to continue processing even while it is retrieving new data from the drive.

DIRTY CACHE: A cache page in which data has been written or modified but which has not yet been copied to the storage device. Once the data has been copied to disk, the page is said to be clean.

DISK ARRAY (or ARRAY): A linked group of small, independent hard disk drives used to replace larger, single disk drive systems. The most common disk arrays implement *RAID* (redundant array of independent disks) technology. (*See also RAID.*)

DISK CONTROLLER: The chip or circuit that controls the transfer of data between the disk and buffer. (*See also DISK DRIVE CONTROLLER* and *INTERFACE CONTROLLER.*)

DISK DRIVE CONTROLLER: The hard disk drive controller electronics, which include the disk controller and the interface controller. (*See also DISK CONTROLLER* and *INTERFACE CONTROLLER.*)

DISK FILE: A file of user data, e.g., the company employee list, with all NAMEs and information. The data in the file is stored in a set of disk *SECTORS* (records).

DISK OPERATING SYSTEM (DOS): A computer program which continuously runs and mediates between the computer user and the *APPLICATION PROGRAM*, and allows access to disk data by *DISK FILE NAMEs*.

DISK OVERHEAD: *See overhead.*

DISK PACK: A number of metal disks packaged in a canister for removal from the disk drive. *WINCHESTER DRIVES* do not have disk packs.

DISK STORAGE: Auxiliary memory system containing disk drives.

DISK SWAP: 1. The act of swapping one optical disk for another. To complete a swap, a jukebox autochanger mechanism must remove a disk from the drive, put it away, retrieve a new disk, and insert it in the drive. The drive then spins-up the new disk and the operation is complete. 2. Changing out a defective or malfunctioning hard disk drive.

DISK PLATTER: For rigid disks, a flat, circular aluminum disk substrate, coated on both sides with a magnetic substance (iron oxide or thin film metal media) for non-VOLATILE data storage. The substrate may consist of metal, plastic, or even glass. Surfaces of disks are usually lubricated to minimize wear during drive start-up or power down.

DISK-TO-DISK (D2D): A two-tier storage architecture.

DISK-TO-DISK TO TAPE (DDT): A three-tier storage architecture.

DISKETTE: A floppy disk. A plastic (mylar) substrate, coated with magnetic iron oxide, enclosed in a protective jacket.

DISTRIBUTED NETWORK: A network that divides data processing, storage, and other functions into separate units rather than having them all handled by a single computer.

DMA: *See DIRECT MEMORY ACCESS.*

DOCUMENT IMAGE MANAGEMENT (DIM): A storage management solution for converting paper documents, photos, and receipts into an electronic format that can be accessed from a computer.

DOS: *See DISK OPERATING SYSTEM.*

DRIVE GEOMETRY: The functional dimensions of a drive, including the number of heads, cylinders, and sectors per track.

DRIVE: A computer memory device with moving storage MEDIA (disk or tape).

DRIVER: A software component or set of file commands that allow an application to communicate with another application, driver, or hardware device. A driver receives I/O requests from higher levels within the operating system and converts those requests to the protocol required by a specific hardware device.

ECC: *See ERROR CORRECTION CODE.*

EFFECTIVE ACCESS TIME: The actual time it takes to access data. In an optical jukebox, it involves variables such as disk swap time, disk spin-up time, seek time, and transfer rates of the host computer and software application.

EISA: *See EXTENDED INDUSTRY STANDARD ARCHITECTURE.*

ELECTROMAGNETIC INTERFERENCE (EMI): Interference resulting from the presence of electromagnetic fields from electrical and/or electronic devices.

ELECTRO-STATIC DISCHARGE (ESD): A cause of integrated circuit (CHIP) failure. Since the circuitry of CHIPs are microscopic in size, they can be damaged or destroyed by small static discharges. People handling electronic equipment should always ground themselves before touching the equipment. Electronic equipment should always be handled by the chassis or frame. Components, printed circuit board edge connectors should never be touched.

ELEVATOR SORTING: A method of sorting records or cache pages by physical location on disk so that the information may be written to disk with less seek and rotational latency.

EMBEDDED SERVO SYSTEM: Servo data is embedded or superimposed along with data on every cylinder. Timing and positioning signals are interspersed in data tracks. These signals provide the information the actuator needs to fine-tune the position of the read/write heads. (*See also DEDICATED SERVO.*)

ENCODING: The conversion of data into a pattern of On/Off or 1/0 signals prior to writing them to the disk surface. (*See also MFM* and *RLL.*)

ENCRYPTION: A security method in which electronic data is scrambled and decoded using a software algorithm.

ENTERPRISE NETWORK: A system of network connections that links all of a company's LANs, allowing enterprises to communicate across many geographic locations and sites.

ENTERPRISE STORAGE NETWORK (ESN): According to EMC Corporation, an integrated suite of products and services designed to maximize heterogeneous connectivity and management of enterprise storage devices and servers. ESN, generically, constitutes a dedicated, high-speed network connected to the enterprise's storage systems, enabling files and data to be transferred between storage devices and client mainframes and servers.

EPROM: *See ERASABLE PROGRAMMABLE READ ONLY MEMORY.*

ERASE: To remove previously recorded data from magnetic storage media.

ERROR: *See HARD ERROR* and *SOFT ERROR.*

ERROR CORRECTION CODE (ECC): An embedded code that allows detection of a mismatch between transmitted and received data in a communications system, or between stored and retrieved data in a storage system. The ECC can correct errors, but within limits.

ERROR DETECTION: A software or firmware algorithm that looks for inconsistencies or errors in a data file as it is being stored. More advanced levels of error detection will not only detect problems, but also correct errors or inconsistencies automatically.

ERROR RATE: The ratio of data that is incorrectly recorded relative to the entire amount of data written.

ESDI: *See ENHANCED SMALL DEVICE INTERFACE.*

ETHERNET: A local area network standard for hardware, communication, and cabling.

EUROPEAN COMPUTER MANUFACTURERS ASSOCIATION (ECMA): An international organization founded in 1961 and dedicated to the standardization of information and communication systems.

EXECUTE: To perform a data processing operation described by an instruction or a program in a computer.

EXTENDED INDUSTRY STANDARD ARCHITECTURE (EISA): An enhanced AT bus architecture designed by nine manufacturers of PC compatibles and announced in September 1988. EISA provides backwards compatibility with existing 8 and 16-bit hardware cards. In addition, EISA supports 32-bit data paths, 33 Mbytes/sec data transfers from Bus Mastering peripheral cards, automatic configuration, and a more sophisticated I/O addressing scheme. (*See also AT* and *ISA.*)

EXTERNAL DRIVE: A hard disk drive mounted in an enclosure separate from the computer system enclosure. An external drive has its own power supply and fan and is connected to the system by a cable.

FABRIC SWITCH: A type of storage area network (SAN) switch characterized by the fact that any port on any switch can provide (subject to bandwidth availability) full speed access to any other port on the network. The network consists of a fabric of linked switches.

FAILOVER: The transfer of operation from a failed component (e.g., controller, disk drive) to a similar, redundant component to ensure uninterrupted data flow and operability.

FAST ATA: Fast ATA is the market identity given to disk drives that support the high-speed data transfers resulting from implementing the industry standard protocols: Programmed input/output (PIO) mode 3, Multiword direct memory access, read/write multiple sectors per interrupt.

FAST SCSI: The original SCSI specification defined synchronous data transmission speeds of up to 5MHz. By assuming transceivers that provide tighter timing margins, the SCSI-2 standard allows synchronous transfers of up to 10MHz. Devices that utilize these faster timings are called Fast SCSI devices.

FAT (File allocation table): A data table stored on the outer edge of the disk and used by the operating system to determine which sectors are allocated to each file and in what order.

FAULT TOLERANCE: The ability of a system to cope with internal hardware problems (e.g., a disk drive failure) and still continue to operate with minimal impact, such as by bringing a backup system online.

FC-AL: *See FIBRE CHANNEL ARBITRATED LOOP (FC-AL).*

FCI: *See FLUX CHANGES PER INCH.*

FCIP: *See FIBRE CHANNEL OVER IP.*

FEEDBACK: A closed-loop control system, using the head-to-track positioning signal (from the servo head) to modify the HEAD POSITIONER signal (to correctly position the head on the track).

FETCH: A CPU read operation from MAIN MEMORY and its related data transfer operations.

FIBRE CHANNEL: A high-speed, serial, storage/networking interface that offers higher performance, greater capacity and cabling distance, increased system configuration flexibility and scalability, and simplified cabling. One can view Fibre Channel simply as a transport vehicle for the supported command set (usually SCSI commands). In fact, Fibre Channel is unaware of the content of the information being transported. It simply packs data in frames, transports them to the appropriate devices, and provides error checking.

FIBRE CHANNEL ARBITRATED LOOP (FC-AL): One of the possible physical topologies of Fibre Channel. In this topology, the Fibre Channel is connected in a loop with devices all connecting to the loop. It can be thought of as a similar structure to a token ring network. Up to 126 nodes can be connected to the loop.

FIBRE CHANNEL CLASS 1 SERVICE: This service level guarantees bandwidth and ordering of packets. It also returns confirmations of transmission.

FIBRE CHANNEL CLASS 2 SERVICE: This service level is connectionless and can deliver packets out-of-order. Delivery of packets is however guaranteed and confirmations are sent.

FIBRE CHANNEL CLASS 3 SERVICE: This is the lowest service level and does not guarantee either ordering or delivery.

FIBRE CHANNEL FABRIC: One of the physical topologies of Fibre Channel. In this topology, the addressing of ports on a network of Fibre Channel nodes is made independently of the physical location or address of the target port. Switches are responsible for passing Fibre Channel packets to the target port regardless of which Fibre Channel loop or switch where the port physically resides.

FIBRE CHANNEL LOOP COMMUNITY (FCLC): An international non-profit organization whose members include manufacturers of servers, disk drives, RAID storage systems, switches, hubs, adapter cards, test equipment, cables, and connectors, and software solutions.

FIBRE CHANNEL OVER IP (FCIP): Fibre Channel over IP (FCIP or FC/IP, also known as Fibre Channel tunneling or storage tunneling) is an Internet Protocol (IP)-based storage networking technology developed by the Internet Engineering Task Force (IETF). FCIP mechanisms enable the transmission of Fibre Channel (FC) information by tunneling data between Fibre Channel fabrics using IP networks. While this capacity facilitates the joining of FC fabric "islands" over a geographically distributed enterprise, it does so at a cost of local SAN identity: all FC fabrics become part of one large fabric.

FIBRE CHANNEL POINT-TO-POINT: One of the physical topologies of Fibre Channel. This topology provides a simple, direct connection between just two nodes, approximating traditional SCSI topology.

FIBRE CHANNEL PORTS: Fibre Channel ports come in a number of types depending on the topology of the Fibre Channel network. N_Ports are simple equipment node ports in a point-to-point connection topology. NL_Ports are node ports connected to an Arbitrated loop. F_Ports are point-to-point ports connected to a fabric. Generally this means that the F_Port is a port on a switch. FL_Ports are ports connecting from one loop to a switch and thus to a fabric. E_Ports are expansion ports used to interconnect switches together. G_Ports are classified by some switch companies as ports that can be either E_Ports or F_Ports depending on usage.

FIBRE CHANNEL PROTOCOL OVER INTERNET or INTERNET FIBRE CHANNEL PROTOCOL (iFCP): iFCP is a mapping of FCP to the Internet Protocol family for use in extending Fibre Channel storage networks across the Internet. iFCP provides a means of passing data to and from Fibre Channel storage devices in a local storage area network (SAN) or on the Internet using TCP/IP. TCP provides congestion control as well as error detection and recovery services. It can either replace or be used in conjunction with existing Fibre Channel protocols, such as FCIP (Fibre Channel over IP). Unlike FCIP, which is a tunneling protocol that encapsulates Fibre Channel data and forwards it over a TCP/IP network as an extension of the existing Fibre Channel network, iFCP operates the Fibre Channel Protocol as an application across an IP network. iFCP gateways can either replace or complement existing Fibre Channel fabrics, and therefore can be used to facilitate migration from a Fibre Channel SAN to an IP SAN or a hybrid network.

FIBRE CHANNEL SAN: An oxymoronic reference to a storage deployment topology more appropriately termed "switched, server-attached storage" or a "Fibre Channel Fabric."

FIBRE CHANNEL SPECIFICATION: A specification for the Fibre Channel serial interconnect, which may be used as the infrastructure for a SAN. FC-0 is the Physical layer of the Fibre Channel protocol stack. This layer includes the definition of all physical components used in Fibre Channel. FC-1 is the Encode/Decode layer in Fibre Channel specification. It covers the byte encoding and character-level error control. FC-2 is called the Framing Protocol Layer. It incorporates the management of frames, flow control, and CRC generation. It also manages sequences of frames comprising a transmission, and exchanges between nodes on the Fibre Channel to accomplish commands akin to the SCSI I/O sequence. This layer also provides the management of the three service classes: Class 1, Class 2, and Class 3. FC-3 is called the Common Services Layer and is currently not used. FC-4 is the Protocol Mappings Layer and is the layer that maps protocols such as SCSI and IP to the underlying layer protocols.

FIBRE CHANNEL TOPOLOGY: A number of possible topologies, or methods for interconnecting devices or nodes, have been specified for Fibre Channel. These include point-to-point, Arbitrated Loop, and Fabric topologies. (*See FIBRE CHANNEL POINT-TO-POINT, FIBRE CHANNEL ARBITRATED LOOP,* and *FIBRE CHANNEL FABRIC.*)

FILE ALLOCATION TABLE (FAT): What the operating systems uses to keep track of which clusters are allocated to which files and which are available for use. FAT is usually stored on Track-0.

FILE RECOVERY: The process of using backup files to replace lost files after a power failure, facility damage, virus infection, system crash, or human error.

FIRMWARE: Permanent instructions and data programmed directly into the circuitry of read-only memory for controlling the operation of the computer. Distinct from software, which can be altered by programmers.

FIXED DISK: A disk drive with disks that cannot be removed from the drive by the user.

FLEXTURE: An extremely pliable plastic circuit which connects the accuator assembly electronics to the base casting. The drive may have access times that move the heads from the outer diameter to the inner as low as 20 milliseconds and this flexture rides along.

FLOPPY DISK: A flexible plastic disk coated with magnetic media and packaged in a stiff envelope. Comes in 8-inch, 5-1/4-inch, and various sub-4 inch sizes. *FLOPPY DISKS* generally exhibit slow *ACCESS TIME* and smaller *CAPACITY* compared to *WINCHESTER DRIVES*, but feature removable diskettes.

FLUX CHANGE: Location on the data track, where the direction of magnetization reverses in order to define a 1 or 0 bit.

FLUX CHANGES PER INCH (FCI): Linear recording density defined as the number of flux changes per inch of data track. The number of magnetic field patterns that can be stored on a given area of disk surface, used as a measure of data density. Also known as flux density. Synonymous with FRPI (flux reversals per inch). In MFM recording 1 FCI equals 1 BPI (bit per inch). In RLL encoding schemes, 1 FCI generally equals 1.5 BPI. (*See also BPI.*)

FLUX DENSITY: *See FLUX CHANGES PER INCH.*

FLYING HEIGHT: The distance between the read/write head and the disk surface, created by the cushion of air that results from the velocity of the disk rotation, which keeps the two objects from touching. Smaller flying heights permit denser data storage but require more precise mechanical designs. Also known as fly height.

FOOTPRINT: The amount of floor space that a piece of equipment (e.g., a rackmount enclosure) occupies.

FORMAT: To write a magnetic track pattern onto a disk surface, specifying the locations of the tracks and sectors. This information must exist on a disk before it can store data. The purpose of a format is to record "header" data that organize the tracks into sequential sectors on the disk surfaces. This information is never altered during normal read/write operations. Header information identifies the sector number and also contains the head and cylinder *ADDRESS* in order to detect an *ADDRESS ACCESS* error.

FORMATTED CAPACITY: The amount of space left to store data on a disk after writing the sector headers, boundary definitions, and timing information during a format operation. Actual capacity available to store user data.

FORM FACTOR: The industry standard that defines the physical, external dimensions of a particular device.

FRICTION: Resistance to relative motion between two bodies in contact; e.g., there is sliding friction between head and disk during drive power up/down.

FULL HEIGHT DRIVE: Winchester 5-1/4" drive which fits in the same space as full height mini-floppy drive (called the full-height form factor), which is 3.25 inches high.

G: A G is a unit of force applied to a body at rest equal to the force exerted on it by gravity. Hard disk drive shock specifications are usually called out in Gs. A shock specification of 40 Gs non-operating means that a drive will not suffer any permanent damage if subjected to a 40 G shock. This is roughly equivalent to a drop of the drive to a hard surface from a distance of 1 inch.

GAP: (1) Part of the disk format. Allows mechanical compensations (e.g., spindle motor rotational speed variations) without the last sector on a track overwriting the first sector. (2) An interruption in the permeable material of a read/write head, usually a glass bonding material with high permeability, allowing the flux fields to exit the head structure to write or read data bits in the form of flux changes on the recording media.

GAP LENGTH: Narrowing the head gap length achieves higher bit density because the lines of force magnetize a smaller area where writing data in the form of flux changes on the recording media.

GAP WIDTH: The narrower the gap width, the closer the tracks can be placed. Closer track placement results in higher TPI.

GIGABYTE (GB): 1 Gigabyte = 1,073,741,824 bytes (or approximately one thousand million bytes).

GUARD BAND: 1. Non-recorded band between adjacent data tracks, 2. For closed loop servo drives, extra servo tracks outside the data band preventing the Carriage Assembly from running into the crash stop.

HALF HEIGHT: A standard drive height of 1.6 inches—the equivalent to half the vertical space of a 5.25-inch drive. (*See also LOW PROFILE.*)

HARD DISK DRIVE: Sometimes called rigid disk drives, or Winchester disk drives. An electromechanical device that can read rigid disks. Though similar to floppy disk drives, the hard disks have higher bit density and multiple read/write surfaces.

HARD ERROR: A data error that persists when the disk is reread, usually caused by defects in the physical surface. Hard errors are caused by imperfections in the disk surface, called media defects. When formatting hard disk drives, hard error locations, if known, should be spared out so that data is not written to these locations. Most drives come with a hard error map listing the locations of any hard errors by head, cylinder and BFI (bytes from index—or how many bytes from the beginning of the cylinder).

HARD SECTOR MODE: A hardware-controlled convention defining a fixed number of sectors per track in any specified zone.

HARD SECTORED: A term describing a hard drive that determines the starting location of each sector from information in the embedded servo. This method is the most common and is newer and more precise than soft sectored techniques. (*See also SOFT SECTORED.*)

HARD ZONING: A method of SAN zoning that uses only WWNs to specify each device. Traffic across the switch is regulated passing requests through the switch's route table. If two ports are not authorized to communicate with each other, the route table for those ports is disabled, and the communication between those ports is blocked.

HARDWARE: Computer equipment (as opposed to the computer programs and software).

HARDWARE ARRAY: A group of disk drives which are all members of the same array and share the same logical name or unit number.

HDA: *See HEAD/DISK ASSEMBLY.*

HDA INTERCONNECT: Connects the drive electronics to the mechanical assembly.

HEAD: An electromagnetic device that can write (record), read (playback), or erase data on magnetic media.

HEAD CRASH: A head landing occurs when the disk drive is turned on or off. This function normally does not damage the disk as the disk has a very thin lubricant on it. A head crash occurs when the head and disk damage each other during landing, handling, or because a contaminant particle gets between them. Head crash is a catastrophic failure condition and causes permanent damage and loss of data.

HEAD/DISK ASSEMBLY (HDA): A sealed Winchester assembly including disks, heads, filter, and actuator assembly.

HEAD LANDING AND TAKEOFF: In Winchester drives, the head is in contact with the platter when the drive is not powered. During the power up cycle, the disk begins rotation and an "air bearing" is established as the disk spins up to full RPM (rotations per minute). This air bearing prevents any mechanical contact between head and disk.

HEAD LANDING ZONE: An area of the disk set aside for takeoff and landing of the Winchester heads when the drive is turned on and off.

HEAD POSITIONER: Also known as the *ACTUATOR*, a mechanism that moves the *CARRIAGE ASSEMBLY* to the cylinder being accessed.

HEAD SKEW: *See TRACK SKEW.*

HEAD SLAP: Similar to a head crash but occurs while the drive is turned off. It usually occurs during mishandling or shipping. Head slap can cause permanent damage to a hard disk drive. (*See HEAD CRASH.*)

HELICAL SCAN RECORDING (HSR): Used widely in VHS formats for video recording, the HSR tape recording method writes at an angle across the width of a tape, allowing higher storage densities on half-inch tape.

HELICAL SCAN: A DAT recording method whereby heads record data at an angle rather than in a straight line (linear), which uses the entire width of the tape.

HEXADECIMAL (HEX): A number system based on sixteen, using digits 0 through 9 and letters A through F to represent each digit of the number. (A = 10, B = 11, C = 12, D = 13, E = 14, F = 15).

HIERARCHICAL FILE SYSTEM (HFS): The file management system in which directories have sub-directories and sub-subdirectories. In MS Windows and Macintosh operating systems, the directories and sub-directories are represented as folders nested within other folders.

HIERARCHICAL STORAGE MANAGEMENT (HSM): A storage system in which new, frequently modified data is stored on the fastest, most accessible (and generally more expensive) media (e.g., RAID) and older, less frequently used data is stored on slower (less expensive) media (e.g., tape).

HIGH-LEVEL FORMATTING: Formatting performed by the operating system to create the root directory, file allocation tables, and other basic configurations. (*See also LOW-LEVEL FORMATTING* and *FAT.*)

HOME PAGE: The main page on a Web site that serves as the primary point of entry to related pages within the site and may have links to other sites as well.

HOME: The reference track of a hard disk, usually the outermost track (track 0), used for recalibration of the actuator.

HOLOGRAPHIC STORAGE: An optical technology that records data as holograms. The hologram is created by two lasers targeted at the media. One laser is beamed into the material through a matrix of LCD shutters, called a "spatial light modulator." The shutters are opened or closed based on the binary pattern of the page of data being stored. For example, using a matrix of 1,024 pixels on each side, the page could hold a million bits. A second reference laser is angled into and intersects with the data laser at the storage unit. If the angle and/or frequency is changed, another hologram can be created overlapping and filling the same space as the first hologram. In fact, 10,000 holograms (pages) can overlap each other. The page is read by directing just the reference laser back into the hologram. The light is diffracted into an original copy of the data, which is sensed by a matrix of CCD sensors. The technology has been in development since the 1960s.

HOST ADAPTER: A plug-in board that acts as the interface between a computer system bus and the disk drive.

HOST BUS ADAPTER (HBA): A hardware card that resides on the PC bus and provides an interface connection between a SCSI device (such as a hard drive) and the host PC.

HOT SPARE: A spare disk drive which, upon failure of a member of a redundant disk array, will automatically be used to replace the failed disk drive.

HOT SWAP: The operation of removing a failed disk drive, which is a member of a redundant array, and replacing it with a good drive.

HUB: A device that splits one network cable into a set of separate cables, each connecting to a different computer; used in a local area network to create a small-scale network by connecting several computers together.

I/O PROCESSOR: Intelligent processor or controller that handles the input/output operations of a computer.

ID FIELD: The address portion of a sector on a formatted hard disk. The ID field is written during the Format operation. It includes the cylinder, head, and sector number of the current sector. This address information is compared by the disk controller with the desired head, cylinder, and sector number before a read or write operation is allowed.

IDE: *See INTEGRATED DRIVE ELECTRONICS.*

IFCP: *See FIBRE CHANNEL OVER INTERNET.*

IMAGE-BACKUP MODE: Used with streaming tape, image-backup mode records an exact copy of the disk, including unused sectors and bad tracks.

INDEX (PULSE): The Index Pulse is the starting point for each disk track. The index pulse provides initial synchronization for sector addressing on each individual track.

INDEX TIME: The time interval between similar edges of the index pulse, which measures the time for the disk to make one revolution. This information is used by a disk drive to verify correct rotational speed of the media.

INDUSTRY STANDARDS: Rules or guidelines, established by independent consortia, to control the development and manufacture of products and devices in the electronics industry. Industry standards for audio CDs, for example, are what assure consumers that any audio CD will work in any CD player.

INDUSTRY STANDARD ARCHITECTURE (ISA): The standard 16-bit AT bus designed by IBM for the PC/AT system. ISA was the only industry standard bus for PCs until the release of IBM's MCA (MicroChannel Architecture) and EISA (Extended Industry Standard Architecture). (*See also EISA.*)

INFRASTRUCTURE: The physical equipment (computers, cases, racks, cabling, etc.) that comprises a computer system.

INITIALIZATION: *See LOW-LEVEL FORMATTING.*

INITIATOR: A SCSI device that requests another SCSI device (a target) to perform an operation; usually a host computer acts as an initiator and a peripheral device acts as a target.

INPUT: Data entered into the computer to be processed, or User commands or queries.

INPUT/OUTPUT (I/O): The process of entering data into or removing data from a computer system. The reception (read) or transmission (write) of computer signals; the entire connection path between the CPU bus and the disk drives.

INSTITUTE OF ELECTRICAL AND ELECTRONICS ENGINEERS (IEEE): The largest technical society in the world, consisting of engineers, scientists, and students. Articulates standards for computers and communications.

INSTRUCTION: The most basic task that a computer performs. A single instruction involves a single, simple calculation processed by the computer. When working on a computer, many instructions are strung together one after another to complete the larger tasks that the operating system or software directs. (*See also MIPS.*)

INTEGRATED DRIVE ELECTRONICS (IDE): A disk drive interface that incorporates the drive controller into the drive electronics. IDE drives are used in IBM-compatible computers. Also known as ATA.

INTELLIGENT PERIPHERAL: A peripheral device that contains a processor or microprocessor to enable it to interpret and execute commands, thus relieving the computer for other tasks.

INTERCHANGEABILITY: The ability to use one brand or type of storage media in a variety of drives. For example, manufacturers of audio tapes and tape players support industry standards for interchangeability, so any tape will work in any player.

INTERFACE: A connection between hardware devices, applications, or different sections of a computer network. A hardware or software protocol (contained in the electronics of the disk controller and drive) that manages the exchange of data between the drive and the computer. The most common interfaces for small computer systems are ATA (also known as IDE) and SCSI. (*See also AT* and *SCSI.*)

INTERFACE CONNECTOR: Attachment point for the interface ribbon cable: 40 pins for ATA; 50 pins for SCSI Narrow, etc.

INTERFACE CONTROLLER: The chip or circuit that translates computer data and commands into a form suitable for use by the hard drive and controls the transfer of data between the buffer and the host. (*See also DISK CONTROLLER* and *DISK DRIVE CONTROLLER.*)

INTERFACE STANDARD: The interface specifications agreed to by various manufacturers to promote industry-wide interchangeability of products such as disk drives and controllers. An interface standard generally reduces product costs, allows buyers to purchase from more than one source, and allows faster market acceptance of new products. (*See SCSI, ESDI.*)

INTERLEAVE: The arrangement of sectors on a track. (*See also INTER-LEAVE FACTOR.*) The interleave value tells the controller where the next logical sector is located in relation to the current sector. For example, an interleave value of one (1) specifies that the next logical sector is physically the next sector on the track. Interleave of two (2) specifies every other physical sector, three (3) every third sector, and so on. Interleaving is used to improve the system throughout based on overhead time of the host software, the disk drive and the controller. For example, if an *APPLICATION PROGRAM* is processing sequential logical records of a *DISK FILE* in a CPU time of more than one second but less than two, then an interleave factor of 3 will prevent wasting an entire disk revolution between *ACCESSES.*

INTERLEAVE FACTOR: The ratio of physical disk sectors skipped for every sector actually written. The number of sectors that pass beneath the read/write heads before the next sector arrives. For example, a 3:1 interleave factor means that the heads read a sector, then let two pass by before reading another, requiring three full revolutions of the disk to access the complete data track.

INTERNAL DRIVE: A disk drive mounted inside a computer either in a drive bay or on a card installed in an expansion slot.

INTERNATIONAL ORGANIZATION FOR STANDARDIZATION (ISO): A worldwide organization that develops, publishes, and promotes international industrial and technical standards. The term ISO is not an acronym, but a derivative of the Greek word *isos*, which means "equal."

INTERNET: A worldwide system of linked computer networks.

INTERNET FIBRE CHANNEL PROTOCOL: *See FIBRE CHANNEL PROTOCOL OVER INTERNET.*

INTERNET SCSI PROTOCOL: *See SCSI OVER INTERNET.*

INTEROPERABILITY: The ability of one computer system to control another, even though the two systems are made by different manufacturers.

INTERRUPT: A signal, usually from a peripheral device to a CPU, to signify that a commanded operation has been completed or cannot be completed.

INTRANET: A computer network, based on Internet technology, that is designed to meet the internal needs for sharing information within a single organization or company.

IOPS (I/Os PER SECOND): A measure of performance for a host-attached storage device or RAID controller.

IP Storage: Storage platforms accessed via IP-based protocols such as iSCSI or iFCP.

ISA: *See INDUSTRY STANDARD ARCHITECTURE.*

ISCSI: *See SCSI OVER INTERNET.*

JBOD: *See JUST A BUNCH OF DISKS.*

JUKEBOX: Also called an optical disk library, a jukebox is a standalone cabinet that holds multiple optical disk drives and cartridges for high-speed, high-capacity storage. It includes a robotic arm to pick an optical cartridge from its storage slot, move it to one of several drives, then return it to the slot when it is no longer needed.

JUST A BUNCH OF DISKS (JBOD): A non-RAID disk array.

KERNEL: The core of an operating system such as Windows 98, Windows NT, Mac OS, or Unix; provides basic services for the other parts of the operating system, making it possible for it to run several programs at once (multitasking), read and write files and connect to networks and peripherals.

KILOBYTE (KB): A unit of measure consisting of 1,024 bytes.

LAN: *See LOCAL AREA NETWORK.*

LANDING ZONE: A non-data position on the disk's inner cylinder where the heads can land when the power is off. In a portable computer, the heads also move to the landing zone after a period of inactivity to save power and extend battery life.

LATENCY, ROTATIONAL: The time for the disk to rotate the accessed sector under the head for read or write. On the average, latency is the time for half of a disk revolution.

LEGACY: A computer, system, or software, that was created for a specific purpose but is now outdated; anything left over from a previous version of the hardware or software.

LIBRARY: *See JUKEBOX.*

LIGHT INTENSITY MODULATION DIRECT OVERWRITE (LIMDOW): An optical recording technology that allows write procedures to be accomplished in one pass of the optical read/write head over the media. LIMDOW accelerates optical performance, but requires somewhat complex and expensive optical media, and involves a more complicated write procedure that leaves less margin for error compared with other optical technologies.

LINEAR TAPE OPEN (LTO): A tape format developed by HP, IBM, and Seagate Technology.

LOCAL AREA NETWORK (LAN): A communications network used to connect computers and other electronic devices within a confined geographical area. For example, a LAN can connect users within a single site, allowing them to share data, exchange e-mail, and share peripherals.

LOGIC: Electronic circuitry that switches on and off ("1" and "0") to perform digital operations.

LOGICAL BLOCK: *See SECTOR.*

LOGICAL FORMAT: Refers to low-level formatting. In relation to DOS-specific format requirements, refers to the translations accomplished by the controller in situations where the hard drive data configurations do not match DOS format limitations.

LOGICAL UNIT NUMBER (LUN): An addressing scheme used to define SCSI devices on a single SCSI bus.

LOOK AHEAD: The process of anticipating events in order to speed up computer operations. For example, a disk drive can use look ahead caching to speed subsequent sequential data requests. When the drive receives a request for data, it reads not only the data requested into the cache buffer but also "looks ahead" and reads data immediately following the requested data into cache until the cache buffer is filled. Once loaded into cache, the information can be accessed almost instantaneously, without the need for additional read operations.

LOOKUP: The action of obtaining and displaying data in a file.

LOW LEVEL FORMAT: The first step in preparing a drive to store information after physical installation is complete. The process sets up the "handshake" between the drive and the controller. In an XT system, the low level format is usually done using DOS's debug utility. In an AT system, AT advanced diagnostics is typically used. Other third party software may also be used to do low level format on both XTs and ATs.

LOW PROFILE: A standard drive height of 1 inch. (*See also HALF HEIGHT.*)

LUN: *See LOGICAL UNIT NUMBER.*

LUN MASKING: A method of masking multiple LUNs behind a single port. By using World Wide Port Names (WWPNs) of server host bus adapters, LUN masking is configured at the RAID-array level. LUN masking also allows disk storage resource sharing across multiple independent servers. A single large RAID device can be sub-divided to serve a number of different hosts that are attached to the RAID through the SAN fabric with LUN masking. So that only one or a limited number of servers can see that LUN (e.g., disk slice, portion, unit), each LUN inside the RAID device can be limited. LUN masking can be done either at the RAID device (behind the RAID port) or at the server HBA. It is more secure to mask LUNs at the RAID device, but not all RAID devices have LUN masking capability. Therefore, in order to mask LUNs, some HBA vendors allow persistent binding at the driver-level.

MAGAZINE: A removable chamber that holds multiple optical disk cartridges or magnetic tapes, often used for high-volume automated backup.

MAGNETIC MEDIA: A disk or tape with a surface layer containing particles of metal, or metallic oxides that can be magnetized in different directions to represent bits of data, sounds or other information.

MAGNETIC RECORDING: The use of a head, recording head, recording media (tape or disk), and associated electronic circuitry for storing data or sound or video.

MAGNETO-OPTICAL (MO): An optical disk storage technology that uses a combination of magnet and laser to alter the magnetic flux directions on a disk's recording surface, much like a magnetic hard disk. The laser heats a small point on the disks' recording surface to 150 degrees Celsius. At this temperature, the polarity of the disk's recording surface can be altered with a magnet, causing a change in reflectivity that is detected during reads. MO is the dominant technology for rewritable optical disks, and meets ANSI, ISO, and ECMA industry standards for interchangeable optical disk cartridges.

MAGNETO-RESISTIVE HEAD (MRH): A special read head technology designed to support data acquisition from media with very high recording densities. Based on materials with special magneto-resistive properties, e.g., whose electrical resistance changes in the presence of a magnetic field, read heads incorporating MR material are more sensitive to changes in the strength of magnetic fields, enabling them to read more densely-packed bits stored on tape or disk media. This mechanism cannot be used for writing, so a conventional thin film inductive write head element is deposited alongside the MR stripe.

MAIN MEMORY: Random-access memory used by the CPU for storing program instructions and data currently being processed by those instructions. (*See RANDOM-ACCESS MEMORY.*)

MAINFRAME COMPUTER: A large computer generally found in data processing centers. (*See MINICOMPUTER* and *MICROCOMPUTER.*)

MANAGED HUB: This is a technique for providing statistics information about the traffic on a hub. Typically, no actual management of the hub is possible using this interface, but information and notification of failures can be achieved. This interface often uses Simple Network Management Protocol (SNMP) Management Information Bases (MIBs) as a standard protocol for providing this information.

MEAN SWAPS BETWEEN FAILURE (MSBF): A measure of reliability specific to optical jukeboxes, usually determined in benchmark testing. MSBF refers to the average number of disk "swaps" a jukebox and its internal mechanisms can be expected to deliver before maintenance is required. A statistical calculation used to predict the average usefulness of a robotic device (e.g., a tape library) with any interruption of service.

MEAN TIME BETWEEN FAILURE (MTBF): The average time before a failure will occur. This is not a warranty measurement. MTBF is a calculation taking into consideration the MTBF of each component in a system and is the statistical average operation time between the start of a unit's lifetime and its time of a failure. After a product has been in the field for a few years, the MTBF can become a field proven statistic. The higher the MTBF, the more reliable the equipment.

MEAN TIME TO REPAIR (MTTR): A measure of the complexity of design in electronic equipment. Highly modular designs—i.e., those that use interchangeable, hot-swappable components—typically have a low MTTR since failed components can be replaced with functioning components.

MEAN TIME until DATA LOSS (MTDL): The average time from startup until a component failure causes a permanent loss of user data in a disk array. The concept is similar to MTBF, but takes into account the possibility that RAID redundancy can protect against loss due to single component failures.

MEDIA: A physical storage medium. Includes optical disks, CDs, magnetic tapes, hard disks, and other technologies used to store computer-based information. The magnetic layers of a disk or tape. (*See DISK/PLATTER.*)

MEGABYTE (MB): A megabyte is 106 or 1,000,000 bytes. One megabyte can store more than one million characters.

MEMORY: Any device or storage system capable of storing and retrieving information.

MESSAGE DIGEST HEADER: A data header containing the results of an algorithm applied to the contents of the dataset. The algorithm produces a unique "fingerprint" for the dataset that may be referenced to determine dataset authenticity and integrity. Several versions of digest algorithms exist, the latest being MD5. MDx hashes may be a useful component of a scheme for ensuring data integrity, authenticity, and self-description-based management.

MFM (Multiple frequency modulation): A method of encoding analog signals into magnetic pulses or bits.

MICROCOMPUTER: A computer whose central processor unit (CPU) is manufactured as a chip or a small number of chips. Personal computers are examples of microcomputers.

MICROINCH: One-millionth of an inch.

MICROSECOND: One-millionth of a second.

MILLISECOND: One-thousandth of a second.

MICROSOFT WINDOWS: An operating system with several variants developed by Microsoft for high-performance processors and networked systems.

MINICOMPUTER: A computer midway in size and processing power between a *MICROCOMPUTER* and a *MAINFRAME COMPUTER*.

MIPS (MILLIONS OF INSTRUCTIONS PER SECOND): A measure of the speed at which a CPU operates. (*See also INSTRUCTION*.)

MIRRORING: A method of storage in which data from one disk is duplicated on another disk so that both drives contain the same information, thus providing data redundancy. A popular term for RAID-1.

MISSION CRITICAL: Any computer process that cannot fail during normal business hours; some computer processes (e.g., telephone systems) must run all day long and require 100 percent uptime.

MISSION CRITICAL DATA: Data or information considered to be so important that its loss would cause grave difficulty to all or part of a business. For example, customer account information at a bank, or patient information at a hospital.

MNEMONIC: A shortened code for a longer term.

MODIFIED FREQUENCY MODULATION (MFM): A method of recording digital data, using a particular CODE to get the flux reversal times from the data pattern. MFM recording is self-clocking because the CODE guarantees timing information for the playback process. The controller is thus able to synchronize directly from the data. This method has a maximum of one bit of data with each flux reversal. (*See NRZ, RLL*.)

MTBF: *See MEAN TIME BETWEEN FAILURE.*

MTTR: *See MEAN TIME TO REPAIR.*

MULTIMEDIA: The combination of several media formats used for the delivery of information. Many commercial CD-ROMs use a multimedia format, combining text, photos, audio, animation, and video on a single disk.

MULTIPLATFORM: The ability of a product or network to support a variety of computer platforms (e.g., IBM, Sun, Macintosh); also referred to as cross-platform.

MULTIPLE SEGMENT CACHING: A technique enabling the division of the cache into segments so that different blocks of data can be cached simultaneously and subsequent commands will have a better probability of a cache hit.

MULTIPROCESSOR: A computer containing two or more processors.

MULTITASKING: The ability of a computer system to execute more than one program or program task at a time.

MULTI-THREADED: Having multiple concurrent or pseudo-concurrent execution sequences. Used to describe processes in computer systems. Multi-threaded processes are one means by which throughput intensive applications can make maximum use of a disk array to increase I/O performance.

MULTI-USER: The ability of a computer system to execute programs for more than one user at a time.

NEAR-FIELD RECORDING (NFR): An optical disk storage technology that combines elements of hard disk and magneto-optical (MO) storage. Though still under development, the technology is expected to deliver hard disk-like performance with greater storage capacities and lower cost storage costs than current technologies.

NEAR-ONLINE STORAGE: A cross between online and offline storage, usually consisting of data stored in optical jukeboxes. Near-online storage is less expensive, more durable, and takes only slightly longer to access than online storage kept on high-speed hard disks. It is significantly faster and easier to access than offline storage.

NETWORK-ATTACHED STORAGE (NAS): A disk array with a thin server operating system optimized for storage and IP network attachement. NAS devices typically present a networked file system in accordance with a protocol such as NFS or CIFS/SMB.

NETWORKING: The ability to interconnect a number of PCs, workstations, servers, and peripherals for the purpose of sharing, sending, receiving and managing information, files, e-mail, and other data.

NETWORK FILE SYSTEM (NFS): A file system originated by Sun Microsystems that will mount remote file systems across homogenous and heterogenous systems. NFS is a client/server application. An NFS server can export local directories for remote NFS clients to use. Typically, NFS runs over IP using UDP, but there are NFS implementations that will work using TCP as the network transport service. NFS has been accepted by the Internet Engineering Task Force (IETF) in certain areas as a standard for file services on TCP/IP networks on the Internet.

NFS: *See NETWORK FILE SYSTEM.*

NODE (or NETWORK NODE): Any device that is directly connected to the network, usually through Ethernet cable; nodes include file servers and shared peripherals.

NOISE: Extraneous electronic signals that interfere with information signals (similar to radio static or TV interference). Sources of noise in computers can be power supplies, ground loops, radio interference, cable routing, etc.

NON-RETURN TO ZERO (NRZ): A method of magnetic recording of digital data in which a flux reversal denotes a one bit, and no flux reversal a zero bit. NRZ recording requires an accompanying synchronization clock to define each cell time, unlike MFM or RLL recording.

NONREPUDIATION: A method for ensuring that a transferred message has been sent and received by the parties claiming to have sent and received the message. Nonrepudiation is necessary to guarantee that the sender of a message cannot later deny having sent the message and that the recipient cannot deny having received the message.

OFF-LINE: Processing or peripheral operations performed while not connected to the system CPU via the system BUS. A collection of data that requires some manual intervention such as loading a disk or tape before it can be accessed. For example floppy disk, tape, CD-ROM.

OFFLINE STORAGE: Infrequently accessed data that is stored offline in a tape archive or file cabinet. Offline storage is the least expensive and slowest storage method, consisting primarily of tape, microfiche and paper media. Restoring offline data to an online environment must be handled manually.

ON-LINE: A collection of data, typically stored on hard disks or arrays, that is immediately accessible.

ONLINE STORAGE: The fastest and most expensive storage alternative, consisting of frequently accessed files found a computer's hard disk.

OPEN SYSTEMS NETWORK: A network comprised of equipment that conforms to industry standards of interoperability between different operating systems (e.g., Unix, Windows NT).

OPERATING SYSTEM: An operating system is a program which acts as an interface between the user of a computer and the computer hardware. The purpose of the operating system is to provide an environment in which a user may run programs. The goal of the operating system is to enable the user to conveniently use the computer's resources such as the CPU, memory, storage devices, and printers.

OPTICAL DISK: A storage medium that generally uses a laser to write and read data. (*See WORM, CD-ROM, CD-R, and CD-RW.*)

OPTICAL STORAGE: A storage alternative to hard disks that provides random-access capability like hard disks. Compared to hard disk storage, optical storage offers higher reliability and a higher degree of removability and transportability. However, optical disk access times are two to four times slower than hard disks, due primarily to the weight of the optical head that reads and writes data. Most optical storage technologies use a read/write laser to store data: to write, the laser heats the recording surface of the media, causing a physical change that is detected during reads.

OPTICAL STORAGE TECHNOLOGY ASSOCIATION (OSTA): An international trade association founded in 1992 to promote the use of writable optical technologies and products.

OUTPUT: Processing data being transferred out of the computer system to peripherals (i.e., disk, printer, etc.). This includes responses to user commands or queries.

OVERHEAD: Overhead refers to the processing time required by the controller, host adapter, or drive prior to the execution of a command. Lower command over-head yields higher drive performance. (*See also ZERO COMMAND OVERHEAD.*) Disk overhead refers to the space required for non-data information such as servo data. Disk overhead often accounts for about ten percent of drive capacity. Lesser disk overhead yields greater disk capacity.

PARITY: A data error checking method using an extra bit in which the total number of binary 1's (or 0's) in a byte is always odd or always even; thus, in an odd parity scheme, every byte has eight bits of data and one parity bit. If using odd parity and the number of 1 bits comprising the byte of data is not odd, the 9th or parity bit is set to 1 to create the odd parity. In this way, a byte of data can be checked for accurate transmission by simply counting the bits for an odd parity indication. If the count is ever even, an error is indicated.

PARITY DATA: A block of information mathematically created from several blocks of user data to allow recovery of user data contained on a drive that has failed in an array; used in RAID levels 3 and 5.

PARKING: Parking the disk drive heads means the recording heads are moved so that they are not over the platter's data area. Many drives have an auto-park feature where the heads are automatically parked when power to the drive is shut off. Other drives require the user to run some kind of parking software to park the heads.

PARTIAL RESPONSE MAXIMUM LIKELIHOOD (PRML): A method for detecting and sampling a signal generated from the reading of a hard disk or tape. Applied in conjunction with *MAGNETO-RESISTIVE (MR) HEADs*, PRML enables extremely high *AREAL DENSITIES* to be achieved on magnetic media.

PARTITION: A portion of a hard drive dedicated to a particular operating system or application and accessed as a single logical volume.

PARTITIONING: Method for dividing an area on disk drive for use by more than one disk operating system or for dividing large disk drives into areas which the File Allocation Table (FAT) can deal with when in use.

PATH: The DOS term "path" has three definitions and each definition involves directories. A PATH may be defined as: (1) the NAMEs of the chain of directories leading to a file; (2) the complete file or directory NAME; (3) a DOS command.

PATTERNED MEDIA: A set of technologies for future storage devices that approach the issue of areal density limitations imposed by superparamagnetism by writing data onto extremely small bit locations on media that is pre-etched with "mesas and valleys" in order to preclude crossover and bit flipping.

PCB: *See PRINTED CIRCUIT BOARD.*

PEER-TO-PEER ARCHITECTURE: A network of two or more computers using the same programs or types of programs to communicate and share data.

PERFORMANCE: A measure of the speed of a hard drive during normal operation. Factors affecting performance are seek times, transfer rate, and command overhead.

PERIPHERAL EQUIPMENT: Auxiliary memory, displays, printers, disk drives, and other equipment usually attached to computer systems' CPU by controllers and cables (they are often packaged together in a desktop computer).

PERPINDICULAR RECORDING: A method of digital recording on a magnetic material in which the bits are arranged vertically rather than horizontally in order to reduce crossover effects of their electromagnetic fields. Perpendicular recording is one method for coping with the effects of superparamagnetism, which imposes a limit on areal density scaling in conventional magnetic media.

PERSISTENT BINDING: Persistent binding is a host-centric method for enabling an operating system to assign specific and non-changing SCSI target IDs and LUNs to certain storage resources. Operating systems and upper-level applications (such as backup software) typically require a static or predictable SCSI target ID for their storage reliability.

PERSONAL COMPUTER INTERCONNECT (PCI): An industry-standard bus used in servers, workstations, and PCs.

PETABYTE: 1,024 terabytes.

PHASE-CHANGE TECHNOLOGY: An optical disk storage technology that uses a plastic disk and metal recording layer to store data. Heat generated by the drive's laser changes the molecular structure of the metal, transforming it from an amorphous to highly reflective crystalline state. The changes in reflectivity are detected during reads. Used for CD-RW and DVD re-writable disks.

PIXIE DUST: A term coined by IBM engineers to describe Anti-Ferromagnetic-Coupled coating for hard disk platters. It refers to a three atom thick layer of ruthenium sandwiched between two magnetic layers. The magnetic layers allow for thinner bits, and the bit above and below are polarized in opposite directions. This technology pushes back the super-paramagnetic limit to between 150 and 200 Gb/in^2.

PLATED MEDIA: Disk platters that are covered with a hard metal alloy instead of an iron-oxide compound. Plated disks can store greater amounts of data than their oxide-coated counterparts.

PLATED THIN FILM DISKS: Magnetic disk memory media having its surface plated with a thin coating of a metallic alloy instead of being coated with oxide.

PLATFORM: A hardware standard, such as IBM, Sun, or Macintosh.

PLATTER: An actual metal (or other rigid material) disk that is mounted inside a fixed-disk drive. Many drives use more than one platter mounted on a single spindle (shaft) to provide more data storage surfaces in a small package.

PLUG AND PLAY: An auto detect method used by the system BIOS to identify and configure peripheral devices. Identification numbers, interrupts and port addresses are set when the system boots.

POLLING: A technique for allocating CPU cycles to specific peripheral devices and tasks.

PORTABILITY: The ability to move storage media from one point to another. Tapes and optical disks are highly portable since they can be easily moved from a working environment to a different location for storage.

POSITIONER: *See ACTUATOR.*

PRECOMPENSATION: A technique used with some oxide media drives to write data bits closer together on the disk in order to offset the repelling effect (bit shift) caused by magnetic recording.

PREVENTIVE MAINTENANCE: A method of doing a scheduled routine observation or exchanging a part, prior to a breakdown of a piece of equipment.

PRIMARY STORAGE: Online storage of electronic data, typically found on a computer's hard disk. This includes frequently used data, work in process, or data that is not frequently used but must be immediately available at all times.

PRINTED CIRCUIT BOARD (PCB): The circuit board with the chips attached to a drive.

PROCESSING (DATA PROCESSING): The handling, manipulating, and modifying of data by a computer in accordance with software instructions.

PROGRAM: A sequence of instructions stored in memory and executed by a processor or microprocessor. (*See also APPLICATION PROGRAMS.*)

PROPRIETARY: Privately developed and owned technology.

PROTOCOL: A set of conventions governing the format of messages to be exchanged within a communications system.

PRML: *See PARTIAL RESPONSE MAXIMUM LIKELIHOOD.*

QUARTER-INCH CARTRIDGE (QIC, pronounced "Quick"): A tape media recording technology that uses a mini-cartridge for tape storage. There are many QIC standards, each defining a method for reading and writing data to tapes.

RACKMOUNT: The cabinet that houses a server/storage workstation (also referred to as a server rack); to mount equipment into a cabinet.

RADIAL: A way of connecting multiple drives to one controller. In radial operation, all output signals are active even if the drive is not selected. (*Also see DAISY CHAIN.*)

RAID (Redundant Array of Inexpensive Disks): A method of combining hard disks into one logical storage unit, which offers disk-fault tolerance and can operate at higher throughput levels than a single hard disk.

RAID ADVISORY BOARD (RAB): An organization of storage system manufacturers and integrators dedicated to advancing the use and awareness of RAID and associated storage technologies; started in 1992, RAB states its main goals as education, standardization, and certification.

RAM: *See RANDOM ACCESS MEMORY.*

RAM DISK: A DOS operation, where part of the computer's random access memory is used to simulate a disk drive. The RAM disk and its contents will disappear if power is lost or DOS MAIN MEMORY is restarted. RAM is far faster (microseconds *ACCESS TIME*) than disks (milliseconds), so *APPLICATION PROGRAMS* that access the disk run faster.

RANDOM ACCESS: The ability to skip randomly from track to track on a storage medium. Optical disks, magnetic hard disks, and audio CDs allow random access to data tracks. Audio tapes, by comparison, allow only sequential access (i.e., fast-forward or reverse) to locate stored data.

RANDOM ACCESS MEMORY (RAM): An integrated circuit memory chip that allows information to be stored and retrieved by a microprocessor or controller. The information can be stored or accessed in any order, and all storage locations are equally accessible. Random access memory usually refers to volatile memory where the contents are lost when power is removed. The user addressable memory of a computer is random access memory.

RDMA: *See REMOTE DIRECT MEMORY ACCESS.*

RDMA OVER IP: Remote Direct Memory Access Over IP is an implementation of RDMA that provides transmission of IP packets from the memory of one computer to the memory of another without involving the CPU. (*See also REMOTE DIRECT MEMORY ACCESS.*)

READ: To access a storage location and obtain previously recorded data.

READ AFTER WRITE: A mode of operation requiring that the system read each sector after data is written, checking that the data read back is the same as the data recorded. This operation lowers system speed but raises data reliability.

READ ONLY MEMORY (ROM): A chip that can be programmed once with bits of information. This chip retains this information even if the power is turned off. When this information is programmed into the ROM, it is called burning the ROM.

READ VERIFY: A data accuracy check performed by having the disk read data to the controller, which then checks for errors but does not pass the data on to the system.

READ/WRITE HEAD: *See HEAD.*

REAL-TIME: Immediate processing of input or notification of status.

RECALIBRATE: Return to Track Zero. A common disk drive function in which the heads are returned to track 0 (outermost track).

RECORD: A record is a single unit made up of logically related fields.

REDUCED INSTRUCTION SET COMPUTER (RISC): A computer processing architecture that requires fewer instructions to run applications, thus increasing processing speed.

REDUCED WRITE CURRENT: A signal input (to some older drives) which decreases the amplitude of the write current at the actual drive head. Normally this signal is specified to be used during inner track write operations to lessen the effect of adjacent bit "crowding." Most drives today provide this internally and do not require controller intervention.

REMOTE DIRECT MEMORY ACCESS (RDMA): A communications protocol that provides transmission of data from the memory of one computer to the memory of another without involving the CPU. InfiniBand, Virtual Interface (VI), and RDMA Over IP are all forms of RDMA. Implemented in hardware on the network adapter (NIC), RDMA techniques have been developed to accommodate the ever-increasing network speeds.

RESOLUTION: In regard to magnetic recording, the bandwidth (or frequency response) of the recording heads.

RESTORE: The act of copying files or data from a backup storage device to their normal location on a computer's hard disk, often to replace files or data that were accidentally lost or deleted.

RLL: *See RUN LENGTH LIMITED.*

ROBOT: A machine that can sense and react to input, and cause changes in its surroundings with some degree of intelligence, ideally with no human supervision.

ROBOTICS: The internal components of an optical jukebox or automated tape library, usually consisting of a mechanical arm that automatically transports media inside the cabinet for use and storage.

ROM: *See READ ONLY MEMORY.*

ROTARY ACTUATOR: *See ACTUATOR.*

ROTATIONAL LATENCY: *See LATENCY, ROTATIONAL.*

ROUTER: An electronic device that connects two or more networks and routes incoming data packets to the appropriate network.

RUN LENGTH LIMITED (RLL): A method of recording digital data in which the combinations of flux reversals are coded/decoded to allow greater than one (1) bit of information per flux reversal. This compaction of information increases data capacity by approximately 50 percent.

SAN HUB: This is a simple connectivity device that allows for devices to be connected to a Fibre Channel loop by being attached to a hub port. The advantage of this is that failures of a single device on the loop can be isolated from the other ports on the loop. The aggregate bandwidth of the hub is still that of a single Fibre Channel loop however.

SAS: *See Serial Attached SCSI.*

SATA: *See SERIAL ATA.*

SCALABLE: The ability of a product or network to accommodate growth.

SCALEABLE LINEAR RECORDING: A tape format from Tandberg Data ASA.

SCATTER/GATHER: A feature which allows data to be transferred to or from multiple discontiguous areas of host computer memory with a single I/O command.

SCSI: *See SMALL COMPUTER SYSTEMS INTERFACE.*

SCSI OVER INTERNET or INTERNET SCSI (iSCSI): iSCSI is an IETF standards-based protocol for operating SCSI as an application across a TCP/IP network. It provides an IP-based alternative to Fibre Channel for interconnecting servers and storage devices in a SAN and may also be used to connect devices to a Fibre Channel fabric via a hybrid iSCSI/FC Fabric switch.

SECTOR: A sector is a section of a track whose size is determined by formatting. When used as an address component, sector and location refer to the sequence number of the sector around the track. Typically, one sector stores one user record of data. Drives typically are formatted from 17 to 26 sectors per track. Determining how many sectors per track to use depends on the system type, the controller capabilities, and the drive encoding method and interface. On Macintosh and UNIX drives, sectors are usually grouped into blocks or logical blocks that function as the smallest data unit permitted. Since these blocks are often defined as a single sector the terms block and sector are sometimes used interchangeably in this context. (*Note:* The usage of the term block in connection with the physical configuration of the disk is different from its meaning at the system level.)

SECTOR-SLIP: Sector-slip allows any sector with a defect to be mapped and bypassed. The next contiguous sector is given that sector address.

SEEK: The radial movement of the heads to a specified track address.

SEEK TIME: The time required to move between tracks when seeking data.

SELF-DESCRIBING DATA: Data that carries with it a header or other mechanism providing descriptive information regarding its origins, criticality, stale date, and other information that might facilitate its lifecycle management.

SERIAL ATA (SATA): SATA is a serial implementation of the Parallel ATA physical storage interface. Serial ATA is a serial link—a single cable with a minimum of four wires creates a point-to-point connection between devices. Transfer rates for Serial ATA begin at 150 MBps. One of the main design advantages of Serial ATA is that the thinner serial cables facilitate more efficient airflow inside a server cabinet and permits smaller chassis designs. In contrast, IDE cables used in parallel ATA systems are bulkier than Serial ATA cables and can only extend to 40 cm long, while Serial ATA cables can extend up to one meter.

SERIAL ATTACHED SCSI (SAS): SAS is a serialized implementation of the parallel SCSI bus. Features include smaller cables and connectors, full duplex connections, the capability of addressing thousands of devices per port, and an initial transfer rate of 3 Gbps. Smaller connectors enable dual-ported SAS drives, reducing the risk of a failing controller and extending the compact 2.5-inch format to enterprise-class drives, with obvious benefits in space and power requirements. SAS will have point-to-point connections; but by using expanders—essentially, fan-out devices—the new protocol makes it possible to address multiple devices from a single port. SAS and SATA devices may be connected to the same controller (but on different ports) enabling the new protocol to consolidate the best characteristics of SCSI, FC, and SATA into a single interface.

SERIAL STORAGE ARCHITECTURE (SSA): A high-speed method of connecting disk, tape, and CD-ROM drives, printers, scanners, and other devices to a computer.

SEQUENTIAL ACCESS: Writing or reading data in a sequential order, such as reading data blocks stored one after the other on magnetic tape (the opposite of random access).

SERVER: A computer that provides access to a network and its resources, runs administrative software controls, and provides services (such as file storage and retrieval) for desktop computers.

SERVER-ATTACHED STORAGE: A storage system that is connected directly to the network server; also referred to as direct-attached storage.

SERVO DATA: *See EMBEDDED SERVO.*

SERVO MOTOR: A motor used to position the actuator arm and read/write heads on hard disk media.

SERVO SURFACE: *See DEDICATED SERVO.*

SERVO TRACK: A prerecorded reference track on the dedicated servo surface of a closed-loop disk drive. All data track positions are compared to their corresponding servo track to determine "off-track/on-track" position. Information written on the servo surface that the electronics of the drive uses to position the heads over the correct data track. This information is written on the drive by the servo track writer.

SETTLE TIME: The interval between the arrival of the read/write head at a specific track and the lessening of the residual vibration to a level sufficient for reliable reading or writing.

SETUP: Program used by at type computers to store configuration in CMOS. This program is sometimes found in the system bios and can be accessed from the keyboard. On other systems, the program is on a diskette.

SHOCK RATING: A rating, expressed in terms of the force of gravity (Gs), of how much shock a disk drive can sustain without damage.

SILICON: Semiconductor substrate material generally used to manufacture micro-processors and other integrated circuit chips.

SIMPLE NETWORK MANAGEMENT PROTOCOL (SNMP): A standard protocol that runs over an IP link to provide management of network type devices without performing continual polling.

SINGLE-ENDED: An electrical signal protocol which transmits information through changes in voltage. Single-ended SCSI uses standard TTL signal-and-ground pairs to transmit information over the SCSI bus.

SKEWING: Some low-level formatting routines may ask for a Head and/or Cylinder Skew value. The value will represent the number of sectors being skewed to compensate for head switching time of the drive and/or track-to-track seek time allowing continuous read/write operation without losing disk revolutions.

SMALL COMPUTER SYSTEM INTERFACE (SCSI): An industry standard for connecting peripherals such as printers, scanners, optical drives, and tape drives to a microprocessor. SCSI covers both hardware and software standards for allowing computers and peripherals to communicate with each other.

SMART: Self-Monitoring, Analysis, and Reporting Technology can help prevent data loss and unscheduled computer downtime. It provides advanced warning of certain types of drive failures, allowing the user of data-management software to backup the data. This technology is not supported by all system manufacturers or hard drive distributors and requires third party software.

SMS: *See SYSTEM MANAGED STORAGE.*

SOFT ERROR: A bit error during playback which can be corrected by repeated attempts to read, usually caused by power fluctuations or noise spikes.

SOFT SECTOR: A convention, defined by software, of setting a variable numbers of sectors per track in direct relationship to the drive's FCI rating in regards to the area of media that passes beneath the head. This schema takes advantage of the fact that, in actual surface area, the outermost tracks are longer than the innermost.

SOFT SECTORED: A term describing a hard drive that determines the starting location of each sector from information stored in data fields. This method is older and results in more overhead than hard sectored techniques. (*See also HARD SECTORED.*)

SOFT ZONING: A method of defining and maintaining SAN zones though software. The zoning process uses the name server database located in the fibre-channel switch, which stores port numbers and world wide names (WWN) used to identify devices during the zoning process. The devices in the database receive Registered State Change Notification (RSCN) when a zone change is made. In order to change related communication paths, each device must correctly address the RSCN. Any device that does not correctly address the RSCN and continues to transfer data to a specific device after a zoning change, will be blocked from communicating with its targeted device.

SOFTWARE APPLICATION PROGRAMS: Disk operating systems and other programs (as opposed to *HARDWARE*). The instructions or programs, usually stored on floppy or hard disks, which are used to direct the operations of a computer, or other hardware.

SOFTWARE PATCH: Software modification which allows or adds functions not otherwise available using the standard software program.

SPINDLE: The drive's center shaft, on which the platters are mounted. A synchronized spindle is a shaft that allows two disks to spin simultaneously as a mirror image of each other, permitting redundant storage of data.

SPINDLE MOTOR: The spindle motor is the electro-mechanical part of the disk drive that rotates the platters.

SPUTTER: A special method of coating the disk that results in a hard, smooth surface capable of storing data at a high density.

SSA: *See SERIAL STORAGE ARCHITECTURE.*

ST-506/ST-412 INTERFACE: One of several industry standard interfaces between a hard disk and hard disk controller. In the ST-506/ST-412 interface, the "intelligence" is on the controller rather than the drive. (*See also INTERFACE STANDARD, ESDI, and SCSI.*)

STEP PULSE: The pulse sent from the controller to the stepper motor on the step interface signal line to initiate a step operation.

STEP TIME: The time required by the drive to step the heads from the current cylinder position to a target cylinder.

STEP: An increment or decrement of the head positioning arm to move the heads in or out, respectively, one track from their current position. In buffered mode (open loop drives), the head motion is postponed until the last of a string of step pulses has been received.

STEPPER: A type of motor that moves in discrete amounts with each electrical pulse. Steppers were originally the most common type of actuator engine, since they can be geared to advance a read/write head one track per step.

STEPPER MOTOR: The stepper motor is the electro-mechanical part of the disk drive that positions the heads by step pulse on the tracks of the disk to read and write data.

STORAGE APPLIANCE: Concept of an intelligent, network-attached, storage device.

STORAGE AREA NETWORK (SAN): A network comprising multiple hosts and storage peripherals, currently conceived as Fibre Channel/SCSI Command Set-based. However, any interconnect and any network protocol could be used, theoretically, to establish a SAN, provided that the strict latency and throughput requirements of storage are met.

STORAGE CAPACITY: Amount of data that can be stored in a memory, usually specified in kilobytes (KB) for main memory and floppy disk drives and megabytes (MB) for hard disk and tape drives. The maximum amount of data that can be stored on a given media.

STORAGE DENSITY: Usually refers to recording density (BPI, TPI, or their product, *AREAL DENSITY*).

STORAGE LOCATION: A memory location, identified by an *ADDRESS*, where information is to be read or written.

STORAGE MODULE DRIVE (SMD): Storage module drive interface. An interface, used in larger disk drives, e.g., 14" drives.

STRIPE: A contiguous region of disk space. Stripes may be as small as one sector or may be composed of many contiguous sectors.

STRIPING: A method of storage in which a unit of data is distributed and stored across several hard disks, which improves access speed but does not provide redundancy. Also called RAID-0.

SUBSTRATE: In disk technology, the material underneath the magnetic coating of a platter. Common substrates include aluminum or magnesium alloys for hard drives, glass for optical disks, and mylar for floppy disks.

SUPERPARAMAGNETISM: In storage technology, when the magnetic energy holding bits in their recorded state becomes equal to the thermal energy generated by the drive itself, random bit flipping can occur. This is referred to as the superparamagnetic effect or SPE. Superparamagnetism imposes a limit on the areal density improvements possible with contemporary magnetic disk technology.

SURFACE: The top or bottom side of a platter, which is coated with the magnetic material for recording data. On some hard drives, one of the surfaces on one of the platters is reserved for servo data.

SURFACE MOUNTED DEVICE (SMD): A CHIP in a smaller integrated surface package, without connection leads.

SUSTAINED MODE: The measured transfer rate of a given device during normal operation.

SWITCH: A network traffic monitoring device that controls the flow of traffic between multiple network nodes.

SYNCHRONOUS DATA: Data sent, usually in serial mode, with a clock pulse.

SYSTEM MANAGED STORAGE (SMS): Software used to routinely back up and archive files. Also abbreviation of DFSMS: enhanced data management software for MVS mainframes from IBM. Introduced in 1988, it provides functions such as automatically allocating data, which prevents most out-of-space errors when disk volumes become full. Also a moniker for Storage Management Services software from Novell that allows data to be stored and retrieved on NetWare servers independent of the file system the data are maintained in (DOS, OS/2, Mac, etc.). It is used to back up data from heterogeneous clients on the network. Various third-party backup products are SMS compliant.

SYSTEMS INTEGRATOR: An individual or company that combines various components and programs into a functioning system, customized for a particular customer's needs.

TAPE DRIVE: A sequential access memory device whose magnetic media is tape in a cassette, reel, or continuous loop.

TARGET: A device that performs an operation requested by an initiator.

TELCO: Abbreviation for "telecommunications company."

TERABYTE: Terabyte equals 1,099,511,627,776 bytes or approximately one trillion bytes.

TERMINATION: A method of matching the transmission impedance of a electrical bus so as to eliminate signal reflections from the physical ends of the bus.

THIN FILM: A type of coating deposited on a flat surface through a photolithographic process. Thin film is used on disk platters and read/write heads.

THIN FILM HEADS: A read/write head whose read/write element is deposited using integrated circuit techniques rather than being manually fabricated by grinding ferrite and hand winding coils.

THIN SERVER: Name given to a network-attached device with an embedded micro-kernel operating system. Storage appliances are thin servers, as are many NAS devices.

THROUGHPUT: A performance measurement indicating the volume and speed of data as it flows from one point to another through a data pipeline. High throughput indicates a system architecture that can carry high volumes of data at high speeds, resulting in high system performance.

TOP COVER: Together with the base casting, creates an airtight, extremely clean environment. Any attempt to remove this top cover outside of a clean room will immediately contaminate and ruin a disk drive. Needless to say, any warranty is immediately voided if the top is removed.

TOPOLOGY: Geometric arrangement of nodes and cable links in a local area network; may be either centralized, and decentralized.

TPI: *See TRACKS PER INCH.*

TRACK: A track is the circular ring traced over the disk surface by a head as the disk rotates under the heads. Also known as a channel.

TRACK ACCESS TIME: *See AVERAGE ACCESS TIME.*

TRACK DENSITY: *See TRACKS PER INCH.*

TRACK FOLLOWING SERVO: A closed-loop positioner control system that continuously corrects the position of the disk drive's heads by utilizing a reference track and a feedback loop in the head positioning system. (*See also CLOSED LOOP*).

TRACK PITCH: Distance from centerline to centerline of adjacent tracks (TPI divided into 1.0).

TRACKS PER INCH (TPI): Tracks per inch. The number of tracks written within each inch of the disk's surfaces, used as a measure of how closely the tracks are packed on a disk surface. Also known as track density.

TRACK-TO-TRACK SEEK TIME: The time required for the read/write heads to move to an adjacent track.

TRACK WIDTH: Width of data track. Also called core width of Read/Write Head.

TRACK ZERO: Track zero is the outermost data track on a disk drive. In the ST 506 INTERFACE, the interface signal denotes that the heads are positioned at the outermost cylinder.

TRACK ZERO DETECTOR: An obsolete technology that *RECALIBRATES* by sensing when infrared beams between a *LED* and infrared sensitive photo-transistor are blocked by the track zero interrupter (TZI).

TRANSFER RATE: The rate of speed at which data travels through a bus or device, typically measured in bits, bytes, kilobytes or megabytes per second. The rate at which the disk sends and receives data from the controller. The sustained transfer rate includes the time required for system processing, head switches, and seeks and accurately reflects the drive's true performance. The burst mode transfer rate is a much higher figure that refers only to the movement of data directly into RAM.

TUNNEL ERASE: An erase scheme where both sides of the recorded data is erased when writing data to eliminate track to track interference. This is primarily used on floppy disk drives.

TURBOCODE: A type of channel coding that uses a convolutional code and a type of Viterbi decoder that outputs a continuous value rather than a 0 or 1. Convolutional coding adds patterns of redundancy to data in order to improve the signal to noise ratio for more accurate decoding at the receiving end. The Viterbi algorithm is used to decode a particular type of convolutional code.

TURN TIME: The constant rate of rotation of a hard disk platter, typically measured in rotations per minute (RPM). Typical disks have rotation speeds of 4,500 to 7,200 RPM, but 10,000 RPM drives are beginning to enter the market.

TURNKEY: A product or system that can be plugged in, turned on, and operated with little or no additional configuring.

ULTRA-SCSI: A variant of SCSI. Doubles the bandwidth of SCSI Fast. It provides 8-bit (SCSI Narrow) data rates of 20 Mbytes per second and 16-bit (SCSI Wide) data rates of 40 Mbytes per second. Shorter cables may be required. Formerly known as Fast-20.

UNFORMATTED CAPACITY: The total number of bytes on a disk, including the space that is required to record location, boundary definitions, and servo data. (*See also FORMATTED CAPACITY.*)

UNIX: An operating system that supports multitasking and is ideally suited to multi-user applications (such as networks).

UPGRADE PATH: Generally, with disk products, a family having multiple products with varying capacities such that the system storage capacity can increase with changing application requirements simply using a different disk drive within the product family.

VAR (Value-Added Reseller): A business that repackages and improves hardware (or software) manufactured by an original equipment manufacturer (OEM).

VCX: A tape technology from Ecrix Corporation.

VERIFICATION: A process of re-reading data just written to disk to ensure the data was written correctly.

VOICE COIL: A fast and reliable actuator motor that works like a loud-speaker, in which the force of a magnetic coil causes a proportionate movement of the head. Voice coil actuators are more durable than their stepper counterparts, since fewer parts are subject to daily stress and wear.

VOICE COIL MOTOR: An electro-magnetic positioning motor in the rigid disk drive similar to that used in audio speakers. A wire coil is placed in a stationary magnetic field. When current is passed through the coil, the resultant flux causes the coil to move. In a disk drive, the *CAR-RIAGE ASSEMBLY* is attached to the voice coil motor. Either a straight line (linear) or circular (rotary) design may be employed to position the heads on the disk's surface.

VOLATILE: Memory that will be erased if power is lost. Typically, *MAIN MEMORY* is volatile, while *AUXILIARY MEMORY* is non-volatile and can be used for permanent (but changeable at will) storage of programs and data.

WAN: *See WIDE AREA NETWORK.*

WEB CACHE: A Web cache fills requests from the Web server, stores the requested information locally, and sends the information to the client. The next time the web cache gets a request for the same information, it returns the locally cached data instead of searching over the Internet, thus reducing Internet traffic and response time.

WEB SITE: A location on the World Wide Web that is owned and managed by an individual, company, or organization; usually contains a home page and additional pages that include information provided by the site's owner, and may include links to other relevant sites.

WEDGE SERVO SYSTEM: A certain part of each *CYLINDER* contains servo positioning data. Gap spacing between each sector contains servo data to maintain position on that cylinder.

WEDGE SERVO: *See EMBEDDED SERVO.*

WIDE AREA NETWORK (WAN): A network that uses high-speed, long-distance communications technology (e.g., phone lines and satellites) to connect computers over long distances.

WIDE SCSI: The Wide SCSI interface provides a 16-bit wide SCSI bus, as compared to the narrow 8-bit SCSI bus. The wider 16-bit bus provides a transfer rate of 20 Mbytes per second compared to 10 Mbytes per second with Fast SCSI 8-bit interface.

WINCHESTER DISK: Former code name for an early IBM hard disk model, sometimes still used to refer to the technology and design of most traditional hard drives.

WINCHESTER DRIVE: A disk drive with a Winchester head and non-removable (fixed) disks sealed in a contaminant-free housing.

WORD: Number of bits processed in parallel (in a single operation) by a CPU. Standard word lengths are 8, 16, 32, and 64 (1, 2, 4, or 8 bytes).

WORLD WIDE WEB (WWW): A global hypertext system operating on the Internet that enables electronic communication of text, graphics, audio, and video.

WORM: *See WRITE ONCE READ MANY.*

WRITE: To access a storage location and store data on the magnetic surface.

WRITE CURRENT: The optimum HEAD write current necessary to saturate the magnetic media in a cell location.

WRITE IMMEDIATE: With host-controlled write immediate, status is returned when data is transferred to the drive buffer instead of waiting until the data is written to the media. The seek, latency, and write times are cut out of the total command completion as seen by the host.

WRITE ONCE READ MANY (WORM): An optical storage technology that burns pits into the recording layer of an optical disk, allowing the disks to be written just once but read without limit. WORM drives write directly to an optical disk from a host computer. Both the drives and disks include built-in safeguards to assure that data, once written, cannot be erased, overwritten or altered. Tape-based WORMs have just begun to enter the market.

WRITE PROTECT: The use of various safeguards to prevent a computer system from overwriting a storage medium. Floppy disks have a sliding tab for "physical" write protect. Hard disks support "logical" write protect in software. Optical disks often use a combination of physical and logical write protect safeguards.

XOR ENGINE: Process or set of instructions that calculates data bit relationships in a *RAID* subsystem.

ZERO COMMAND OVERHEAD: To reduce command overhead to zero, processing traditionally done through software can be placed in the hardware, where it is completed almost instantaneously. Zero command overhead yields a substantial improvement in system performance.

ZERO LATENCY READ: This reduces the delay in transferring data from the drive to the initiator due to rotational latency delays. Data is read out of order from the disk and transferred to the host where the requested order is restored.

ZONING: This is the term used by some switch companies to denote the division of a storage area network or fabric into sub networks or fabrics that provide different levels of connectivity or accessibility between specific hosts and devices on the network. In effect routing tables are used to control access of hosts to devices. This zoning can be performed by cooperative consent of the hosts or can be enforced at the switch level. In the former case, hosts are responsible for communicating with the switch to determine if they have the right to access a device.

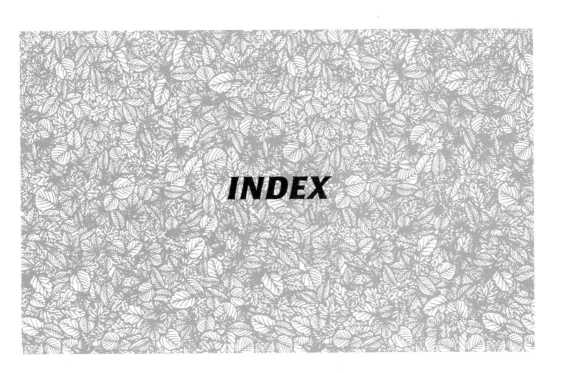

INDEX